LIVERPOOL
SHADOWS

© Richard Whittington-Egan 2002

Published by The Bluecoat Press, Liverpool
Book design by March Design, Liverpool
Printed by MFP

ISBN 1 904438 05 9

RICHARD WHITTINGTON-EGAN

LIVERPOOL
SHADOWS

The Bluecoat Press

CONTENTS

Historic Shadows

Literary Shadows

Shadows of the Past

PROLOGUE

IN THE DEPARTURE LOUNGE

I grow old ... I grow old ... soon, like Eliot's J Alfred Prufrock, I shall wear the bottoms of my trousers rolled. Or the top under my armpits!

To grow old is not all bad. When that redoubtable Scottish lawyer and superlative criminous scribe, the late William Roughead, Writer to the Signet, whose biography I wrote, was once, in his octogenarian days, toddling happily along the treacherous, ice-spattered pavement of Princes Street in his native Edinburgh, he encountered an equally agèd legal luminary. "Och, Willie," his friend greeted him, "we're getting auld!" Riposted Willie, quick as a flash: "Aye, thank God for that, otherwise we'd be deid."

There is, as they say, no answer to that. And no argument about it.

Thank God, I am still here. There are so many beautiful birds in the wild woods of the world whose songs I do not yet know. And I want to. But I am on the wing. On the wrong side of the hill, with darkness below me.

Here, away in Great Malvern, looking out from my high-perched study window, up on the Worcester Beacon, across the Severn Plain, or the Plain of the Seven Ages of Man, past Housman's Bredon, to where the sky falls to meet the land, I am in waiting. I am in the departure lounge, waiting with my obolus in my palm for the ferry-boat, not the *Royal Daffodil* to cross the Mersey, but that of Charon, who will oar me safely over the dark Styx, or the salvatory aeroplane to fly me up, up and away into the inscrutable, limitless sky beyond the scattered light of stars.

As time lengthens, accumulating mornings' breaks and evenings' falls, so does the focus of one's view; presbyopia, but not, I hope, presbyophrenia, set in. Scenes like those magic lantern slides of one's youth, form and dissolve. Were they ever really there? Was I? Is old age all delusion?

It is a short day's journey now into night. Perpetual darkness. This Liver bird is, as I have said, on the wing. But before the circle which I fly decreases into the final vortex of nothingness, I have wanted to scatter a few more feathers of memory, that those who knew not either me, or my Liverpool, may know that I – and it – once upon a time were. Hence this book.

Soon, I shall be remote as the quaintest, bewhiskered and mustachioed, mutton-chop Victorian, as far 'Beyond the need of weeping, beyond the reach of hands,' as Julius Cæsar. Yet my eyes saw, and my ears heard, the sights and sounds, and my tongue sang the praises of the beloved city that, in time, bore and shaped both you and me.

> Liverpool the lovely ...
> For I in thy heart had dwelling,
> And thou hast in mine for ever.

Time is of the essence – and the accident. It is the accident that divides us: the wilfulness of non-chiming coincidence. My grandfather can never be me: nor my consciousness yours. But my grandfather and I, and you and I, can share a vision – even after it has faded – by the magic of words, spoken or written. I can, if you will but permit me, conduct you along with me into the pleasaunces of the past. I can bring you into a Liverpool that was as real, and as enduringly insubstantial, as the sunshine and shadow on the Church Street pavement of the here-and-now today:

> The sunlight on the garden
> Hardens and grows cold
> We cannot cage the minute
> Within its net of gold ...

For the strange fact which you must learn is that, contrary to conventional belief, it is not the brick-and-mortar city that is the permanent survivor, but its image in the flickering memory of sick-and-mortal man. Phantoms we may all, *sub specie æternitatis*, be, but it is our ghostly presences that linger after the dust and rust, moths and mildews of Time have eaten away the solid struts that bore the bridges of our pilgrimage.

If ghosts there be, I shall surely be at least an earthbound spirit, like the old Irishman of whom my father used to tell me. The man had lived all his life in Mullinabro, near Waterford, County Kilkenny, and loved every square millimetre of the place. Lying on his deathbed, he was heard muttering and repeating like a mantra:

> Heaven's above and Hell is below, but how can I leave
> you sweet Mullinabro?

And, my father would say:

> Sure he never did! His ghost was seen time after time
> after time, and without the aid of poteen I may tell you,
> by sober men and women, and even innocent children,
> beating the bounds of his earthly paradise.

If, I say, there are such things as ghosts, well then, I shall hover on autumn afternoons over timeless Hadassah Grove, and linger on long summer's evenings about Childwall churchyard, and the Gateacre that was – and no more is – where I stood beside the market cross in the lane and listened to the cuckoo, where now rears the concrete row of shops. In the spring evenings I shall walk the parks, Prince's, Sefton, Calderstones, and ascend to Mossley Hill's summit, beside the beautiful old church and Great Aunt

Emma's Sudley. On winter nights I shall be listening to catch through the misty dusk, spattered with sputtering street lamps, strong and plangent, the newspaper-sellers' cries of yesteryear, "Liverpool ... Exy-Echo!" And see again, as though in life, the wraith of a poor, threadbare man, upturned collar, down-turned cap, crying his paper-thin wares into the knife-sharp wind, for slow-falling pennies in the fast-falling dark.

All these are the slants and accents of my Liverpool past.

I shall in the fulness of appointed time be back in Liverpool, never again to depart. After more than seven decades of wandering, I shall have come finally home.

It will all end for me in the petrified stone forest of Allerton Cemetery – that massive dormitory of the dead, the largest in Europe, so I am told – a tombstone's throw from the leaf-bound place of my birth and golden youth. My father, Cyril Whittington-Egan, the learned attorney, has lain, full soil's depth six, awaiting me there these sixty-odd years. My marbled bed is of best Carrara, pinkish and blue veined. The stone, already erected and carved with my name and year of birth, stands attendant. It needs only the inscription of the date of my demise.

And if I am remembered at all, let that memory be that the heart that lies below, mouldering gently back into the Liverpool earth, loved that fair stretch of land and water called Liverpool life-long, and rests well content deep bedded in its soil's embrace.

To adopt and adapt the words of Rupert Brooke: in that rich earth of Allerton is richer dust concealed, a dust that Liverpool bore, shaped, and made aware, her streets to walk and flowers to pluck, washed by the waters of Mersey, lying now, until the day breaks, among the fungi and the greenery, under the wide bright arc of the Liverpool sky.

SHADOWS
OF MURDER

THE HUNTING OF RAY BEECH

It was late afternoon when the telephone rang in Liverpool's Prescot Road police station. The desk sergeant picked it up.

"Hallo."

"Hallo. Hallo." The voice on the other end of the line was urgent. "Police? This is Jimmy Hatton speaking. I'm the landlord of the Princes Park Hotel in Upper Stanhope Street. I think I've seen Beech. Beech, you know, the bloke you're looking for for the murders."

The desk sergeant stiffened to attention and clamped the receiver closer to his ear.

"Just one minute, Mr Hatton." Then, covering the mouthpiece, turned to the group of young policemen chattering away by the counter. "Hey! Shut up you lot," he snapped. "This is important."

The chattering subsided.

"Hallo. Right Mr Hatton. Now what were you saying?"

"I had a chap in this afternoon the dead spit of Beech. I'm sure it was him. Had a girl with him. Young piece, about twenty-four. Now look, I don't want any trouble, I keep a respectable house, but I heard the bloke say to her that they'd be coming in again this evening. I reckon it might be worth your while looking in."

The instant he had put the receiver down the desk sergeant rushed round to the CID and told them what Hatton had said. Seconds later, Hatton's message was being relayed to the Murder HQ that Superintendent Herbert Balmer had set up at the Lawrence Road police station.

Patrolling the Upper Stanhope Street area that afternoon, studying every face in the way that policemen do, were Detective Sergeants John Beaverstock and Joseph Gillbanks, and when they rang in a routine check call to Lawrence Road, they were told the score and ordered to 'proceed forthwith' to the Princes Park Hotel. So they looked at their watches, saw that it was getting on for six o'clock, and wheeled round in the direction of Upper Stanhope Street.

Jack Beaverstock and Joe Gillbanks were both 45, a couple of old-timers, beginning, at least, to think in terms of retirement and pensions. Both, too, were family men. Beaverstock was the father of four young sons. Gillbanks had a lad of 16. They were big, burly men, tall, clean-shaven and, despite greying hair, not the type you'd choose to pick a barney with! Not that they were the sort to look for trouble – though they were not the sort either to shirk it if it happened to come their way.

And now it had – with a vengeance. This was it.

They knew that the man they were looking for had a partly-loaded revolver in his pocket. They knew, too, that he had already killed twice, and wasn't likely to be worried about notching up a third murder – particularly that of a 'Jack'.

It was just after 6pm when the two detectives with eyes in the backs of their heads reached the Princes Park Hotel. It was a very ordinary, rather shabby, public-house, all frosted glass and drab brown wood, just like any one of a hundred other slightly seedy Liverpool pubs. Quiet, too, at this time of the evening. It would be hours before it livened up.

The two CID men drifted gently in through the swing doors into the front parlour. No noise. No fuss. They fanned out slightly. At the same time their trained eyes took in the details of the six people in the bar. Five were eliminated in seconds. But the sixth …

There, standing at a corner of the counter, a glass of beer in front of him and a girl beside him, was a dark, wavy-haired six-footer, with blue eyes and a fresh complexion. It was Beech all right.

Slowly exchanging a significant glance, Beaverstock and Gillbanks moved forward. You would have called their movements sluggish if you didn't know the reason. They didn't want to set off a shooting match. They didn't want innocent bystanders to catch a bullet, let alone catch one themselves.

Very quietly then, they sidled up to Beech, one on either side. It was Beaverstock who spoke.

"We're police officers. We'd like to have your name and address and some evidence of your identity," he said.

The tall young man between them hesitated. Old hands like Beaverstock and Gillbanks sensed that he was concocting a story. But that wasn't the point. The thing was, was he going to come quietly? Or was he going to go wild? At that moment there was one nasty, persistent thought ticking away at the back of both of their minds.

If he chose to, the man could probably kill them both where they stood.

~

The hunting of Walter Richard 'Ray' Beech had begun a few minutes after the people who lived in Underley Street, Wavertree, had heard shots and screams coming out of Number 32. That had been at about half-past six on the evening of 16 April 1951. Heads popped out of windows, women left their cooking, men in shirt-sleeves rushed out into the road. Respectable yellow-brick Underley Street suddenly buzzed like an upturned beehive.

The two boldest men, 56-year-old Arthur Barber and 42-year-old Gladwin Field, didn't hesitate. They rushed round to the back of Number 32, up the entry, into the back yard, and peered through the kitchen window.

Both blanched at the scene of bloodshed that met their eyes.

Two women were lying close together on the floor. Both had been shot through the head. The face of one of them had been battered in. Beside her body lay the broken half of a gun butt. In a far corner was a little fat dachshund, piteously whining and whimpering.

Barber kicked in the back door. The two men tore through the house, every minute expecting another shot. But there was nothing. No one. Just those two splayed and very dead bodies in the kitchen. Stillness. Eerie silence, pierced only by the thin, high whinings of the dachshund.

The front-door of the house was swinging open. The killer had vanished into the network of alleyways which criss-cross that part of Liverpool. The jiggers … a labyrinth of escape.

Within a matter of minutes, a cavalcade of cars had converged on normally quiet Underley Street, spewing out police. A cordon of uniformed officers had sealed off the street and a dozen grim-faced plain clothes detectives were shepherding the bewildered inhabitants back into their houses.

It did not take the police long to identify the murder victims. They were Mrs Lilian Harriet Parr, a 55-year-old widow who worked as a domestic servant at nearby Sefton General Hospital, and her 24-year-old married daughter, Mrs Lilian Beryl Beech. She was living apart from her husband, 29-year-old Ray, and was working as a night sister in the maternity section of the same hospital as her mother.

While detectives and forensic experts were going over the murder room inch by inch, searching for fingerprints and taking photographs of the bodies, others were questioning the neighbours.

It was Mrs Eleanor Barber who was able to give them the vital information that they needed. That day had, she said, been Beryl Beech's 24th birthday, and she had popped into Number 32 to see her. She had found Beryl and her mother in the back kitchen. They were very upset and both crying. While she was there Ray Beech came into the kitchen and told Mrs Barber that there had been a quarrel. He had wanted his wife, who was expecting a baby, to return to him, to leave her mother's and join him in the couple of rooms where he was then living, but she was refusing to do so. Upset and embarrassed by the family row, and not wanting to get involved, Mrs Barber had left. That was shortly after 6pm.

So, within an hour the police knew who they were looking for and why he had done it.

Out went the order – "Find Beech!"

In a teeming cosmopolitan seaport of some 800,000 people it is not hard for a man to disappear. There are a thousand out-of-the-way nooks and crannies to hide a fugitive. There is, too, a vast twilight world, a tight-lipped community that wouldn't raise a finger to help the 'scuffers'. But this time the police were in luck. Raking through the criminal records down at their Dale Street HQ, they found that they had plenty on file about Ray Beech.

A former Merchant Navy steward, he was a known violence merchant.

And he was no stranger to the feel of a gun. He had had one in 1946. With it, just three months after he had married Beryl, he had held up a house in Waterloo. He had got five years for that. And it wasn't his first conviction either.

When he came out, a couple of months before the Underley Street shooting, Beryl had told him that she still loved him.

"I'll go straight this time, love," he swore.

He meant it, too. He even took a job as an acetylene welder with a firm of shipwrights.

Then Ray Beech acquired another gun.

"Find Walter Richard Beech. Bring him in for questioning." Then, grimly, murder hunt chief Balmer added the ominous warning. "And be careful, he may shoot."

The massive manhunt was mounted. A cordon was thrown round all the roads leading out of the city. Sharp eyes watched from the shadows at rail and bus stations, and at the docks. Big, bulky men, treading like cats, moved through the night. Detectives with pictures of Beech in their pockets visited the spielers, the sleazy clubs that he was known to frequent. In the back streets the constables shone their torches and peered through windows. The radio squad cars moved into action.

More than 300 detectives, uniformed police and tracker dogs raked the territory – the waterfront pubs, the midnight coffee stalls, the all-night cafés, the doss-houses of Sailortown. When dawn came they were still at it, still searching, footsore and weary from pounding the pavements. And all the following morning … and afternoon … a hopeless, needle-in-the-haystack quest … in which they drew blank after blank after blank.

Until, in the late afternoon of 17 April 1951, the phone shrilled in Prescot Street police station.

~

And now the whole vast operation was to boil down to the quiet courage of two greying detectives facing death in a seedy, backstreet pub.

Beaverstock and Gillbanks moved nearer to Beech. For a second or two he looked at them in silence. Then he spoke.

"I'm off a Dutch ship," he said. "I haven't got my papers with me. They're just across the road. I'll slip over and get them."

But the CID men weren't falling for that one.

"There won't be any need for that," said Beaverstock.

Over Beech's shoulder he caught the landlord Jimmy Hatton's eye. Almost imperceptibly a nod of understanding passed between them. Hatton gestured towards the back parlour. That was where the old dears used to settle down nursing their bottles of stout. At this time of the evening it was empty.

"Would you mind stepping in there with us for a minute?" asked Beaverstock, and they led him into the unoccupied back parlour. Beech went quietly.

"We're not satisfied with your explanation," Beaverstock told him. "We have reason to believe that you are Walter Richard Beech, and I must ask you to accompany us."

As Beaverstock and Gillbanks moved forward to close with him, Beech suddenly whipped a revolver out from under his coat. Pointing it at them, he shouted: "Stand back or you'll get it. You're not taking me in."

Beaverstock and Gillbanks froze. Their minds raced. What were they to do? Back away? Unthinkable. Stand their ground? Move nearer? Neither spoke, but as one man they began to edge nearer.

"Stop! Stop!" Beech screamed. "It's loaded and you're going to get it."

Beaverstock felt the sweat prickle behind his ears. Gillbanks felt, like palpable blows, the the punchings of his heart.

"Don't be a fool, man. Put that gun away."

Beaverstock's voice sounded distant and unreal in his own ears.

"Don't be stupid," shouted Gillbanks.

Then, the gun pointing at their stomachs, the detectives advanced, stepped inexorably nearer, nearer.

There was a flash. A terrific bang that echoed and re-echoed ringingly, deafeningly, in that tiny room. A wisping puff of blue smoke. An acrid burning smell.

"I thought he'd shot Joe," said Beaverstock afterwards.

"I thought Jack had got it," said Gillbanks.

But, dropping his bluster, changing his mind in those final seconds, Beech had fired the sixth and last bullet in his .45 Colt into his own brain.

Still dazed, not making much sense, Jack Beaverstock bent down to where Beech lay slumped on the floor, the gun still in his hand. The butt was broken in half.

It was precisely seven minutes later that the first big shiny car pulled in at the kerb outside the Princes Park Hotel. Out leapt Superintendent Balmer. He hurried into the pub. Balmer took from his pocket the half of a gun butt found beside the bodies of the women in Underley Street. He bent down, matched it with the weapon in Beech's stiffening fingers.

It fitted exactly.

"Call off the hunt," he said.

DEATH AT THE GRAVEYARD OF CHAMPIONS

It was known in the élite circles of boxing and wrestling aficionados as 'The Graveyard of Champions'. Its official name was the Empire Stadium. It was situate at the top of Bixteth Street. The style 'graveyard' had come to be attached to it by reason of the slaughterings and 'deaths' that took place in the square – or squared – ring. The champs all seemed to take the tumble, lose their titles there. But for those *outside* the ropes it was a well-beloved sporting venue, and there are to this day, rheumy-eyed veterans who remember Friday nights as Jack Pye nights –Jack Pye, the 'Uncrowned King of the Mat', Jack Pye, the Doncaster Panther *v* Everybody.

Less happy, though, is the memory of one Sunday night in August 1961, and the death that occurred well away from the sporting arena of the Empire ring. The protagonists were unequally matched – a well-muscled 23-year-old man and a slender 19-year-old girl. He was John Christopher McMenemy, a labourer, who lived with his parents in Lorne Street, near Newsham Park. She was Valerie Sellers, who worked as a waitress in Rhyl, and lived, also with her parents, in the nearby hamlet of Gronant.

What was to turn into tragedy began as delight, joy in each other's company when Chris and Val first got to know one another in the summer of 1960. It did not take Val long to decide that the romantic young man from Liverpool was Mr Right for her. That July she took him proudly home to meet her parents.

Mr and Mrs Isaac Sellers found the pale, red-headed young Liverpudlian presentable and likeable enough, but they could not see much future in the relationship the way the couple's finances were. Nevertheless, not wishing to upset Valerie, when she sought their permission to marry Chris, her father gave her a qualified 'yes'. What occasioned his hesitation was his failure to see how the pair could possibly hope to set up house together on such low wages and with the slender resources they possessed.

Nothing discouraged, fully animated with the optimism of youth, the impecunious young couple carried on courting, toing and froing between their respective parents' houses in Liverpool and North Wales. Although far from wanting to precipitate things, nudge the youngsters into a rash marriage, by the time Christmas came, Isaac Sellers could not help feeling that it was a bit odd that Chris and Val were showing no signs of making any practical plans. He decided, however, to say nothing. Bide his time.

The first months of 1961 slipped by. Still no sign of any movement in the active sphere of matrimonial preparation. Isaac's misgivings returned to surface with even greater force. But Val seemed happy. The last thing that he wanted was to upset her. So he bit his lip and kept mum. In the end, though, he simply could not help himself. He had to speak out.

It was summer again. Almost a year had gone by. On Sunday 30 July, when Chris was spending the weekend with them, Mr Sellers raised the awkward issue. And yes, yes, they chorused, *of course* they still wanted to get married. And yes again, it was only the problem of money that was stopping them.

Taking Chris to one side, Mr Sellers had a quiet word with him, and, in response to his rather anxious questioning, Chris was bound to come out in the open and agree that there really was very little prospect of his being able to support a wife in the foreseeable future.

Obviously thoroughly put out by that piece of home truth talking, Chris and Val had gone upstairs to her room, and Mr Sellers had heard Chris shouting angrily to his daughter, "I'll never marry you!"

She and Chris had been planning to have a night out in Rhyl, but that flew out of the window, and a bitterly weeping Valerie came rushing downstairs to tell her father what Chris had said. And Isaac Sellers told her: "It's probably all for the best." With exemplary tolerance, Mr Sellers told Chris McMenemy that he could stay the night. With placatory intent, no doubt, Chris told him that he was starting work at Mostyn Ironworks in the morning. He then betook himself off to bed. The following morning Mr Sellers gave him half-a-crown for his bus fare, and he left.

Nothing more was heard of him for the best part of a fortnight. Then, suddenly and unexpectedly, at ten o'clock on the evening of 12 August he knocked at the Sellers' door. He was received coldly. He said that he had come to repay Mr Sellers the three pounds and ten shillings that he owed him, and was about to launch into an account of how he was getting on at the ironworks, when he was told that he was no longer welcome in the house, was asked to leave, and told not to call again. After McMenemy had departed, Mr Sellers told his daughter, who had been upstairs in her room throughout, who it was that had called. He also said that he would wake her at 5.30 next morning to go to work in Rhyl.

But when he went in to give her that early call on 13 August, he found her bed empty, and no sign of her anywhere in the house. It was not hard to guess that she had gone off to join McMenemy. Indeed she had, and the pair of them were living rough, wandering about the rural outskirts of Liverpool, sleeping in the barns and outhouses of farms.

On Friday morning – 18 August – they were walking along the Liverpool-Warrington Road. It was at half-past eleven, when they were about eight miles from Warrington, that a car stopped, picked them up, and the driver, a Mr Edward O'Sullivan, took them to a transport café near Warrington.

Over welcome cups of tea and a bit of a snack, O'Sullivan said that he would drive them up to Glasgow. They arrived there the following afternoon. It was while they were in Glasgow that McMenemy produced a sheath knife, which he carefully and secretively salted away under the dashboard of O'Sullivan's car. After spending only four hours in Glasgow the trio drove back to Liverpool, where O'Sullivan dropped them off. The sight of McMenemy quite openly retrieving his sheath knife from its hiding place, not unnaturally, gave O'Sullivan alarmed pause, and he decided that in the circumstances he was not sorry to see the backs of his late travelling companions.

The next recorded sighting of the lovers is at around 1.40am on Sunday 20 August, when two patrolling policemen saw a couple walking up Bixteth Street towards the Stadium. They had their arms around one another and the woman seemed to be distressed.

It was shortly after this that the lovers had a tiff that rapidly turned into a lethal quarrel. A stupid row over money. A fight for a very different sort of purse from the kind usually on offer at the Liverpool Stadium. It had less than three pounds 'prize money' in it. A fight that rapidly escalated out of all proportion, and ended in death.

The trouble started when Chris demanded some money from Val to buy rum with, and she wouldn't give it to him.

"You can have your own [money], but you're not having mine," she told him.

But he was determined.

"I *am* having it," he said, and grabbed her purse.

She grabbed it back.

McMenemy, who had been trimming a match with his sheath knife, told Val that if she didn't give him the purse he'd stick the knife in her. The girl continued to defy him, hung on to her purse, and quick as a flash McMenemy plunged his knife into her stomach and seized the purse. She caught hold of his hand. The hand holding the knife. They were standing at the top of a flight of stone steps leading up to a side entrance to the Stadium. They struggled, and fell together, still struggling, down the steps. Val was desperately calling out his name, and, in a state of frenzy, he stabbed her again and again, until she lay still. Then, he took off his tie and wound it round her throat, before covering her head and body with her macintosh.

Leaving her there where he had laid her, Chris McMenemy walked smartly off into the night.

He made his way down to the Pier Head and went to the coffee stall there, where he used the money in Val's purse to buy cigarettes and a succession of cups of coffee. Realising with horror that he was now a murderer, McMenemy thought at first of making a run for it, but he knew that it would be hopeless, he would be caught anyway. He walked round and round, frantically thinking what to do, and finally came to a decision. At precisely 3.48am, he stepped into a telephone box and dialled 100.

An operator at Liverpool Central GPO exchange answered the call.

"What number do you require?" he asked.

The man on the line told him that he wanted him to take a message:

"There's a body by the steps behind the Stadium."

"Where are you speaking from?" asked the operator, but the caller hung up without another word.

The telephone operator contacted the police. The Post Office went into immediate action, and traced the location of the box from which the call had been made.

Meanwhile, despatched by a radio message, Constables Smith and Walton sped in their Land Rover to the scene where the body was alleged to be. It had been no hoax call. There lay the heavily bloodstained corpse of Valerie Sellers, the raincoat draped over her legs. On the ground beside her was a man's tie.

It was now just after 4am.

McMenemy was still hanging about near the Pier Head coffee stall when Smith, Walton, and another police officer arrived there. As they approached, him, they instantly spotted that he was not wearing a tie. They noticed, too, a curious reddish coloured staining on his right hand, and a bloodstain on the cuff of his right sleeve. Constable Smith told him that they were making enquiries into the very recent murder of a young woman, and asked him to account for his movements during the past hour.

"I've been walking about," said McMenemy.

As he was being conducted round behind the coffee stall for further questioning, he suddenly blurted out:

> She was my girlfriend. I stabbed her once and she
> groaned, so I kept on to put her out of her misery. It's in
> my back; in my waistband.

'It' was the sheath knife. The murder weapon. One of the policemen withdrew it from where it was positioned at the base of McMenemy's spine.

Constable Smith, having cautioned McMenemy, arrested him, and he was whisked off to the bridewell in Dale Street. There, he was interviewed at length by Detective Inspector Wade. Searched, he was found to have several of Valerie's belongings in his pockets – a bracelet engraved with the words 'Chris and Val', a cigarette case, and her purse, which was empty. He explained:

> When I knew I was getting picked up I didn't want to
> have any of her money on me, so I threw a note and some
> silver into the Mersey.

Making a full confession, he told Inspector Wade:

It's my fault. I want everyone to know what happened.
First, I didn't mean to kill her, I only meant to hurt her,
but when she started gurgling, I decided to finish her off.

On 24 August, Mr Sellers was taken to the Liverpool City Mortuary, where he had to undergo the harrowing experience of identifying the body as that of his daughter.

John Christopher McMenemy came up for trial before Lord Chief Justice Parker at Liverpool Crown Court on 1 November 1961, charged with murder in the furtherance of theft, which was then a capital offence, so that he stood in danger of being hanged if found guilty. Even so, he offered no defence. Mr JS Watson, QC appeared on his behalf. Counsel for the prosecution was Mr David Carpmael, QC.

Opening for the Crown, Counsel described the discovery of Valerie Sellers' body, and disclosed the fact that she had been two months pregnant at the time of her death. He went on to outline the couple's aimless wanderings about the Lancashire and Cheshire countryside, after she had fled from home; their days of rough living and nights of rough sleeping. He told of McMenemy's confession to the police.

Isaac Sellers went into the witness-box to speak of his daughter's relationship with McMenemy. Asked if he knew what she was doing after she left home, he replied: "We did not even know where she was." He had, in fact, feared that the couple had gone off to Scotland, where the law allowed anyone over the age of 16 to marry without their parents' consent.

Dr Charles Arthur St Hill, the pathologist who had carried out the post-mortem on Valerie Steers, gave the cause of death as multiple stab wounds. He testified to having found twelve stab wounds in the centre of her chest, one in the right side of her chest, and a five-and-a-half-inch-deep stab wound in her stomach. Four of her ribs had been severed. Great force, he opined, would have been needed to inflict some of her injuries.

McMenemy elected not to go into the witness-box, neither did he call any witnesses in his defence. He chose rather to rely upon his counsel's speech in mitigation.

Mr Watson challenged the prosecution's contention that Valerie had been stabbed in the furtherance of theft and asked the jury:

Are you really satisfied that that was so? Because you
have to be convinced of that before you convict this man
of capital murder. He may have taken some of her
property, but these two people were in love. They
wanted to marry each other. Persons in love regard each
other's property as their own.

The judge seemed to be summing up in favour of the accused:

> The prisoner and the girl were loving friends. They intended to get married. Apart from one quarrel of which we have heard, they remained a loving couple.

But the jury were unimpressed. Doubtless they were appalled by the savagery of the attack. They found McMenemy guilty as charged, pointedly making no recommendation to mercy, and he was duly sentenced to death.

He fared no better at the Appeal Court. His appeal was heard on 17 November 1961. Mr Watson asked the Court to substitute a verdict of manslaughter on grounds of diminished responsibility. He contended that evidence on that score had been available at the time of the original trial. McMenemy had, however, despite the pleas of his family and the strong recommendation of his legal advisers, refused to allow it to be heard. This conduct was surely, said Counsel, indicative of mental abnormality.

Their Lordships disagreed. Dismissing the appeal, Mr Justice Ashworth said that they could hear only new evidence. In this case the evidence had been previously available. It could not be regarded as new. McMenemy could not now be allowed to submit it. He had only himself to blame for his present predicament. But, Mr Justice Ashworth added, any misgivings that the Appeal Court might have were set at rest by the fact that McMenemy's mental responsibility would be carefully examined in other quarters.

And so indeed it turned out. Doctors appointed by the Home Office found that he was not fully responsible for his actions, and he was reprieved.

After serving 12 years, John Christopher McMenemy was released in 1973.

THE STRANGLING TEDDY BEAR

"Oh, Teddy Bear," the widow murmured reproachfully, "I am dying. You must always take care of your Boofie."

She smiled up at the young charmer who had just strangled her. And expired. The cup of tea she had brought him minutes before sat, untasted and going cold, on the table.

Now it was Boofie's turn. He had to take care of her. He selected a knife from the sideboard. There was always the pyjama-cord in his pocket – just in case. As he slipped silently up the stairs of the little house in Liverpool's Northbrook Street, church bells, outside, were ringing, chiming for the Sabbath: inside, they were booming in his ears, calling him to a second act of murder.

Softly he turned the handle of Boofie's bedroom door, and saw that she was dressing for church. He put his hands on her shoulders, looked straight into her face, and said flatly: "You know how much I love you. That's why I am going to do this."

He seized the girl by the throat. She struggled free and screamed for her mother.

"You needn't call for your mother," he said, "I've already killed her."

The tragedy of which this was the awful climax had started six months before, early in 1928 …

It was one of those pouring wet days that every son and daughter of Liverpool knows so well. A ceaseless deluge. Coming down moggies and doggies, as if a gigantic hand had up-ended the Mersey and swamped the city.

Mary Agnes Fontaine, typist, aged 19, stood sheltering and shivering in a shop doorway. A pretty girl, rather frail looking, like a piece of porcelain, but below the frailty was a coolness, a resourcefulness, which was to save her quarter-spent life one nightmare Sunday in the following November.

At first she blushed and ignored the young man who dashed under the dripping eaves into the dry haven of the doorway beside her. They were alone, and she was embarrassed by his presence. He was like a drowned rat, or a sleek water vole.

If only she had left him there shivering in the cold. Instead she took him into her home and her heart – and he devoured everything there within. It was like harbouring a stray puppy that grew into a wolf.

The young man, Joseph Reginald Victor Clarke, alias Reginald Kennedy, was decidedly not shy. He could never resist an opportunity of ingratiating himself with a pretty girl, and long before the fury of the rain had abated he had introduced himself in the name of Kennedy. By no stretch of the imagination could he be described as handsome with his slight build, clean-cut features, fair hair slicked back, and horn-rimmed spectacles. He soon confided that he was a wireless operator on one of the Atlantic liners plying regularly between Liverpool and New York. This was not quite accurate, but the seed of glamour was sown, and one thing followed another in time-honoured fashion.

Mary lived alone with her 47-year-old, widowed mother, Mrs Alice Fontaine, at 110 Northbrook Street, Princes Park – oddly enough, almost opposite the house from which Victor Grayson, the vanishing MP, had disappeared almost a decade before. Life was somewhat bare for the two women, and they were only too willing to accept this well-spoken, lonely orphan of 21 into their home. He infiltrated their cosy cocoon like a deadly virus.

He came first for tea; then – it would have been about the June – he moved in as a paying guest, or rather as an *unpaying* guest, since it was soon Mary and her widowed mother who were not only doing all the paying out – he never paid a single penny towards his keep – but were also continually lending him sums of money which he never repaid. He finally achieved undisputed security of tenure as a suitor, when he and Mary became officially engaged. There would – or so the duped Fontaines believed – have undoubtedly been a wedding, if, that is, the gallant fiancé had not been careless with an ardent letter from a former flame, who clearly believed that the fire was still burning brightly. It was Mrs Fontaine who found it.

The Fontaines should have shown him the door then. For their 'Teddy Bear', as they pet-named him, was really a grizzly bear of the most ferocious and evil *mien*.

'The boy with the hundred sweethearts', as the newspapers were later to call him, was in fact a highly experienced Don Juan. He lived by his wits, or other people's lack of them, and had made a career of sponging off vulnerable women. Like the mistletoe, that parasite of love, he clung and he sucked until his host was dry and empty. His laser-hard, unblinking gaze turned young girls, and older women too, to jelly. "Somehow I could not resist him, and would do anything he suggested," one victim confessed later. "I used to find myself feeling tired and sleepy when he looked into my eyes."

This sounds as if he had hypnotic powers – and that is exactly what he wanted people to think. Hypnotism was still a novelty, strange and exciting, in 1928. Amateur hypnotists abounded and party tricks were the fashion.

But Reginald Clarke had a head start over those who picked it up, like Pelmanism, from a pamphlet. He had learnt it scientifically in a psychology laboratory at Princeton University, in America, where he had acted as a volunteer subject. Do not, though, imagine that he was a student there. He was a pantry-boy. For Joseph Reginald Victor Clarke was a fraud from start

23

to finish. Nor was he an orphan. He simply used the ploy as a sympathy-seeking ruse to ensnare his victims.

Like Münchhausen or Louis de Rougemont, he spun many yarns of adventure in steaming jungles and coconut islands, but the truth was that he was born in King's Lynn, Norfolk. His parents separated, and he was brought up by a female relative. When he was 16, she died, and he sailed to rejoin his mother in Virginia. His stint in the cool pantries of Princeton provided the needed exotic polish. He migrated to Halifax, Nova Scotia, and went too far with the daughter of a rich businessman there. Pursued by threats from her enraged father, in 1927 he worked his passage back to England – as a pantry-boy.

He scarcely had to leave the dockside at Southampton before entrapping a young girl shop assistant, who fell for his charms and chat line. Not only did she dole out money to him, but she also provided him with a becoming wardrobe out of her meagre savings. "Only the best is good enough when I am with you," he told her. Thus immaculately attired, he fed his new bevy of admirers with the old romantic lie that he was the 'sparks' on one of the big Atlantic greyhound liners.

Inevitably, it was not long before he managed to blot his copy-book yet again. Things became a little too hot for him, and, deserting his young benefactress, he migrated to Liverpool, whither his thoroughly starry-eyed Southampton admirer went on sending him money, her heart wrung, no doubt, by his puling letters:

> *Oh girl! Can you imagine wearing the same underclothes for six weeks with never a change? Of not having a bath for three weeks? Or sleeping in a nook of the wall of a warehouse with a sack for mattress, sheets, blankets and counterpane?*

Clarke knew how to write with a fine rhetorical flourish and his pleadings always had the desired effect.

The tale of his ripest conquest in the new northern territory of Merseyside reads like a story straight out of the pages of *Decameron Nights*. He wooed four sisters at once, and such was his amatory skill and cunning that, incredibly, none of the girls suspected what was going on. Each thought that he was hers alone. He stole some of their mother's jewellery, including a valuable ring, which he gave as a present to the youngest girl, who was his favourite, and produced the purloined birth certificate of her 22-year-old sister when giving notice to marry the 17-year-old at the Birkenhead Registrar's Office.

His malfeasances discovered, he attempted to strangle the girls' mother, and was forthwith banished from his Mormonic Garden of Eden. Whereupon he waylaid his favourite betrothed in the street.

"If I can't have you nobody else shall," he informed the shrinking girl, as he pulled a pyjama-cord from his pocket like a snake, and tightened it around her neck. But the rabbit broke free from the stoat and ran off screaming, "Police!"

The family, anxious to avoid unpleasant publicity, promised not to press charges against him providing that he made no further attempt to contact them, and he moved on.

If only he had been stowed away safely then.

It was Mrs Fontaine's chance discovery of the letter from Teddy Bear's old sweetheart in Nova Scotia that shipwrecked his new idyll with the family in Northbrook Street. Outraged, his benefactors ordered him to leave at once. But he refused to sling his hook. He lurked sullenly upstairs and whiled away the time in his lair composing obscene anonymous letters to the Fontaines, mother and daughter.

Uncuddly Teddy Bear had turned savage.

Mary and Alice Fontaine went to the police. Detective Sergeant Tomlin, having prosecuted 'certain enquiries', felt it his duty to warn them that their sitting lodger was notorious for 'other girls' and 'other things'. Meanwhile, a paranoid notion was growing fast, like a tiny cactus seed into a prickly plant, in Clarke's beleaguered head. It was that Tomlin fancied his girl, his very own Mary, for himself. If only the detective had been in a position then to eject this ticking bomb, lock, stock and barrel, on to the street. But he was not. And Teddy Bear stayed on, growling and licking his wounds.

The Fontaines, *mère et fille*, tried everything they could to reform him. They nagged. They cajoled. They preached. Oh, how they preached!

It was the mother that he sprang at first that Sunday, 4 November, morning as her voice, mingling with the clamour of the iron-tongued church bells, yammered on at him – Get a job. Pay your debts. Face up to your responsibilities. Improve. It did not take much resolution to respond to this demeaning tirade. He choked Mrs Fontaine to death in one minute flat. It turned out that her lungs were weak anyway.

Mary Fontaine was a tougher proposition. Like a Hydra with many heads, she fought back, defying this bloodied bear. He continued producing more and more weapons. He used his powerful thumbs … a pyjama-cord … some electric light flex. He seized her by the hair and repeatedly banged her head on the floor. She kept passing out. Imagine the horror of coming to and finding someone still trying to kill you. Once, he seemed to repent, and revived her. But she screamed again. She would keep screaming. He cut her throat. There was silence – except for the gonging church bells outside, or in his head, he did not know which.

Then, suddenly, she was alive again, and this was probably her last chance of survival. For the moment he was exhausted. She thought hard: it had to be the right approach or it would all be over. She caught his hand and said quietly: "Let us sit on the bed, Teddy Bear. You know I love you. Why have you done all this?"

"I thought you meant to give me up."

"How can you think that?" she said, trying to keep her voice even. "I love you still. Let us go and see Mother."

"For God's sake, don't go now," he begged her.

"You must, Teddy Bear, and tell her you are sorry."

Very, very gently she inched out of the room. He shambled after her. She forced herself to go slowly down the stairs. The front-door came nearer and nearer. She ran at it. It opened. And she was out in the street, with people and the air full of bells. She was screaming and covered in blood, and they had to cut a cord from her neck.

When the police arrived, Clarke was calmly combing his hair in front of a mirror in an upstairs room. He made no attempt to escape. Nor did he defend himself at Liverpool Assizes, on 4 February 1929. He refused to plead insanity, pleaded guilty to murder and attempted murder, and was sentenced to death by Mr Justice Finlay. It was as if the violence of his crimes had sapped all his energy and with it his compulsion to deceive.

"Thank you, my Lord," he rapped curtly.

All who watched were struck by the coolness of his demeanour and his hypnotic gaze. His trial had lasted four and a half minutes.

Later, he wriggled and tried to appeal. He claimed that his full confession was false. His counsel, Basil Nield, sought leave to appeal against conviction. However, the three judges of the Court of Criminal Appeal – Mr Justice Avory, Mr Justice Horridge and Mr Justice Rowlatt – found nothing to justify interference with Clarke's conviction and sentence. In giving judgment, Avory J said that although since Clarke had been under sentence medical evidence had emerged which showed that Mrs Fontaine's lungs had been in a badly diseased condition, and that the prisoner's attack on her had only hastened her natural death, due to asphyxiation by causes beyond Clarke's control, that afforded no answer to the charge, and the application was dismissed.

Clarke made one last bid to save his own life. He decided to make a direct personal appeal to the Home Secretary, Sir William Joynson-Hicks. On the afternoon of 9 March, the news was brought to his cell that his appeal for a reprieve had been carefully considered but no grounds upon which to grant it had been discovered.

Joseph Reginald Victor Clarke was accordingly hanged at Walton Gaol on 12 March 1929. A crowd of some 200 people had gathered outside the prison gates, and most of those sighing figures that bleak Tuesday morning were young women.

Footman with a Handgun

Ambrose Bierce it was, the American author, who, in 1913, mysteriously vanished off the face of the earth, whose collected works were – quoting from the *Introductory Rubric* in *The Order For The Burial of the Dead*, in *The Book of Common Prayer*, – entitled *In the Midst of Life*.

And nowhere is the implication of that sobering observation – 'In the midst of life we are in death' – better borne out than in the bizarre happenings which took place in the ancestral hall of the Earls of Derby on the night of 9 October 1952.

Four years before, on 22 July 1948, 28-year-old Lady Isabel Milles-Lade, the sister of the 4th Earl Sondes, had married Edward John Stanley, aged 30, who, earlier that year, had succeeded his grandfather as 18th Earl of Derby. The wedding took place in Westminster Abbey, and King George VI, Queen Elizabeth, and the Princesses Elizabeth and Margaret Rose, were present. And afterwards, there had been a glittering reception, with more than a thousand guests, at the Savoy Hotel.

The newly-weds took up residence at Knowsley Hall, the stately mansion standing magnificent in its great park, between Liverpool and St Helens. Crammed with treasures and works of art garnered-in and accumulated here by the Stanleys since the fifteenth century, their seat near the Lancashire village of Knowsley, had always been the place where, traditionally, kings and princes stayed when they visited the north of England.

Now, this October Thursday evening, Lady Derby was sitting alone in the smoke-room there … and death was soon to enter unbidden through the door.

The Earl was away that night, attending as a guest a Territorial Army dinner at nearby Altcar, and his wife was having her evening meal at a small table in front of the television set. The clock had just struck a quarter past eight, when, suddenly, betrayed by just the click of its catch, the smoke-room door slowly began to open. No knock. That was disturbingly unusual. It gave Lady Derby not only quite a start, but also a simultaneous irritation at the intrusion. She was not accustomed to people walking in on her without knocking.

Mild puzzlement escalated rapidly into acute alarm, when her eyes, initially dazzled by the brightness of the television screen, having adjusted themselves sufficiently to the circumambient gloom, she saw the young footman, Harold Winstanley, standing, tall and gaunt, framed in the doorway. From his lip a cigarette dangled insolently, in his hand he was holding a gun, pointing straight at her.

The startled Lady Isabel jumped to her feet.

"What are you doing?" she asked. "What do you want?"

He ignored her questions. All he said was: "Turn round, my lady."

Numbly, she obeyed. An instant later there was an explosion. She felt a violent blow on the back of her neck. It blasted her crashing to the floor. She lay there, beside the television set, feeling the warm blood running out and seeping into the rich pile of the carpet on which she was lying. Some life-preserving instinct, some sixth sense, made her lie there motionless, as one dead. It called for nerve, for rare presence of mind, but it was that brave, prolonged feigning of death that was to save her life.

A terrible silence descended upon the room. Gradually, her ears became attuned to the faint noise of Winstanley's breathing, and she could hear him moving stealthily around. A little while later, her anxiously cocked ear caught the sound of other footsteps entering the room, followed by a voice she recognised as being that of the butler, Walter Stannard, a 40-year-old Yorkshireman. He was asking Winstanley what he was doing in the smoke-room. In answer, he received a short burst of gunfire, and fell dead, thudding on to the carpet close to where, mouse-quiet, her ladyship stretched prone.

Winstanley's restless pacing resumed.

In the midst of life …

Another eternity of stifling stillness passed. Then, from the adjoining room, the library, came voices. It was the under-butler, a 29-year-old Londoner, Douglas Stuart, who, worried by the noise of the unusual commotion, had come hurrying along to see what was the matter. Going first into the library, and finding there Winstanley, who had wandered in from next door, he was asking him, in rapid succession, what all the rumpus was about, where was Lady Derby, and, as the pair came through into the smoke-room, why had he a gun in his hand?

But seeing then with horror the bodies of her ladyship and his fellow-servant, Stallard, the chilling realisation of the nature of the situation came tardily to him, and, playing for time and opportunity, he turned to Winstanley:

"Take it easy, Harry. I'll do anything for you, and I'll not tell anybody what I've seen."

The verbal olive branch availed him nothing. Winstanley advanced grimly towards him. Panic rising from his chest into his throat, Stuart, galvanised, made a great leap over a sofa and crouched behind it. Winstanley tripped off a few shots, then stopped. Stuart, believing that the automatic's mechanism had jammed, made a bound for the library door. He was aware of Winstanley following him. He turned, and cried out a final pitiful appeal:

"My wife … my wife!"

But the gun barked again, the fatal bullets lodged in him, and he collapsed, wounded, dying, against the door through which he had hoped to escape with his life.

Up on the floor above, His Lordship's valet, William Sullivan, busy tidying the place, had also been disturbed by what he recognised as the unmistakable sound of shooting coming from below. He ran out into the corridor, where he was joined by two frightened young housemaids. All three peered warily over the banister, and saw Winstanley emerging, gun in hand, from the smoke-room.

Automatically, without pausing to think about any possible danger, Sullivan went rushing headlong down the stairs to confront Winstanley.

"What's happened? What are you doing with that?" he asked. "What was the noise we heard?"

"I'll tell you when the girls come down," answered Winstanley.

Anne Mitchell, one of the maids, called out to Winstanley: "Why do you want us to come down?"

"I'll tell you when you come down," he said.

The girls shook their heads. They weren't going to be caught like that.

Sullivan did not at all care for the way things were shaping, either. He knew nothing, in fact, of the fate of Lady Derby, Walter Stallard and Douglas Stewart, but having heard the shots and seeing Winstanley's agitated state, decided that discretion can indeed be the better part of valour, and took off as fast as his legs would carry him down the stairs, with Winstanley in hot pursuit and firing from the hip.

Reaching the ground floor, he scorched along the servants' corridor, an iron spray of death-dealing bullets whining and screeching and tearing splinters from the woodwork all about him, and found temporary refuge in a recess beside the lift shaft at the foot of the staircase – but not before one of the bullets had struck him in the hand.

During this phase of the uproar, Lady Derby's personal maid, Elizabeth Doxford, curious to find out the cause of the furore, came out of her room on the second floor. Winstanley was still prowling the servants' corridor, leading off from which was the housekeeper, Mrs Hilda Turley's, room, where she and the assistant-housekeeper, Miss Mary Campbell, had been peaceably watching television. After hearing what Mrs Turley described as a "fearful noise, as if the light bulbs were bursting", the two women had emerged into the perilous corridor just as Winstanley, chasing Sullivan, came hurtling towards them. As Sullivan went to ground in the corner by the lift, Mrs Turley and Miss Campbell ran across to help him. Mrs Turley was bent over the badly bleeding and hysterical man when she felt a sharp, tingling pain in her leg. Another of Winstanley's wild, ricocheting bullets had found its mark.

Winstanley himself approached, his pointing gun menacing the crouched and trembling Sullivan. Brave and cool, Mrs Turley stepped forward, interposed herself between them, laid a gentle hand on the gunman's shoulder and said: "Come on, Harry, what's wrong?" then adding, as surely only an Englishwoman would, "Would you like me to get you a cup of tea?"

Turning to her, Winstanley said: "I won't shoot you, you have been so kind to me."

He turned then to Mary Campbell, nodded towards the shrinking Sullivan.

"Pick him up," he said.

But Miss Campbell, too terrified, just ran helter-skelter off down the corridor, and Sullivan, by dint of a mammoth effort of will, rose to his feet and tottered unmolested after her.

The last person in that feudal stronghold to attempt to divert Winstanley from his fell purpose was the Derbys' French chef, Monsieur Paul Dupuy. He walked along the corridor at Winstanley's side, chatting amiably and comfortingly to him, trying to introduce him to reason, until, yielding to impulse, he made his fatal mistake. He tried, as a tactic of surprise, to wrest the gun from Winstanley's grasp. An ill-judged act which triggered instant reaction. Winstanley lashed out, landing a pulverising blow on the Frenchman's head and releasing a nonuplet of bullets that pocked the wall around him like a circus knife-thrower's pattern of deliberate near-misses.

The time had now come for Winstanley's exit. He left by a side entrance to the Hall, walked with brisk movement and firm intention out of the park by Ormskirk Lodge, went into the Coppull House Inn in Knowsley Village, downed a pint of beer, bought a bottle and a packet of crisps to take away – and took them away, to an old barn he happened to know on a nearby lonely country road.

Brooding in the barn, reviewing the terrible events of the last couple of hours, Winstanley came round to the inescapable realisation that so gross and irreversible had been his conduct and its consequences, that no alternative was left to him other than to give himself up. Having, however, no wish to return to the scene of his engineered disasters, he headed for the main road and caught a late bus into Liverpool.

And there, at precisely 11.42pm, from a telephone box in North John Street, Harold Winstanley put a 999 call through to the Liverpool police, and within minutes a police car had sped round to the call box wherein the man who claimed responsibility for what he called "the Knowsley Hall affair" was still standing. He was arrested, lodged in Walton Gaol, and put up for trial before Mr Justice Jones at Manchester Assizes on 16 December 1952.

Defended by Miss Rose Heilbron, instructed by Mr Rex Makin, Winstanley pleaded not guilty. Called by his counsel, Dr Francis H Brisby, Senior Medical Officer at Walton, testified that, in his view, Winstanley had not been responsible for his actions, being at the time unable to distinguish between right and wrong, or to know the nature and quality of his acts. He was, in Dr Brisby's diagnostic opinion, suffering from "a grave disease of the mind, in the nature of schizophrenia and gross hysteria."

Following the indications of the learned judge's summing-up, the trial jury, without leaving the court-room, found Winstanley guilty but insane, and it was ordered that he should be kept in custody at Broadmoor Special Hospital.

To discover the transaction whereby Winstanley became possessed of the gun with which he wrought so inordinate an amount of damage is of interest. The weapon in question was a Schmeisser 9mm automatic pistol, which was a type of hand gun issued to German paratroopers. On Tuesday 7 October 1952, Winstanley had gone over the water to Hoylake to meet a lad he knew. Well, this lad told Winstanley that he'd managed to get hold of "a smashing Schmeisser", and he was willing to swap it for a leather jacket. They argued and bargained and hummed and hawed, finally agreeing on the platform at Hoylake station to exchange the gun, about 400 rounds of ammunition, and some spare magazines, for £3 and a pair of grey gabardine trousers. The exchange took place the following evening in the toilets at James Street station, in downtown Liverpool.

There is good evidence that Winstanley was very proud of his new acquisition. Answering the front-door bell at Knowsley Hall at about a quarter past nine on the Wednesday (8 October) evening, Winstanley's fellow-footman, Terence Cooke, found Winstanley standing there clutching an expensive bottle of cocktail, which he thrust into Cooke's hand as a present, but Cooke said he did not want it.

A bit later that same evening, Winstanley had asked Cooke if he wanted to see a gun.

"Don't talk daft," Cooke retorted, "you've not got a gun."

"All right," said Winstanley, "I'll go and fetch it."

Which, to Cooke's surprise, he did. He said that he had bought it for £120 from a Pole, and that he would be selling it for double that.

The gun was proudly exhibited, too, to the housemaid, Anne Mitchell, at around five o'clock on the day of the shootings. She was told that he had paid £110 for it, and would be selling it on at a handsome profit.

Everyone was at a total loss to account for Winstanley's homicidal episode. All spoke well of him. He had been a very popular member of the household – "A normally very jolly and good-humoured man," was how Anne Mitchell described him. He was also thought well of by his superiors. Captain McKinney, Lord Derby's comptroller spoke of him as ...

> ... an excellent worker who carried out his duties in a
> very efficient manner. [He] was jolly and he was easy to
> get on with. He was a very willing hard worker.

He was 19 years old when he arrived at Knowsley Hall, in December 1951, as a trainee footman. He came, highly recommended, with a good reference from the Royal Liverpool Golf Club, at Hoylake, where he had worked as a wine steward before his brief military service with the Scots Guards, in which he had enlisted at the age of 17. He had been invalided out within a year, because his physical condition fell well below the promise of his impressive six-foot stature.

Winstanley said that he had been happy at Knowsley Hall. He had been well treated by Lady Derby and all the staff.

"I have had no reason to do anybody any harm," he said.

The sole explanation he could offer for his outrageous outburst was panic. When he first went into the smoke-room he had, he said, intended to ask Lady Derby to help him to get rid of the gun. But ...

> When she looked at me, I was frightened. I said, "Turn round," because I did not want to shoot her while she was looking at me.

The fact of the matter is that none of it makes sense. But there is one, surely significant, clue which emerged when the psychiatrists looked more closely into Harold Winstanley's family's medical records. They found a history of insanity on his mother's side.

Lady Derby recovered from her injuries. She lived on to die a natural death at the age of 70, in 1990.

THE CLUE OF THE THREE WISE MONKEYS

If at Christmastime, that festive season of the year when the pre-lunch sherry tastes sweet – or dry – upon your palate, and the brown and sizzling image of the turkey hovers on the near horizon, I were to invite you to play with me the old word-association game, I would hazard that the word 'sack' would bring to your mind a vision of that cornucopian bag slung traditionally over the broad, red shoulders of that beamingly benevolent, white-whiskered old gentleman, Santa Claus. Or, possibly, if the children are all grown up, and the stamp and patter of tiny feet no longer punctuate the pattern of your Yuletide, the word sack might ally itself in your mind to the word dry – and from this combination would flow the golden stream of a certain, and delectable, variety of sherry.

For myself, however, and no doubt the psychiatrists would draw some very sinister conclusions from this, I have only to hear the word sack and the theatre which lies beneath the vaulted white dome of my skull is instantly set with a very different series of images.

It begins, this grisly charade within my head, in total darkness. Then ... gradually ... out of the blackness grow glow-worm points of flickering light. They shape themselves into gas-lamps, and, in their fitful yellow radiance, I see a long, dark street. Along this street something is moving. It comes more clearly into focus. It is a hand-cart, and pushing it, two shadowy figures. My vision pans in, as the television people say, on to the hand-cart, and I see upon it a sack. There is something about the contours of that sack that shocks me. For a moment or two I am puzzled, then, suddenly ...

But let me begin my winter's night tale at the beginning, for the shades that haunt this Christmastide reverie are no mere marionettes of fantasy. They are the ghosts of flesh and blood, who moved about their nefarious business through the murk of a long-ago December night in Liverpool. Let us turn back the leaves of the calendar. Back through other Christmases. Back beyond the anxious Decembers of the First and Second World Wars. Back to the night of Wednesday 10 December 1913.

It is a night of high wind. A full moon rides among the scudding clouds. A solitary figure is pacing slowly the deserted pavement of Old Hall Street. All around are locked, bolted and shuttered shops and offices. Tall, Dickensian clerks' stools stand forlorn in dark and empty counting-houses. Up and down the aeolian canyon of the wind-loud night street the patient sentinel moves.

He is Walter Musker Eaves, a young ship's steward on shore-leave from the *Empress of Britain*, and he has an appointment to meet his sweetheart, Miss Mary Catherine Shepherd. She is exercising the lady's privilege of being late. He glances at his watch. Half-past seven.

An extra violent gust of wind blusters up from the nearby river, sweeps along the narrow street and, with a clatter, clouts a wooden shutter from the frontage of a shop that Eaves is passing. It strikes him a glancing blow on the head, denting the brand-new bowler he has proudly donned in honour of Miss Shepherd. And, as he stands there ruefully contemplating his damaged headgear, a boy emerges from the shop and picks up the fallen shutter.

"Hey! Just a minute," shouts Eaves. "Your shutter's ruined my new hat."

Quick as a lizard, the boy darts back into the shop. Comes out again seconds later accompanied by a young man in a grey suit. There is some conversation between Eaves and the young man in the grey suit. A reiterated complaint. An apology. Some talk of compensation. A florin is pressed into Eaves' hand. A cordial "Goodnight". The boy and the young man step back into the shop.

Eaves resumes his pacing. Presently he sees the shop-boy walking up the street, pushing a hand-cart. He is followed, several yards behind, by the young man in the grey suit. They disappear in the direction of the Lock Fields – and the Leeds and Liverpool Canal.

In the year 1913, the shop premises at 86 Old Hall Street was occupied by a Mr John Copeland Bradfield, a tarpaulin manufacturer, who also owned a factory in nearby Great Howard Street. Bradfield himself spent the greater part of his time at the works. The shop was managed for him by his 40-year-old spinster sister, Christina Catherine Bradfield.

Miss Bradfield exercised a sensible no-nonsense dominion over a staff of three: Miss Margaret Venables, a typist; George Sumner, a 22-year-old assistant-cum-packer; and an 18-year-old lad rejoicing in the somewhat ornamental name of Samuel Angeles Elltoft.

When I met her, fifty-eight Decembers on, Miss Venables was an old lady of 79. As I sat with her and her husband in the bright living-room of their house in Maghull discussing the strange events of all those years ago, she told me that, although she was not exactly a tartar, Miss Bradfield was certainly a severely conscientious woman, on the prim side (as befitted a Sunday School teacher), dedicated to her brother's interests, and scrupulous in seeing to it that her tiny staff worked as hard and as honestly as she did.

The hours of business were from half-past eight to six o'clock, and Miss Bradfield was always the first to arrive and the last to leave. It was, said Miss Venables, about ten minutes past six on the evening of 10 December 1913, when, amidst the clutter of rope and twine and piles of horse-cloths and sacks, she put on her hat, coat, and mittens. She was in a hurry as she had a train to catch. She left behind Miss Bradfield, who was busy counting the day's takings, Sumner, who was sweeping the floor, and young Elltoft, who was putting up the shutters.

What was about to be done behind those shutters in that dimly lit shop after Miss Venables had gone safely home, was sheer *Grand Guignol*.

Had Miss Bradfield, one cannot help wondering, any inkling, any fleeting clue, as she sat there beneath the gas-jet, ranging the sovereigns, the half-sovereigns, the silver and copper in neat piles, of the awful thing that hovered in the air of that dusty, old-fashioned shop? Did she, perhaps, glancing up as she shovelled the money – seven pounds and one penny – into the little leather satchel which it was her custom to take home with her each night to her lodgings over the water in Tranmere, see the glittering eye of George Sumner fixed upon her?

Or was it, when he pounced, a total and terrifying surprise?

Imagine, if you can bear to, the split-second of horror, the unspeakable terror, that must have gripped her as she saw that young man, over whom she had ruled with kindly severity for four years eight months, change without warning into a different, an utterly menacing, creature. It was as if the docile shop-cat had, by some nightmare magic, been transformed into a ravening tiger. The sudden and terrible unfamiliarity of the familiar must have nearly stopped her heart.

With ferocious bestiality, this 'quiet' young man fell upon her. He clawed the clothes from her back, humiliated her, assaulted her, and, in a frenzy that surely slipped temporarily over the border of sanity, beat her to death with a rope-splicing fid.

It was only when the prim Miss Bradfield, half-nude, trussed up like an obscene, plucked chicken, had been reduced to a bloodied pulp that he finally came to his senses – and found himself standing athwart a corpse.

And where was young Elltoft while all this was happening? We do not know for sure. Nor do we know precisely how the labours of disposal – the cleaning-up, the packaging – were apportioned between the man, Sumner, and the boy, Elltoft. All that we do know, is that the roped and doubled-up body was sewn into a sack (Elltoft was a dab hand with a needle), laid upon the improvised hearse of a hand-cart, and trundled half or three-quarters of a mile through smiling moonlight and wind-rinsed streets.

Up Old Hall Street … turn right into Leeds Street … left into Pall Mall. Past lifeless warehouses, depots and manufactories. Not another living soul. Not a single moving vehicle. The universe empty – save for themselves, their dead-weight burden of meat, and a solitary starveling black cat streaking, startled by the rumble of their approach, under a railway arch.

Pall Mall narrows and becomes Love Lane – 'Sugar Land', dominated and overshadowed by the towering bulk of Tate & Lyle's. Then, Love Lane leads, straight as a die, to where, in 1913, the Lock Fields began. And across the clinging clay of this stark and rubble-strewn stretch of industrial no-man's-land they bore the body of Miss Bradfield. There stand the locks. White-painted. Heavy brown timber gates. Slabbed stone basins filled with dark and brooding water.

The moonlight boys tumble the corpse in its sackcloth shroud into the cold, wet grave of the Leeds and Liverpool Canal.

At five minutes to nine the following morning, when Miss Venables arrived, bright and neat, at the shop, she found Sumner and Elltoft already there, busily sweeping. But – unprecedented occurrence – of Miss Bradfield, the early bird manageress, there was no sign. She later told me:

> When Miss Bradfield didn't come in that Thursday morning, I never in my wildest dreams thought that she had been murdered. And I certainly didn't think that the boys had anything to do with her disappearance. I always liked George Sumner. He was a good-looking, polite, cheerful young man, and very keen on music. He used to lend me gramophone records. I found it hard to believe he was a murderer. Young Sammy Elltoft was a good boy, too. Very much under George's thumb, though. They were both so calm and collected that morning Miss Bradfield was missing, you'd never have guessed they were involved.

There was still no sign of her when, around eleven o'clock, Mr Bradfield came into the shop in Old Hall Street. And to make matters even more mysterious, her landlady, Miss Holden, had telephoned from Tranmere. Miss Bradfield had not come home last night. Was she all right?

Hearing this, Mr Bradfield thought that she might have gone to stay with her married sister, who lived in Wavertree. He made enquiries. No, she had not seen Christina. Worried now, he got in touch with the police.

Meanwhile, shortly after midday, Francis Robinson, master of the barge, *William*, was on the verge of picking the key to the mystery from the lock – Number 3 Lock of the Leeds and Liverpool Canal.

Arriving at the eastern end of Number 3 Lock, he found himself experiencing unusual difficulty in opening the gates. He put his boat-hook down to investigate, deftly snared the obstruction and drew it up – a large waterlogged bundle. Then, turned pale. Protruding from the dark and dripping sack was a black-stockinged leg. And when the sack had been slit open, and the body which it enshrouded fully revealed, there, suspended, like an identity disk, by a thin silver chain around the neck of the female corpse was … the Clue of the Three Wise Monkeys.

Later that day, Mr Bradfield and Miss Holden went along and identified the body at the Prince's Dock Mortuary. Among other things, there could be no mistaking the silver medallion on the chain. It was a Japanese charm. The Three Wise Monkeys:

Swazaru who speaks no evil;
Mizaru who sees no evil;
Kikazaru who hears no evil.

Christina Bradfield had always worn that lucky charm.

That night, or rather at half-past one on the morning of Friday 12 December, the Liverpool police arrested young Elltoft. They found him sleeping peacefully in bed at his parents' house in Windermere Street, Anfield. They went also to Sumner's lodgings, in Boundary Lane, West Derby. But that young gentleman had already flown.

Throughout the next eight days the greatest manhunt that had ever been seen on Merseyside was mounted. Christmas was still a week or so away, but distinctly gathering its festive shape out of the murk of the December dusk. In the bright-lit streets and shops townsfolk were packing their shopping bags and baskets with gaily-papered parcels.

But while the people of Liverpool went merrily about their seasonal preparations, anxious policemen, with no time and little inclination for festal frivolities, went grimly about their vital search for the man they believed to be the killer. They combed the gigantic warehouses around the docks, the seamen's boarding-houses, the seedy Sailortown pubs and cafés. On the Saturday, squads of detectives mingled with the Christmas shoppers and the crowds at local football matches, for George Sumner was known to be mad about football. His photograph was projected on to the screens of the city's 'electric picture palaces'.

Rumour, that lying jade, had it that he had stowed away on the *Majestic*, bound for New York. The liner was searched at Queenstown, and, yet one more coincidence was uncovered in this chance-riven saga, a steward was discovered aboard whose name happened to be George Sumner.

Spurred on by the offer of £50 reward, Liverpool became a city of peeled eyes and bounty-hunting amateur detectives. But of Sumner – or Ball, as the police had now discovered his real name to be – there was absolutely no trace.

Christmas was only five days away now when, pure chance again, Ball (as we must now call him) was run to earth. It was an old schoolfellow who eventually spotted him in the street. Ball was disguised. He had shaved his thick eyebrows, bought himself a pink eye-patch and a pair of cheap spectacles. But his friend knew George's distinctive shuffling gait. He followed him and saw him go into the Mersey Lodging House Company's establishment at 84 St James' Street, where, it transpired, he had been staying for a week. Then George's friend told a policeman.

In the lodging-house hall, just before midnight on Saturday 20 December, his 23rd birthday, George Ball, alias Sumner, was arrested. His first question to the constable who took him in charge was as to the result of that day's big football match. *Plus ça change!*

The trial of Ball and Elltoft took place in St George's Hall, and opened on 2 February 1914. The prosecution was led by Mr Gordon Hewart, KC, who, in 1922, was to become Lord Chief Justice of England. Ball was defended by Mr Alfred Tobin, KC, who, four years before, had defended Crippen. Elltoft was represented by Mr Lindon Riley.

Ball's defence was a complicated cock-and-bull story about a man with a dark-brown moustache who had suddenly materialised in the shop and held him at gun-point while he clubbed Miss Bradfield to death, then snatched her money-satchel before running off into the night. Left with a corpse on their hands, he and Elltoft had panicked: they had decided that the only thing to do was to get rid of the body.

But when Elltoft went into the witness-box he put paid to any faint chance that Ball might have had. The latter's story simply fell apart. It was a case of hanging together – or being hanged one by one! Elltoft testified:

> I was just leaving the shop at about seven or seven-fifteen, when George said, "Stand outside. I won't be long." I waited a quarter of an hour on the corner of Virginia Street. Then I went back to the shop. George came to the door. Just then a shutter fell. I put it back. Then George appeared with a hand-cart. I asked him what was in it, and he said a bag of rubbish. I wheeled it to the canal, and George dumped it. When I heard next morning of the disappearance of Miss Bradfield, I had not the slightest idea that anything was wrong.

The jury did not, however, have to rely upon these discrepancies alone. By any common-sense yardstick the evidence against Ball was overwhelming. Accordingly, they brought in a verdict of guilty.

So far as Elltoft was concerned, they felt that there was some measure of doubt – a doubt of which they decided to give him the benefit. He was found guilty of being an accessory after the fact, with the rider of a strong recommendation to mercy, and was sentenced to four years' penal servitude.

While George Ball was waiting at Walton to be hanged, he made a full and frank confession of his guilt.

One of the things that weighted the balance in Elltoft's favour was the fact that not a shred of evidence could be adduced to show that he had in any way profited from the death of Miss Bradfield. However, a detective subsequently examining Elltoft's bedroom had a sudden hunch. He unscrewed one of the brass knobs on the boy's bed, and there, nestling inside it, glinted two and a half gold sovereigns. The price of his co-operation? Had the jury known about the cache, things might have gone very differently for young Sammy Elltoft.

It was pure chance that the money was discovered at all.

Indeed, so much in this extraordinary case boiled down to the workings of chance.

It was pure chance that that shutter blew down when it did, and fell on Walter Eaves' new hat. If it had not, Eaves very likely would not have noticed, and been able to identify beyond any reasonable doubt, the pair who pushed the hand-cart with its macabre load, to the Lock Fields that night. And his evidence is vital.

It was pure chance that Christina Catherine Bradfield's body fouled the lock-gates and lay there awaiting discovery, instead of being swept out by the swirl of the waters into the Mersey, as Ball had calculated.

But chance is a two-edged sword. While it saved the life of Samuel Angeles Elltoft, George Ball justly perished beneath its avenging blade.

Sammy Elltoft has been dead these many years now, but it is a safe bet that every Christmas of his life thereafter he must surely have remembered that long, long ago Yuletide, when, but for his youth and a prodigal gift of luck, he might well himself have ended up decorating not the Christmas, but the fatal gallows, tree.

And What About Liverpool Jack?

In August 1993, Stewart Evans, one of the world's leading authorities on the Jack the Ripper murders mystery, paid me both a visit and a compliment. At a time when it was top secret, he confided to me his completely new evidence as to the possible identity of one who was, without question, a prime contender for the bloodstained laurels of that Victorian bogeyman, the Whitechapel murderer, who passed by the nom de meurtre of Jack the Ripper. I can still recall walking up the zigzag path to bosky St Ann's Well, with its perpetually bubbling fountain of crystal-clear Malvern water, while he unfolded his startling discovery. He knew then that it was going to be big, and indeed it was.

Back in my study, he also laid before me for my inspection his newly-acquired treasure – a letter written, on 3 September 1913 by former Detective Chief Inspector John George Littlechild, who was at the time of the Ripper murders head of the Special Branch at Scotland Yard, to the celebrated journalist, George R Sims, author, incidentally, of that famous sentimental Victorian ballad, *It is Christmas Day in the Workhouse*. In that letter, Inspector Littlechild names a man whom he describes as 'a very likely' suspect. And that man had very strong Liverpool connections.

The first association of Jack the Ripper with Liverpool can be traced back to 1927 – thirty-nine years after the East End crimes – when a London journalist, J Hall Richardson, who covered the Whitechapel murders for the *Daily Telegraph*, published his autobiographical volume, *From the City to Fleet Street*. It is here that we can find the following:

> The Police and Press received many letters from the 'Ripper', mostly written in red ink, and I give one:
>
> *Liverpool*
> *29th inst.*
>
> *BEWARE I shall be at work on the 1st and 2nd*
> *inst. in "Minories" at 12 midnight and I give the*
> *authorities a good chance but there is never a*
> *Policeman near when I am at work.*
>
> *Yours,*
> *Jack the Ripper*
> *Prince William St., L'pool.*

What fools the police are I even give them the name
of the street where I am living.

Yours,
Jack the Ripper

Prince William Street, by the way, still exists. It escaped the bombs of the Second World War in the Great May Blitz of 1940, and stands, very little changed, running between Hill Street and Warwick Street, in Liverpool 8.

We next come upon reference to this letter in *The Identity of Jack the Ripper*, by Donald McCormick, published thirty-two years later, in 1959, when McCormick refers to what Richardson described as *one* letter ('and I give one') as *two* letters from Liverpool. He also dates that which he identifies as the first letter as having been written on 29 September – the month being gratuitously substituted for the abbreviation 'inst'.

In Stewart Evans and Keith Skinner's definitive volume, *Jack the Ripper: Letters From Hell*, Evans, who has examined and recorded every one of the 210 letters and postcards 'which purport to have come from the murderer' in the Metropolitan Police files, and the 'substantially fewer in the preserved City of London Police letters file', states that the original Liverpool letter, or letters, cannot be traced. He adds:

> The only mention of this Liverpool correspondence prior to McCormick was by J Hall Richardson. The inevitable conclusion is that McCormick *must* have used Richardson as the source for the Liverpool letter(s).

McCormick further complicates the matter by his assertion that 'Dr Dutton … confirms that the Liverpool letters were in his [the Ripper's] hand.' For the said Dr Dutton and his 'lost' diaries constitute a very dubious factor in the whole equation! This Dr Thomas Dutton, of Westbourne Villas, Bayswater, is claimed by McCormick to have …

> …compiled over a period of sixty years three volumes of handwritten *Chronicles of Crime*, based on his experience as a doctor. Prior to the East End murders he had been a leading figure in the Chichester and West Sussex Microscopic Society and had specialised in micro-photography.

Possibly with the exemplar of the sleuthing doctor as represented by the very genuinely concerned and involved Dr Forbes Winslow in mind, McCormick proceeded to develop Dutton as a leading protagonist in his book, according him especial stature as a student of the Ripper correspondence. He quotes Dutton's alleged statement:

> I made micro-photographs of 128 specimens of the alleged correspondence of 'Jack the Ripper' to the police and other institutions and individuals. Of these at least 34 were definitely in the same handwriting.

As a result of all this, Tom Cullen, in good faith, perpetuated in his *Autumn of Terror: Jack the Ripper His Crimes and Times* (1965), the McCormick myth of *two* letters from Liverpool – and another Ripper legend was born!

One of the keenest proponents of a Liverpool lad for the rôle of Jack the Ripper was a Mr John Morrison, of Leyton, East London. It was back in 1986 that I paid him a visit, and sitting in his Ripper Murder Hunt HQ – the living-room of 21a Goodall Road – surrounded by books and gruesome wall-charts of victims and slaying sites, the then 60-year-old, out of work lorry driver told me, "'Mad Jack' has kept me sane". For when, four years before, he lost his job, he remembered the Duke of Edinburgh's glib advice to the mounting thousands of work-hungry unemployed: "Don't just waste the time on your hands. Use it to do something you've always wanted to do." And what John had always wanted to do was to discover the identity of Whitechapel Jack. After four years of dedicated ferreting, he was convinced that he had solved the mystery, run the Ripper to ground.

A fanatical enthusiast, eyes shining, tongue flailing, he rocket-launched into a breathless monologue on the topic that had become the most important thing in his life. As I stood by, he feverishly excavated a paper mountain of research data 'filed' under the sideboard, and surfaced triumphantly waving a single page document. "Here's a quote from the private notes of Inspector Joseph Chandler, who was actually on the case." He read it out to me, voice trembling with excitement.

> The man we are seeking once murdered in a house in Liverpool, was sent to an asylum and escaped just prior to the commencement of these crimes. I doubt if we'll catch him, he's such a cunning devil.

John Morrison told me: "Chandler was talking about a man named James Kelly." That, he said, was the name of the Ripper ... and it came to John in a dream.

> I dreamt I was in court. They were trying Jack the Ripper. Lord Hailsham was the judge. He called for the evidence, and they produced a *Guinness Book of Records*. And it was

a dream that came true! Next morning I went along to the library and looked it up in the Guinness book. And there it was. James Kelly was listed as the longest-ever escapee from Broadmoor. He had murdered his wife in Liverpool and been declared insane.

Wife-killer Kelly went over the wall on 28 January 1888. Just 65 days later, the Ripper murders began.

The story that John Morrison pieced together was one of "terrible vengeance" and "a scandalous cover-up in the highest places". He told me:

> The name of Jack the Ripper's last victim was Mary Kelly. She came from Liverpool, where she had had a passionate affair with a man so infatuated with her that he killed his wife. This man was James Kelly. He and Mary were lovers. She even took his surname. By the time he was convicted of wife-murder, Mary was carrying his child. Desperate to erase all traces of him from her life, she fled to London, had an abortion, and went on the streets. It was a mistake. Kelly found out where she was.

But why would he have wanted to kill and mutilate her? Morrison explained:

> The insane Kelly saw Mary's desertion and rejection of him as vile treachery. Getting rid of their child made it worse. And he couldn't bear the thought of her selling herself to other men. He escaped, made his way to London, started to scour the East End. He killed ten women before he finally tracked Mary down. He would ask each prostitute victim if she knew where he'd find Mary Kelly – then slay her to silence her. By the time the last of the ten died – a woman named Kate Kelly – the police were hot on the Ripper's trail. For a while the killings stopped. Then Scotland Yard received a letter from Liverpool admitting the murders. It was signed 'Jack the Ripper'. James Kelly had gone home. He returned to London soon afterwards, went straight to Mary Kelly's Whitechapel hideout, and, literally, ripped her to pieces. This last killing was the absolute confirmation the police needed. Now the Yard *knew* that Kelly was their man. They wanted to raise the alarm, put

out a hue and cry for him. Then, to their amazement, the Home Office said, 'No'. Why? I'll tell you. Because officialdom was embarrassed by its own incompetence at having failed to make the obvious connection between the dangerous homicidal lunatic at large and the Whitechapel slayings. Police Commissioner Sir Charles Warren was ordered either to obey the clam-up command, or resign. He resigned.

Sheer fantasy?
"I have proof," said John Morrison:

> Inspector Chandler's mistress wrote a book about the case. It is disguised as fiction, but it reveals so much of the mechanics and details of the police work that it just has to be the inside story of the truth.

Morrison said that he knew the identity of the woman. She was a well-known person, highly connected and married to an eminent writer on The Times. Her name and all the facts were, he informed me, in the safe-keeping of his solicitor.*
Morrison continued:

> Early in 1889, the New York City Police complained to Scotland Yard that they had experienced a couple of murders identical to those in Whitechapel. And, later, Paris police reported Ripper-style killings.

Then he brought out what he clearly regarded as the clincher: after an adventurous life in New York, Paris, and at sea, James Kelly surrendered to the police in April 1927, and after an absence of thirty-nine years was returned to Broadmoor, where he died in 1930, but, according to Morrison, "not before confessing that he was Jack the Ripper".

There are, I have to say, glaring inaccuracies in John Morrison's more detailed narrative, but it was nevertheless accepted in principal by James Tully as the basis for his book on the case, *The Secret of Prisoner 1167: Was This Man Jack the Ripper?* (1997).

Tully got the facts right. In the second half of 1859, Sarah Kelly, an illiterate, 15-year-old, working-class Liverpool girl found herself pregnant without benefit of matrimony. The father of her, as we now less barbarously

---

* I can reveal that the woman in question is Mrs Marie Belloc-Lowndes, and there is not a jot or tittle of evidence for any of these allegations that have been made against her. For a full consideration of the justification for regarding James Kelly as Jack the Ripper, see my The Quest for Jack the Ripper (Patterson Smith, New Jersey, 2002).

term it, love child, was a free-ranging clerk by the name of John Miller, who promptly abnegated his responsibilities and deserted Sarah. Fortunately, her family stood loyally by her, and she was despatched by her mother to Preston, most likely, the home of her aunt, Mary Motler, to have her baby. The child, a boy, named James, was born on 20 April 1860, at 43 St Mary's Street, Preston. Mother and son returned to Liverpool, where James was handed over to be brought up by his grandmother, who, Sarah having gone off, he believed to be his mother.

In 1870, the missing Sarah suddenly turned up with a husband, John Allan, a master mariner with a share in his ship, who lived at 76 Aubrey Lane, in Everton. After their marriage the couple moved out to Southport, where they occupied 95 Manchester Road. Their union was childless, and on 16 May 1874, while voyaging to foreign parts, John Allan died, at Pisagua, in Peru.

The widowed Sarah returned to Liverpool. She was ailing, in constant pain from an affliction of the liver, and was looked after by John Munro, a victualler and friend of her late husband's, at his home, 10 Walker Street, Low Hill. Her health deteriorated rapidly, and on 29 July 1874, she died. In a will she made provision for the future of James. He had left school at 13 and been apprenticed to a firm of upholsterers, Messrs Ray & Miles, of London Road, but now, in accordance with the terms of his mother's will, he went over the water to attend Dr Robert Hurworth's Commercial Academy, at 1 Albert Terrace, Egerton Street, New Brighton. He left the Academy when he was 17, found a position with the pawnbroker, Isaac H Jones, at 102 West Derby Road, and went into lodgings at 49 Fielding Street. It was while he was there, lonely and brooding in the evenings in his room, that he began, gradually, to exhibit symptoms of mental instability. There was madness on his mother's side. A cousin had become insane. James developed a positive obsession that he must get out of Liverpool. He moved to London, and it was there that he was to meet the girl whom he was to marry and to murder, Sarah Brider. It was as a result of his furious and fatal knife attack upon his wife that James Kelly was to be sent, in August 1883, to Broadmoor Criminal Lunatic Asylum.

That, as John Morrison, reports, Kelly escaped from confinement there, and remained at liberty for nearly four decades, is indisputable, but that he was, as Morrison and Tully affirm to be their belief, the veritable Jack, seems, after a careful study of all the concommitant circumstances, highly unlikely.

Let us turn now to the very different constellation of suspicious factors surrounding the man with the very strong Liverpool connections whom Detective Chief Inspector Littlechild put tentatively in the frame.

He was Dr Francis J Tumblety. His family origins were Irish, and he was born, the youngest of 11 children, in Ireland in 1833, although the family moved very shortly afterwards to Rochester, New York. He seems early to have displayed a streak of sexual disreputability, for at the relatively tender age of 15 he was, as they say, turning a fast buck, peddling pornographic books and papers on the local canal boats. His first taste of medical practice was only slightly less dubious, doing odd jobs for the highly suspectable Dr WC Lispenard, specialist in a gallimaufry of sex nexus afflictions. Following in the good doctor's somewhat scabrous shoe-prints, Tumblety had, by the time was 24, established quite a reputation for himself as a great herbal healer. The path of the true pioneer is never, or seldom, straight, and Tumblety's corkscrew progression was pock-marked with deaths and brushes with the police, but his footwork was of the finest, and his agility as a side-stepper truly remarkable. Setbacks set adroitly aside, his fortune grew.

Coffers bulging, his first descent on the Old World would seem to have been in 1869. He was back again across the herring pond in 1874, and that was the year when, in his rôle as herbal doctor, he set up his therapeutic tent in Liverpool. Here he met, and enjoyed a Uranian relationship with, a young bisexual writer, Hall Caine, who was to achieve outstanding literary success as the author of such novels, set in the Isle of Man, as *The Deemster* and *The Manxman*. Caine suffered from chronic neuralgia, and it was as a patient that he first came into contact with Tumblety.*

Throughout the next dozen or so years, Tumblety was constantly back and forth between America and England, and on Friday 31 August 1888, when Ripper-shed blood fell on the cobbles of Bucks Row, he was assuredly in London. That was the very day that he committed an act of gross indecency there with one Arthur Brice. Twice more he was similarly caught out, on 14 October and on 7 November, when he was arrested. He was out on bail on the night of 8-9 November, when Mary Kelly was unpicked at the seams in Miller's Court. He appeared again before the magistrate at Marlborough Street on 16 November, was further remanded on bail, and fled from England, sailing on 24 November from Le Havre to New York.

Supporting the theory that Francis Tumblety was the Whitechapel murderer, Stewart Evans and Paul Gainey** have discovered that when he reached New York, two American detectives shadowed him to his lodgings, and, in December, Inspector Walter Andrews, one of the original three Ripper hunters, arrived in Manhattan in quest of Jack the Ripper. But nothing came of it.

Tumblety lived on for another fifteen years, dying on 28 May 1903, a Roman Catholic, ultimately groomed and garnered for salvation by the nuns who ran the institution where he breathed his last, St John's Charity Hospital, St Louis.

---

* See: Hall Caine: Portrait of a Victorian Romancer. Vivien Allen (Sheffield Academic Press, 1997).

**See: Jack the Ripper: First American Serial Killer (Kodansha International, 1996).

He left a living link in the Liverpool area – Mrs Margaret Brady, who resided at 20 Frederick Street, Widnes. She was the daughter of Dr Tumblety's sister, Bridget. Another tie with Liverpool was a namesake uncle Tumblety, who had been connected for more than twenty years with the Cunard Line. By an odd coincidence, it turned out that a Captain Anderson, serving in the Royal Navy, whom Dr Tumblety, when he was living in Boston around 1863, had got to know, knew Tumblety's Liverpool relatives. They had got it into their heads that Dr Francis had joined the United States Army and been killed in action. On one of his trips, Captain Anderson took a daguerrotype of Tumblety to his Liverpool uncle to convince him that Francis was still in the land of the living.

But was Francis Tumblety Jack the Ripper? Evans and Gainey are of the opinion that he very likely was. But what was the official police conclusion at the time? Littlechild wrote to Sims that there was a large dossier on him at the Yard. There is absolutely no trace of it. It has simply vanished into thin air. And, here is the oddest thing of all. There is a total absence of the name of Francis Tumblety, not only from the English newspapers, but also from the official documents. He rates not a single mention in the police files or in those at the Home Office. Tumblety's name exists nowhere amid the acres and acres of bureaucratic paperwork. What are we to make of this blanket of silence – a deliberate shroud for the Liverpool Ripper?

THE BLOCKHOUSE MURDER

It was back in my fledgling medical student days that I first met Dr James Brierley Firth. He was not a doctor of medicine. Director of the Home Office North Western Forensic Laboratory at Preston, he held a doctorate in science, was a Master of Science, a Fellow of the Royal Institute of Chemistry, and a Member of the Institution of Chemical Engineers. All of these skills he brought to bear in the service of forensic science, which he defined as science applied to the interests of justice.

And very often Dr Firth's expertise was called upon to help in the solving of cases of murder. Among the celebrated ones in which he was significantly involved were those of Dr Clements, the Southport wife-murderer; Mrs Merrifield, the Blackpool poisoner; and that of the two larcenous Liverpool thugs, Burns and Devlin.

It was Firth's recondite ingenuity which contributed to the solution of the riddle of the Man in the Iron Cylinder,* and that of the Girl with the Lungful of Diatoms.**

His assistance was also of vital importance in the unravelling of the mystery of the Blockhouse Murder.

At precisely 6.40pm on the evening of Saturday 2 November 1940, James Hagan sent his 15-year-old daughter, Mary, out from the family home in Brookside Avenue, Seaforth, to buy him a packet of cigarettes and a *Liverpool Echo*, giving her two shillings to cover the purchases. The trip, to the newsagent's in nearby Sandy Road and back, ought not to have taken her more than ten or, at the outside, fifteen minutes. But as the time ticked by, and after two hours there was still no sign of Mary, her worried family contacted the local police, and PC Dixon came to the house. Friends and neighbours hearing of the Hagans' plight rallied round to help, and were soon organising search parties to scour the district for the missing girl.

It was a wild, wet night, and black as pitch, for it was wartime, and with the Great May Blitz etched in unforgettable flames in Merseyside's recent memory, the blackout in Liverpool was one of the most strictly enforced in the country. And very necessary that stringency was to prove, for a little over three weeks later, on 28 November 1940, came Liverpool's horror night of land-mines, 30 of them floating slowly down to earth, swaying sinisterly below green parachutes, one of them razing the Junior Technical School in Durning Road, Edgehill, in what Churchill was afterwards to describe as

* See my Liverpool Colonnade (Philip Son & Nephew, 1955) and my Tales of Liverpool Murder, Mayhem and Mystery (The Gallery Press, 1985).

** See A Scientist Turns to Crime, by JB Firth (William Kimber, 1960).

"the worst single incident of the war". Two hundred men, women and children died that Thursday night.

Very cautiously, then, with carefully doused torches emitting no more than an occasional glow-worm point of light, the searchers crept through the darkness.

At the spot in Seaforth where Brook Vale joins up with Cambridge and Sandy Roads, a railway bridge crosses the Waterloo-Lime Street line, and beside that bridge there had been erected at that time a small and rather ugly concrete structure, a miniature military pillbox-style fortress, or blockhouse, designed to function as an anti-invasion obstacle for *in extremis* use as a strong-point by the local defence unit of the Home Guard.

It was a search party led by a local ARP warden that came stumbling up to this dank, soot-stained, and rather forbidding-looking little building. Negotiating as best they could the ankle-deep puddle of dirty water standing in the entrance, they found themselves wrapped in an overwhelming, almost palpable blackness. Safely under cover, it was, however, all right to switch on a torch and rake the surrounding interior of the blockhouse with full beam. Its yellow radiance revealed a filthy floor littered with a detritus of old tins and cigarette packets, tossed in through the gun-slits, bits of rag, crumpled sweet-papers, cigarette butts, spent matches and a carpet of myriad winds' sweepings of dead leaves. But … wait … there was something else. The hairs on the napes of the searchers' necks prickled. There, lying on the floor just beyond the circle of the torch's light, was a vague human shape. The hunt for Mary Hagan had ended. Her clothing was torn and disarranged. She had been raped and strangled.

It was 1.30am when Dr Firth, who had been summoned by the Seaforth Division of the Lancashire Constabulary, arrived by police car at the blockhouse. Pending the arrival of the forensic expert, nothing had been touched since the discovery of the body. Electric arc-lights had been installed, and after a police photographer had recorded the scene, Firth made a careful examination of the dead girl.

She had, he decided, died at about 7pm. He found blood and dirt inside her nose and lips, and a bloodstained bruise and some dirt over the left eye. There were bruises on both sides of the neck. He noted particularly one bloodstain on the left side of the neck. It was composed of hard, dried blood. It seemed to him to be a thumb impression that had been made in fresh blood. It could, he thought, have been made by someone with a cut thumb from which blood was still flowing.

A soiled white handkerchief with a blue border, found under the body and marked with the name 'G Rimmer', was hailed by the detectives with considerable optimistic excitement. Rimmer is a very common name in West Lancashire – originating, so I have been told, in its application to those who lived and worked around the rim of reclaimed Martin Mere – but, disappointingly, all the Rimmers traced and interviewed after searches of nominal rolls, visits to Army camps in the region, and ships docked in the Mersey, yielded no result.

On the ground, underneath the body, was the copy of the *Echo* that Mary had bought, but of the cigarettes or the change from the florin which she had been given there was no sign anywhere.

With the aid of a stirrup-pump – such pumps were common wartime issue for dealing with incendiary bombs – the water was sucked up from where it had pooled on the blockhouse floor, and from the resultant quagmire a number of potential clues were recovered and carefully laid out for examination on blotting-paper.

Among them was a wrapper from a bar of chocolate. Significantly, as it was later to prove, it bore on it traces of zinc ointment and an antiseptic substance. A tiny matching piece from this wrapper was subsequently discovered in a fold of Mary's clothing, and particles of milk chocolate, found, *post mortem,* in her teeth, showed that she had eaten a bar of chocolate shortly before her death.

Also recovered from the water was what was described as 'a piece of soaked fabric'. It was this which, in Firth's skilled hands, was to provide the all-important key to unlock the mystery. He identified this piece of fabric as a strip of gauze made from materials very similar to those normally included in an Army field dressing. His analysis disclosed that it was impregnated with antiflavine. It revealed, too, a substance which he identified as a zinc compound. The gauze also exhibited bloodstains, the positions of which indicated that it had been used to bandage a wounded finger or thumb.

Everything about this fragment of bandage set warning bells ringing in Firth's mind. To begin with, the presence of zinc ointment puzzled him. No military medical orderly would have put zinc on a field dressing. It was quite unnecessary. He felt certain, moreover, that no serving soldier would have opened his field dressing packet to bandage something so slight as a thumb injury. Then there was the fact that he had found traces of zinc and antiflavine on the chocolate wrapper. They were sure proof that the wearer of the bandage had been in contact with Mary Hagan.

So, based on Firth's findings and deductions, the detectives reasoned that if they could track down the owner of the bandage, the chances were that they would also have found the killer. It would be a mammoth task, though, for there were literally thousands of troops stationed in wartime Lancashire.

A start was made visiting hospitals, doctors and chemists. No luck. No one remembered a serviceman with an injured finger or thumb. Next, a radio appeal was put out asking anyone who had seen Mary Hagan before 7pm that night of 2 November, or who had noticed anybody acting suspiciously in the neighbourhood to contact the police.

Several witnesses came forward saying that they had seen a young soldier with a Lancashire accent and a cut face. One woman witness told of a soldier with a cut on his face who had approached her just as she was going into her house. He had asked her if he could use her bathroom to clean himself up, as he had been involved in a fight with another soldier. She had refused to let him in because she was alone in the house.

Detectives descended *en masse* to give saturation coverage to the streets around the Brookdale area, questioning people:

"Were you in the vicinity of the blockhouse that night?"

"Did you see a man thereabouts?"

"Have you ever seen a man loitering near it?"

This last question because there was reason to believe that the lock on the blockhouse door had been deliberately broken several days before the murder.

Uniformly the answers to all the detectives' questions seemed to be "No".

Then, at last, "Yes" – from a young married woman.

"Several days ago a soldier tried to trip me up on the bridge."

And "Yes" – from a schoolgirl.

"There was a soldier on the bridge who looked at me and walked towards the blockhouse. I waited till some people came up before I dared cross the bridge."

And again "Yes" – a barmaid in a local pub remembered a soldier with a damaged thumb coming in on the night of the murder. A tallish young man in the Irish Guards, his right thumb was bleeding and there was blood on his cap. He looked as if he had been running and asked for a cigarette in an agitated sort of way. He had taken a field dressing from his tunic pocket and tried to bandage his thumb himself, but witness had done it for him.

All this was good, sound, informative stuff, but it was still a needle-in-a-haystack operation trying to find the thumb-sore killer.

On 4 October, Anne McVitte had been cycling along the bank of the Leeds and Liverpool Canal, a mile or so from the scene of the Mary Hagan murder, when she was attacked by a young soldier. She had escaped from his menacing clutches by jumping into the water and swimming across to the opposite bank. He had stolen her purse, containing just under two pounds, and her bicycle. Other witnesses had reported seeing a soldier on the canal bank shortly before the attack. Their descriptions of him sounded uncannily similar to that of the soldier described by witnesses in the Mary Hagan case.

What the frustrated detectives needed was a stroke of luck. It came when they received a telephone call from the police at Streatham, telling them that, on 13 November, they had arrested a soldier who had been found loitering suspiciously in a doorway on Streatham Hill, and who, asked for identification, had run off. He was subsequently identified as Samuel Morgan, of Seaforth.

Detectives hurried to London to interview the soldier. He was 28 years old.

He was serving with the Irish Guards, and his home was in Berkeley Drive, Seaforth. He had a freshly-healed scar on his right thumb.

Morgan was brought back to Liverpool for questioning, and the police surgeon at Seaforth police station, who, on 15 November, thirteen days after the murder, examined the inch-long, semi-circular wound on his thumb, said that it could be anything from seven days to a fortnight old, and that it might have been caused by a blunt instrument, such as barbed wire, or possibly by a bite.

A search was made at Morgan's mother's house, and there, in the bathroom, officers found a quantity of field dressing, which was being used as a face-cloth.

One is inevitably reminded of the case of the 11-year-old London girl, Vera Page, who, in December 1931, was found lying raped and strangled in the shrubbery just inside the driveway of the tradesmen's entrance to 89 Addison Road, Kensington. In the crook of the child's right elbow, detectives found a finger-stall covering a piece of lint smelling strongly of ammonia. Only one person who knew Vera had been wearing a finger-stall. His name was Percy Orlando Rush. Aged 41, married, he lived just a few minutes away from Vera's home, was employed at Whiteley's laundry, and worked with ammonia.

Rush, questioned by the coroner, Ingleby Oddie, stated that he had discarded his finger-stall two days before the murder was committed, and bandages and lint removed from his home were not identical with those of the finger-stall taken from little Vera's body. There were certain other clues, too, which seemed to point to Rush, but neither individually nor collectively did they present with the sort of secure evidence required for a committal. The murder therefore remains officially unsolved. Unofficially, Percy Orlando Rush is regarded as the killer.

In Samuel Morgan's case, the field dressing found at his mother's was sent to Dr Firth for comparison with the piece that had been recovered from the blockhouse. They matched exactly.

Witnesses were able to identify Morgan as the soldier seen in the blockhouse area shortly before the murder. His boots were compared with a heel print that had been discovered in the blockhouse. Again, a perfect match.

A soil sample collected by Firth from the blockhouse floor presented marked agreement, both microscopically and spectrographically, with soil removed from Morgan's clothing.

Put up at Liverpool Assizes in February 1941, Morgan admitted that he had robbed Mary Hagan of some cigarettes and a few pennies, but denied murdering her.

The jury did not believe him. He was hanged at Walton Gaol on 9 April 1941, by Thomas Pierrepoint. He made no confession.

LETHAL BIRDS OF PASSAGE

For the delectation of those whose fancy, like that of Thomas De Quincey, tends to the appreciation of murder as a fine art, there was inaugurated in Edinburgh, in the fifth year of the last century, a wonderful sequence of volumes which was to become justly famed as the *Notable British Trials* series.

Between their covers – scarlet for English, green for Scottish – are embalmed full accounts, complete with High Court proceedings transcripts, of what have come to be regarded by those learned in the forensic field, as classic cases of murder.

By no means all of the famous trials of the past are, or indeed could be, represented in the series' 83 volumes, but there are sufficient to furnish an exemplary education in an acknowledgedly recondite subject.

In the annals of celebrated crimes, the name of Liverpool is writ large as the scene of two outstanding murder cases. The first is that of Mrs Florence Elizabeth Maybrick, tried at St George's Hall in 1889 for the poisoning with arsenic of her husband, James Maybrick, at Battlecrease House, in Riversdale Road, Aigburth.

The second, is that of William Herbert Wallace, the Prudential Assurance Company collector, who, occupying the same dock as Mrs Maybrick earlier, was tried in 1931 for the battering to death of his wife, Julia, in the front parlour of their modest home at 29 Wolverton Street, Anfield.

While Mrs Maybrick's case is included in the *Notable British Trials* series, inexplicably, that of William Herbert Wallace has been omitted from the canon.

As it happens, I can boast personal connections with both of these affairs. The Maybricks were acquaintances of my grandparents, frequently dining at each others' homes, and my grandfather and grandmother actually went with them as their guests in the horse-drawn bus which they had hired for the occasion, to the 1889 Grand National, and were present when, on 29 March, gallant old Frigate, with Tom Beasley up, won, and the Maybricks had that quarrel on the course over Alfred Brierley which is alleged to have precipitated the murder.

I have myself been into Battlecrease House on a couple of occasions. Both were during the days of the Second World War when the place was standing empty, several of its windows bomb-blasted out and boarded-up. One of the window boardings was loose, and I remember clambering in on impulse, at dead of night, and exploring the empty, echoing house with its looming grand staircase throwing eerily moving shadows in the flickering light of my torch. My second visit was in broad daylight and was alarming in a different way. I had ascended to the floor where James Maybrick's death had taken place fifty-three years before, when I distinctly heard the sound of someone coming up the stairs. Thinking that it might be a tramp who had wandered in to find shelter in the deserted house, I went out on to the landing to look. No one. Nothing. I thereafter searched the place from top to bottom. There was no other living being anywhere in the house. But I did, I remember, find, in a small anteroom upstairs, a dressing-room to a bedroom I suspect, a quite extraordinary heap of dead moths, flies, and bluebottles, forming what looked like a thickish carpet on the floor, as well as a liberal deposit of their dried bodies on the window-sill.

Rather more tenuous is my 'connection' with the Wallace affair. It is simply this: that I was a small boy living in a house in Mossley Hill which Wallace passed closely by on the night of his Qualtroughean Odyssey, and six years before, Dr CG Mort, the Liverpool City Coroner, who held the inquest on Julia Wallace, was the doctor who brought me into the world. Later in life I came to know Mr Hector Munro, Wallace's solicitor, and the Wallaces' next door neighbour, Mr John Sharpe Johnston, with his amazing cupboard full of 57 assorted varieties of truss, still living in Wolverton Street, and still as firmly convinced as ever of Wallace's innocence.

Later still, with my old friend Jonathan Goodman, author of that first-rate monograph, *The Killing of Julia Wallace*,* I met, and subjected to severe cross-examination, Richard Gordon Parry, the man whom Wallace named as the killer of his wife.

I was also, through the courtesy of the occupants of the Wallaces' old house, permitted to visit both the murder room and the kitchen, where night after night Mr and Mrs Wallace used to sit. Standing in the small front parlour, my feet beside the very spot where poor Julia's body had lain, I was surprised to find how little an after-shock that terrible event has left behind. Of course, the new owners have done a great deal of decorating, and brought about numerous changes in the place. The old gas-fire and the mantel-side gas-brackets have gone, but the contours of the room are as they always were. The kitchen and scullery, on the other hand, have undergone a complete face-lift. No trace of the old atmosphere of one's imagining remains.

And, finally, I found myself acting as defending counsel for Wallace in a mock trial, held under the auspices of the Merseyside Medico-Legal Society in 1977, at the Liverpool Medical Institution, where, arguing against the Liverpool barrister, Mr RH Montgomery, who appeared for the prosecution, I won my case.

What has struck and surprised me, thumbing through my collection of the *Notable British Trials*, is the considerable number of celebrated murderers who, in the course of their abbreviated passages through the world, have, in

* George G Harrap, London, 1969.

one way or another, come to rest, or nest, in Liverpool. The contact of some has been fleeting, using the city as a mere staging post.

Oscar Slater, for example – incidentally the subject of William Roughead's meticulous treatment in one of the early, green-bound volumes of the *Notable Scottish Trials* – is associated with Liverpool in this sort of way. He was the dandified German-Jewish immigrant, professional gambler and whoremaster, wrongly convicted in 1909 of the murder of the wealthy, 82-year-old, Glasgow spinster, Miss Marion Gilchrist, and who was to languish for more than eighteen years in the bleak granite fastness of Peterhead Convict Prison, on the iron lip's edge of the German Ocean, before, in 1926, Sir Arthur Conan Doyle helped to bring about his belated release. Slater and his French mistress, Andrée Antoine, spent the night of 25-26 December 1908, in Room 139 at the North Western Hotel, in Lime Street, before embarking for New York on the *Lusitania*.*

Then there is Crippen, who is to crime, as Sherlock Holmes is to detection, universally generic. He is remembered as the mild little doctor from Coldwater, Michigan, Hawley Harvey – Peter to his friends – Crippen. Leaving his filleted wife, the former Kunigunde Mackamozki, transmogrified into the latterday music-hall non-star, Belle Elmore, beneath the coal-cellar floor, at 39 Hilldrop Crescent, Holloway, North London, he set sail, with his *inamorata*, Miss Ethel Le Neve, hair cropped, decked out as Master Robinson, and himself posing as the 'boy's' father, Mr John Philo Robinson, aboard the *SS Montrose*, outward bound from Antwerp for Quebec.

Liverpool, in the shape of the ship's master, Captain Henry George Kendall, who lived when ashore at 8 Moss Lane, Aintree, brought about the capture of the fugitive. For his was the lynx eye that spotted the Robinsons', *père et fils*, true identity as Crippen and Le Neve, and sent the first-ever wireless message to catch a murderer. And it was to Liverpool that Chief Inspector Walter Dew, who had overtaken the *Montrose* in the faster White Star liner, *Laurentic*, out of Liverpool, brought the wanted pair back to stand trial in London, at the Old Bailey.

They arrived at the Pier Head in the early afternoon of Saturday 27 August 1910, aboard the White Star liner *Megantic*, and travelled to London by the boat train. Le Neve was found not guilty of being an accessory after the fact, and was discharged. Crippen was sentenced to death, and hanged at Pentonville. I have in my 'Black Museum' collection the crucifix ring which Crippen, a devout convert to Roman Catholicism, wore, and the rosary beads which were entwined in his fingers when Mr Hangman Ellis came to fetch him.

A celebrated murderer who spent the earlier part of his career in

---

* See *The Oscar Slater Murder Story: New Light on a Classic Miscarriage of Justice*. Richard Whittington-Egan. Neil Wilson, Glasgow, 2001.

Liverpool was Seddon the Poisoner. Frederick Henry Seddon was a greedy, grasping man. He was also a miser. He worked, and there are those who would say most appropriately, as an insurance superintendent, and in the first years of the last century he was practising the art and artifice of his calling in Liverpool, living, in 1900, at 60 Brunswick Road, and in 1901, at 88 Belmont Road, Anfield, just round the corner from where, in Wolverton Street, William Herbert Wallace, another insurance man, with whom Seddon has often been compared and likened, was to come to live fourteen years later.

The Liverpool period of Seddon's life was, of course, long before the time that fame, or, more accurately, infamy, descended upon his balding head. It was in 1910, that, diamond cut diamond, miser met miser, with ultimately mutually tragic results. The female niggard was one Eliza Mary Barrow, a 49-year-old spinster who came to lodge as top-floor tenant of the 14-room house at 63 Tollington Park, Islington, North London, where the Seddon family – Margaret, his wife, their five children, and his father – had taken up residence in 1909, and where Seddon ruled like a tyrant, everyone in the household being frightened of him.

Miss Barrow moved in July 1910, and throughout the succeeding 12 months, Seddon, playing upon her cupidity, systematically mulcted her of her assiduously garnered gold, promising mouth-watering future returns on handed over here-and-now hard cash.

Miss Barrow, it must be said, was a decided oddity. Suspicious, selfish, quarrelsome, badly dressed, and exceedingly parsimonious. She was also densely ignorant, and had a previous history of overfondness for the bottle. She was fond, too, of a 10-year-old orphan boy, Ernest Grant, who lived with her. When, later, she became ill with the classic vomiting and diarrhoea of arsenical poisoning, she quirkily insisted that little Ernie should sleep with her in her distinctly noisome bed.

There is small doubt that Seddon poisoned Eliza Barlow, and having done so, running true to form, gave her a cut-price funeral, not failing into the bargain to dun the undertaker for twelve shillings and sixpence commission for having introduced the business.

Miss Barrow's relatives, the Vonderahes, extremely put out at having received no intimation of cousin Eliza Mary's demise until after the funeral, came truffle-snuffling after her gold. Seddon superciliously dismissed them with the unwelcome tidings that she had parted with her scraped-together life-savings to him, in exchange for a guaranteed life-long annuity.

In these misfortunate circumstances, frustrated greed and need generated mistrust in the Vonderahe bosoms. Suspicion arose. So did Miss Barrow, exhumed from Islington Cemetery, and delivered into the probing scientific hands of Doctors Spilsbury and Willcox. They found arsenic. Seddon was arrested and put, with his 37-year-old wife, into the dock of star-rated

Number One Court at the Old Bailey.

In the event, he scuppered himself by his demeanour in the witness-box. A hard-headed Lancashire man of business, flinty cool and callously clever, answering every question plausibly, he was described as 'cold and hard as a paving-stone'. He displayed such a jaunty, overweening self-satisfaction in regard to his fiscal acuity and business acumen, was so obviously preposterous and unsympathetic a character, that the jury's backs were arched like cats', and he seemed to them at least capable of being culpable insofar as the crime of calculated acquisition with which he stood charged was concerned. And that, when it came to it, was the verdict of them all. Mrs Seddon was found not guilty – upon hearing which, her husband exhibited his solitary demonstration of human emotion throughout the entire proceedings. He turned to his wife beside him in the dock and planted upon her a resounding kiss, loud and echoing through the tense stillness of the court.

When the time came for Mr Justice Bucknill, who was a freemason, to pronounce sentence of death, Seddon, making a secret masonic sign and declaring to his fellow-mason that "before the Great Architect of the Universe" he was not guilty, so upset the judge that the tears were coursing down his face as he spoke the words of the dread sentence of the law.

Frederick Seddon's overwhelming obsession with money stayed with him right up to the edge of eternity. On his last afternoon on earth he sent out from the condemned cell at Pentonville for his solicitor. He wanted him to tell him what sort of prices his furniture had fetched at auction. On hearing that they had fallen considerably short of his expectations, he showed great rancour, struck the table at which he was sitting with some viciousness, and said, "That's done it!"

To the end, which came on 18 April 1912, he went on insisting on his entire innocence, and met that end pallid but proudly erect, and refusing to join in with the chaplain's prayers.

My friend, Donald Rumbelow, showed me a copy he possessed of the *Notable British Trials* volume on the case. It had belonged to Sir Edward Marshall Hall, who defended Seddon. Beneath the photograph of Seddon which it contained, the Great Defender had written:

Perhaps the cleverest and certainly the worst scoundrel I ever appeared for.

More Murderous Merseyside Migrants

Liverpool's actual production of home-grown killers is vastly inferior to its deliverance of comedians, but there is one whose name is enshrined high on the dishonourable scarlet roll of renowned murderers.

Having first seen the light of day under the Mersey sky at Edgehill on 23 September 1889, Herbert Mahon, Monday's child and fair of face, was by birth and birthright a son of Liverpool, albeit with a fairly vigorous spray of shamrock somewhere in his blood, and chippings from the real rock of the Blarney Stone in his tongue. Although christened solely Herbert, it was, doubtless, in favourable acknowledgement of this ancestral Irish blood of his that he adopted the name of Patrick, by which he came to be known, and by which we shall henceforth refer to him.

His family was large – he was one of six – struggling, working-class, and God-fearing. They were regular attendants at St Mary's Church, Edgehill, and entered wholeheartedly into the social side of church affairs. Indeed, one of Patrick's brothers took religion so seriously that he became, in the fullness of time, a duly ordained clergyman, and was, in 1930, Rector of Carnforth, in Lancashire.

Patrick seems to have led a blameless, or at any rate unrecorded as blameworthy, childhood. The zealous profiler would discover a history of keen attendance at St Mary's Church and Sunday School, where later he taught, and a vivid interest and passionate involvement in church activities. At St Mary's School, Edgehill, he showed some small scholastic talent, and rather more athletic prowess, especially on the football field. Taken all in all, the entire *modus vivendi* of his salad days has been described as having set 'a model for all young men'.

He presented, moreover, a pleasing façade, which made him popular at school, particularly with one pretty, dark-haired girl, Jessie Hannah, a couple of years younger than himself. He grew tall and handsome. And didn't he have plentiful endowment of all the old Hibernian charm!

He left school at 14, and his father apprenticed him to a Liverpool bookseller. I happen to know that he worked at Henry Young's shop, then in South Castle Street, as I was a regular purchaser of books there in the 1940s and one of the old, long-serving assistants confided to me that recondite morsel. And it was there that the fatal flaws, below the superficially engaging characteristics which were eventually to lead him to the scaffold, started to show themselves. He began to pilfer, was found out, and sacked.

With his disarming, boyish smile, his frank eyes, and shy, innocent-seeming charm, he soon got another job … and another … Moving on, he gradually climbed up a somewhat rickety ladder from tea-making office boy to the status of full-blown clerk.

On 6 April 1910, circumventing the family's opposition on the grounds of his total fiscal inadequacy for the taking of such a step, he clandestinely married Jessie Hannah, the dark-haired beauty from St Mary's School, now aged 18 and living at 110 Walton Village, at West Derby Registry Office. It is said that he was then working as an invoice clerk with a Liverpool firm of produce merchants, but on his marriage certificate he entered his occupation as 'Literary publisher's book-keeper'. Whichever, within less than a year it was discovered that he had been forging and uttering cheques on the firm to the tune of £132. An obsessional womaniser from the start, he used this money to take the current girl of his adulterous fancy off to the Isle of Man. As a first offender, he got away with being bound over. Even so, his reputation was tarnished in the church and social circles in which the Mahons moved, and, in 1911, he and his forgiving wife left Liverpool, and went to live in Sheffield.

Apart from the fact that the young couple's parents insisted on their going through a religious marriage ceremony at St Luke's Church in Sheffield in 1911, nothing more is heard or known of Mahon until 1912, when he was in trouble again. Working then as a milk salesman at Sherborne, in Dorset, he vanished with £60, creamed off money collected on behalf of his employer. Arrested in Salisbury, he attempted suicide, swallowing the contents of a phial of veronal, which had been hidden in one of his socks. This time he was given a 12-month sentence at Dorchester Assizes, and, going to prison, left behind a recently born little daughter.

He came out plausibly verbalising good intentions – which are said to pave the road to Hell. In his case, they assuredly did, for in relatively no time at all he was back in the dock, facing on this occasion a formidable Red Judge, Mr Justice Darling, on a charge of bank robbery at Sunningdale, Berkshire, in the course of which he had struck a servant-girl, Olive Kate Wickens, a rain of hammer blows on the head. When she came to, the seedy Romeo was holding her hand, kissing and fondling her, all sweetness and apologies for having struck her down.

His Irish charm weighed not at all in the scales held by Darling J. Neither did his proposal to join the Army and be off to the trenches. "The Army does not want men like you," the judge told him. "They are not so hard-up as that. The Army dislikes arch-thieves. Not only are you a burglar, not only a coward; you are a thorough-paced hypocrite, and the time has come when you must go to penal servitude."

And his lordship passed sentence of five years. During the time of this spell of incarceration, a second child, a son, was born to his wife. Sadly, he died when he was two years old, without ever seeing his father.

Prison proved in no wise remedial. Mahon came out in 1920, to take up where he had left off – an appalling philanderer, hopping from bed to bed; an incorrigible villain, going from bad to worse. His little Liverpool wife stuck by him and cherished their child.

On the surface, and Mahon was nothing if not a man of surfaces – superficies, length and breadth, but no depth – he began to do well. His wife, who was working as a clerk with Consols Automatic Aerators Ltd, at Sunbury-on-Thames, secured him a job as a traveller for the firm, and his easy, confident, and engaging manner, and laughing Irish eyes, did well for him – so well that he was made up to manager.

The outlook now would seem to the onlooker to be at last set fair for the couple's future happiness, but he would be reckoning without taking into account Mahon's worst enemy – his personal vanity. That was both his predominant characteristic and his Achilles heel. It led him to easy conquests, which, in turn, led him to difficult escapes. Most terrible of all was his easy conquest of 38-year-old Emily Beilby Kaye, and the superlatively difficult escape that cost both of them their lives.

He met her, in the course of business, at the office of the Copthall Avenue firm of chartered accountants where she worked as a shorthand typist. She lived in a bachelor-girl apartment at the Green Cross Club, at 68-69 Guilford Street, in Bloomsbury. She fell passionately in love with this 'Broth of a Bhoy', to quote a favourite description of him by him, who cheerfully responded by impregnating her.

According to Mahon, she knew of the Liverpool female fly in the romantic ointment, his wife, but had nonetheless made up her mind to marry him. To this end, she proposed an arrangement, a "love experiment", whereby they spent some time together, just the two of them, in a suitably remote spot.

Apparently compliant, Pat, as she called him, selected for them the ideal isolated place, a small, whitewashed habitation, the Officer's House. It had previously been the residence of the coast guard, alternatively known as Langney Bungalow, situated on the Crumbles, a lonely stretch of shingle between Eastbourne and Pevensey Bay. A sinister coincidence: close by was the spot where, four years before, Field and Gray had murdered 18-year-old, holidaying typist, Irene Munro.

According to Mahon, and he was the only living witness, things had not gone idyllically at the experimental love-nest. A sharpish quarrel had blown up, and Emily Kaye, in a paroxysm of feminine fury, had hurled a coal axe at his head. He had closed with her in self-defensive combat, they had fallen, and she had hit her head on a coal cauldron, which had killed her.

Ironically, it was his long-suffering, ever loyal and loving wife, Jessie, who brought about the capture of Patrick Mahon. Back in the single furnished room which she and Patrick shared in the boarding-house at 2 Pagoda Avenue, Richmond, she had of late become both exercised and troubled by the increasing constancy of his absences from home in connection with alleged business trips.

Feeling pretty certain that he was "at it again" with another woman, she, uncharacteristically rummaging through his pockets in search of clues, had come upon a ticket for a deposit in the cloakroom at Waterloo Station, and asked a friend, John Beard, a former detective inspector in the Metropolitan Police, for advice and help. They went together to Waterloo, presented the ticket, and received a Gladstone bag. Forcing the side and peering into it, Beard saw masses of bloodstained material and a big, wicked-looking knife. Without revealing what he had seen, Beard returned the bag to the cloakroom, and told Jessie to replace the ticket where she had found it. He then got in touch with his contacts at Scotland Yard. A watch was mounted on the left luggage office. Mahon turned up, claimed the Gladstone, and was promptly detained.

He admitted dismembering the body, and, thoroughly unmanned, told how at midnight, with a storm raging above, he was burning the head on the living-room fire, there had been a tremendous clap of thunder, a flash of lightning, the dead woman's eyes had opened and her hair flared into flame among the glowing coals. In his shirt-sleeves, he had fled in terror out on to the rainswept shingle.

Included in the Mahon archive is a most interesting photograph of the renowned Home Office pathologist, Sir Bernard Spilsbury: interesting for two reasons. Firstly, because it shows him in the garden of the bungalow on the Crumbles actually in the process of examining the piecemeal remains of Emily Kaye, from which he subsequently fitted her together 'like a three-dimensional jigsaw'. Secondly, because, uniquely, it shows the unheard of tolerance of the presence of a woman beside Sir Bernard while he worked. In fact, the woman in the fur coat is Mrs Hilda Bainbridge, widow of Professor Francis Arthur Bainbridge (1874-1921), occupant of the Chair of Physiology at St Bartholomew's Hospital. It is known that Sir Bernard entertained romantic feelings for Hilda Bainbridge, and that his 16-year marriage to Edith Horton had failed.

An eerie thing happened during Mahon's trial at Lewes. As he was being cross-examined about the disposal of Miss Kaye, there was a sudden terrific clap of thunder, and, remembering no doubt that other storm which broke over the Crumbles when he was burning his victim's head, a clearly shaken Mahon cowered fearfully in the box.

The jury brought in an unhesitant verdict of guilty, and on 3 September 1924, just 20 days before his 35th birthday, Mahon kept an unwilling appointment with Thomas Pierrepoint at Wandsworth Prison. A lifetime's habit of avoiding the consequences of his acts prevailed to the very end. On the scaffold he hopped backwards in an instinctual last stand against fell circumstance, striking the edge of the trap with such force in the process that, pre-empting the hangman, the Broth of a Bhoy snapped his spine.

~

Although not, unlike Mahon, a native of the city of Liverpool, Herbert Rowse Armstrong, the Hay Poisoner, the only British solicitor ever to hang, arrived here at the age of two. He came with his parents – William Armstrong and Eleanor Cole Rowse – from Plymouth in 1871, the family settling at 6 Durning Road, Edge Hill.

In the *Liverpool Directory* for 1872, the firm of Armstrong & Rowse, lard refiners, soft soap manufacturers and oil merchants, is listed as occupying premises at 79, 81 and 83 Rose Place, off Cazneau Street.

The Armstrongs moved, in 1882, to another house – Number 52 – in Durning Road. Doubtless, it was from here that, through the generosity of two maiden aunts, young Herbert was enabled to go up to St Catherine's College, Cambridge, where he read law. He served his articles in the office of the Liverpool solicitors, Alsop, Stevens and Cook, and in 1895, was duly enrolled as a solicitor and notary public.

He left Liverpool in 1901 and went to work in Newton Abbot, in Devon. Seeking to improve his prospects, he moved, in 1906, to Hay, on the Welsh border, and by June 1907, was in a position to marry Katharine Mary Friend. In the course of the next few years, business prospered, the couple had three children, and, in 1912, moved into a splendid old house called Mayfield, in Cusop Dingle.

But all, it was said, was not well with the Armstrongs. The loudish whispers of local Welsh gossip had it that the little man, who should have been master in that fine house, was much tried, driven to the brink of uxoricide by the henpecking tongue of a naggart wife.

The Great War came … and Mr Armstrong left for the front. He came back *Major* Armstrong, strutting dapper with swagger stick, in British Warm and high-polished riding boots. But however much *he* might have changed, *she* had not. Folk in Hay could not help but notice that for all his military advancement, the little Major still seemed to be under the thumb of his domineering wife, and after the freedom and camaraderie of base camps and officers' messes, the petty restrictions imposed at Mayfield must have irked him.

Smoking *verboten* – he was permitted to smoke his pipe or savour a cigar in one room only, and positively never out of doors.

Alcohol *verboten* – a rule enforced with some humiliation and erosion of his ego when, out with his wife as dinner guests and the bottle passed around, the voice of the naggart was heard to exclaim: "No wine for the Major."

At a tennis party, as the little major skipped merrily about the court, Madam materialised and, peering through fierce, metal-rimmed spectacles, issued the peremptory summons: "Come, Herbert! It's six o'clock. How can you expect the servants to be punctual if the master is late for dinner?"

Or, on another highly public occasion, even more embarrassingly, the steely voice of the iron lady calling out: "Herbert! It's your bath night."

One can well imagine him, like Dylan Thomas' Mr Pugh in *Llaregyb*, reading with intent *Lives of the Great Poisoners*.

On 22 February 1921, returned from recent sojourn in Gloucester's Barnwood Private Asylum, Katharine Armstrong was dead, of what, upon her exhumation, proved to be arsenical poisoning.

In the course of the first year of his grass-widowerhood, the mourning major was able freely to enjoy the occasional spree in the company of a lady whom he had met when stationed at Christchurch in 1915 – Miss Marion Glasford Gale, of Bournemouth. He was also gainfully employed during that time in plotting the strategy and tactics for the elimination of one whom he saw as being, as Katharine had been, a threat. This was his fellow-solicitor and professional rival in Hay, Oswald Martin.

One October afternoon in 1921, Armstrong invited Martin to tea, and with a polite, "'scuse fingers!", handed him an arsenic-buttered scone. He ate it and nearly died.

On New Year's Eve, 1921, Armstrong was arrested and charged with attempted murder. Two days later, Katharine Armstrong's prematurely resurrected corpse yielded lethal quantities of arsenic, and the charge was changed to murder.

He was to all appearances an unlikely murderer – a diminutive figure, weighing a mere seven stone, standing just about five feet in height, with a straw-coloured moustache, carefully waxed at the ends, *pince-nez* glasses, with a long, slender gold chain and anchored behind his right ear by an encircling gold hook. The high starched collar, sober tie and invariably discreet *boutonnière* seemed to hall-mark his professional quality and respectability.

When he was arrested a curious little twist of paper had been found in his pocket. It contained a white powder which, on analysis, proved to be a fatal dose of arsenic for a human being. Armstrong had an ingenious explanation. The bane of his life – Katharine and Martin apart, one must surely add – had been the dandelions that infested his much-prized lawn. He hated them *en masse*, he hated them individually, so much so that he carried about with him dandelion-sized doses of arsenic, each precisely calculated for lethal administration to the root of just one dandelion. It was too much for even the keenest gardener on the jury.

But there are those who, to this day, believe that Armstrong was not guilty. It was at Hay, one day in 1993 that I met Martin Beales, and he told me that he was writing a book in which he would present a strong case for Armstrong's innocence. And he was, indeed, uniquely placed for the undertaking of such a task. Not only was he, like Armstrong, a solicitor, but he was practising in Hay from Armstrong's old office, living in Armstrong's old house, Mayfield, and, in further off reduplication, had, again like Armstrong, a family of three children.

In due course his book, *Dead Not Buried: Herbert Rowse Armstrong**
appeared. Well-researched, coruscantly argued, it held up a blinding mirror of
doubt.

Is Armstrong really entitled to stand up there with the looming Titans of
twentieth century venenation – Crippen and Seddon? What emerged was like
nothing so much as a Simenon novel of small-town Gallic jealousies, spite and
cupidity; a strange *huis clos* up at the Big House, where, even on fine days of
open windows to blue skies, one could sense the heavy atmosphere wrapping
it about like an invalid's shawl. And at the centre of the leaden air, blanketing
the many rooms of Mayfield, was the frail, distracted woman, Katharine
Armstrong, moving like a whirling cloud of ectoplasm, a nebula, in her busy
vacuum of voices and insulatory presences of imagined guilt. Through those
rooms and passages, landings and hallways, there surely blew zephyrs of true
madness.

In a fluxional world of shifting certainties, sundry anchorages of generally
accepted fact have provided one with a stable basis of received information.
One such previously indisputable-seeming fact was the toxicological
turpitude of the little Major of Hay. Mr Beales succeeds in throwing partial
doubt upon it. But the central crucial riddle remains, raising its ineradicable
dandelion-head: Who weighted Mrs Armstrong with her fatally heavy
grainage of arsenic? It could, surely, have been only her husband or, by
accident or design, herself. Mr Beales calls into evidence Katharine
Armstrong's truly psychotic melancholia. Was she not certified and confined
for a while in Barnwood Asylum? Did she not display to several witnesses
clear signals of a certain preoccupation with considerations of suicide? He
suggests that she may have been suffering from Addison's disease, which
might have accounted for the coppery tone of her skin. Equally, though, it
could have been the effect of arsenic, producing a toxic jaundice as a result of
its presence in the liver. Mr Beales also paid close attention to Armstrong's
business affairs and is able convincingly to refute the suggestion that their
balance was such that the elimination of Martin was of salvatory moment.

I remember attending a party to mark the occasion of the publication of this
importantly fascinating book. It was the perfect, blue-skied, sunshine-
drenched afternoon of Sunday 28 May 1995. There was a marquee and we sat
on Armstrong's lawn, not a dandelion in sight, and no one offered me a
buttered scone with a 'scuse fingers *politesse*.

It was here, though, that I met Armstrong's only surviving child, his
daughter, Margaret. She was then 75 years old, and had not set foot on
Mayfield's lawn since she was six. A mathematician – I discovered that she
had read mathematics at the same Cambridge college as my wife, Newnham
– she had obviously inherited her father's good brain. She was also totally
convinced that he had not murdered her mother.

---

* *Robert Hale, 1995.*

~

In the summer of 1889, when Armstrong was a 20-year-old Cambridge undergraduate, two young men went up a hill, and only one came down. The hill was Goatfell, the 2,866-foot peak of the Isle of Arran. The men were John Watson Laurie, a Glaswegian pattern-maker, and Edwin Robert Rose, a London clerk, both holiday-making.

The two men struck up an acquaintance on the Rothesay steamer. Laurie, who, for some reason which was never clarified, was calling himself John Annandale, invited Rose to share his digs. Ignoring sound advice proffered by a fellow-holiday-maker, Rose agreed to climb Goatfell with Laurie.

When Rose failed to return to his Tooting home at the end of his holiday, his family became alarmed. His brother travelled up north to hunt for him, and Rose's body was found concealed beneath a cairn of stones on the mountainside. He had been bludgeoned to death and robbed.

When news of the discovery of the body broke, Laurie took flight from Glasgow, and hid himself amid the citizenry of that other no mean city, Liverpool, where he lodged with a Mrs Elizabeth Ennitt, at 10 Greek Street. Leaving Liverpool after a couple of days, Laurie, listing to the irresistible whistle of the thistle, headed back to Scotia, was spotted by a golden-eagle-eyed constable at Ferniegair railway station, and after a chase, arrested.

His trial – fully reported by William Roughead in the *Notable British Trials* series – took place at the High Court of Justiciary in Edinburgh. He was found guilty on a majority verdict – by one vote. It was decided to hang him at Greenock, where the grumbling magistrates put out the money on a flagpole and a black flag, but thriftily borrowed the Glasgow scaffold. Mr Hangman Berry was booked. Two days before the execution date, a Medical Commission found Laurie to be of unsound mind. He was reprieved. The scaffold was despatched back to Glasgow, and he was despatched to penal servitude for life at Perth Penitentiary.

In April 1910, Laurie was transferred to Perth Criminal Asylum, whence twenty years later, on 4 October 1930, he was removed by that capital sentence under which we all lie deferred, and from which there is no reprieve.

~

On the evening of Tuesday 12 April 1977, I took part in a unique murderous 'celebration', when a party of five of us – Edgar Lustgarten, the well-known barrister and crime writer; Joe Gaute, the publisher; John Hill, of Wildy's Lincolns Inn Law Bookshop; our American host, Lee Berckman; and myself – sat down to supper in an upper room at Stone's Chop-House, in London's Panton Street, with the infamous Tony Mancini as guest of dishonour.

According to the whispering leaves of the calendar, the man sitting opposite me was old, but his appearance was such that it made one think that the calendar's whisperings might be lies. With his raven-black, Marcel-waved, brilliantined hair and neat, black, Ronald Colman moustache, he looked not only anachronistically young, but also extraordinarily like a film star of the Hollywood heyday. And, indeed, his name, like that of one of those now forgotten celluloid shadows, had once blazed famously the length and breadth of Britain. Not for acting ability – although perhaps it should have been – but as the notorious Brighton Trunk Murderer. Neither was Mancini his name. Nor were those other assumptions of his, Hyman Gold and Jack Notyr. The son of a Deptford, South London, shipping clerk, he was really Cecil Lois England, but bedazzled by the lives and styles of the Italo-American gangsters of Chicago, he became self-styled Tony Mancini, self-styled, *ersatz*, hood.

It had been on Sunday 28 November 1976, that that peerless organ of social documentation, the *News of the World*, revealed that …

> … a man acquitted of killing his mistress, after one of the most famous murder trials in British history, has now confessed … that he was guilty.

The man was Mancini, who, in 1934, was charged with the murder of Violette Kaye. Now, forty-two years later, he was, the article disclosed, living under an assumed name – in Waterloo, near Liverpool, as I was to discover – and planning to write his autobiography, *I Got Away With Murder*.

Fresh out, in August 1933, from a spell inside following his last disastrous enterprise in petty theft, Mancini got a bread-and-margarine job at an eating-house in the Leicester Square hinterland. It was here that he met Mrs Violet Saunders, *ci-devant* vaudeville toe-dancer Violette Kaye, now, at age 42, playing the streets. He, with his dark Italianate façade and carefully projected Valentino-Novarro aura, caught her fancy. He was twenty-six. She invited him to share a new life.

So they set out, the erstwhile *soubrette* and the fledgling *souteneur*, to set up shop together in the shoddy underworld Greeneland of Pinkie and Brighton Rock. She established her seedy clientele. Things settled into a flyblown pattern. She paid the rent, bought the food, doled out the pocket-money. He danced attendance upon her, did the household chores, including the cooking, warmed her bed, made himself scarce when she brought gentlemen home to occupy it. On free evenings, he, an expert dancer, too, escorted her to the dance-halls.

Then Mancini got himself a job. Nothing spectacular. Just as a waiter-cum-washer-up at the Skylark Café, underneath the arches, at shingle level, just below the point where West Street meets the promenade. And then the trouble started. Violette grew jealous. There were rows. A final crescendo public row in the Skylark, over a waitress. That was on Thursday 10 May 1934. Next morning Mancini announced that Violette had left him, which was true – but she had not gone to Paris.

Tidings of the basement drama enacted at 44 Park Crescent came about as the result of Brighton Trunk Murder Number 1 – a headless, legless female torso found in the left luggage office in Brighton Station. This triggered off a massive police search, which led to the finding of a big, black, evil-smelling trunk, abandoned by Mancini in his last lodgings in Kemp Street. Inside it was the body of Violette Kaye.

Mancini was tried at Lewes. He was magnificently defended by Norman Birkett – and set free by the jury. When they delivered their not guilty finding, all that Mancini, open-mouthed in amazement, could say was, "Not guilty, Mr Birkett! Not guilty!"

Over the supper table that April night in 1977, I heard his version of the true tale from Mancini's own lips he told me:

> After the scene Violette made in the Skylark, I came home filled with an awful anger. I found her lying on the bed drunk and under the influence of morphine. She glared at me and shouted: "Come here, you. You belong to me, d'you hear?" Suddenly I hated her. I was disgusted by her. I turned to go to the kitchen, felt a blow on the shoulder. She'd launched herself at me like a wild cat, clawing and scratching at my eyes. I struck out at her. She reeled backwards into the fireplace. I went to pick her up and she spat full in my face. That's when things went blank. Next I knew, she was limp in my arms, head lolling back, blood coming from her nose and mouth. I realised she was dead. I had thought that I was banging her head on the floor. I'd been banging it on the knob of the fender. I crouched there for some time, nursing her head in my arms. I was in a daze. Couldn't think straight. And I knew the police wouldn't believe I hadn't intended to kill her. I lifted her on to the bed. Suddenly I had to get out of that room. I walked down to the sea. And that was when I decided the only thing to do, the only way out, was to hide the body. I put her in the corner cupboard we used as a wardrobe. I spent the night cleaning up the flat. A few days later I bought that big black trunk, and …

At that moment, most timeously, the waiter set down two large brandies beside our coffees.

MYSTERIOUS
SHADOWS

The Fate of the Gingerbread Town Sisters

Ormskirk, the little Lancashire market-town 13 miles north east of Liverpool, is a quiet place. Nothing much happens there. Births, marriages and deaths are the alpha to omega of its dramas. The neighbours are plain-speaking, kind-hearted, red rose folk. It is a good place to live. The town has long been famous for its gingerbread and its Church of St Peter and St Paul, which from a distance looks like two churches, because it has both a spire and a separate tower, side by side. Two tales are told of how this oddness came about. One version is that the tower was added in 1540 to house the bells from Burscough Priory after its dissolution. The other is that there were two sisters of Ormskirk who bequeathed goodly sums of money to the church on the condition, said one of them, that a beautiful steeple be built; said the other, providing that a noble tower be raised. And the story goes that, animated by the greed of Vitellius and the wisdom of Solomon, the incumbent of the time, determined to lay hands on both ladies' legacies, erected both a tower and a steeple.

It is, however, with the tale of two other sisters of Ormskirk that we are here concerned, the Misses Margaret and Mary Ormesher.

In the late evening of Saturday 5 May 1956, Police Constable George Mellor, on duty, cruising alertly in patrol car Z-Quebec-Two, was somewhat disturbed to spot his neighbour, 67-year-old Miss Mary Ormesher, walking home on her own, carrying what he knew to be the day's takings from her sweet and tobacconist's shop in Church Street in a battered brown attaché-case under her arm.

It would, according to his reckoning, have been all of six years back that the police had advised her for her own good, either to put her money safely away in a bank, or, at the very least, to have someone walk with her at night the three-quarters of a mile from the shop to her house – Ivydene, 8 Asmall Lane. Miss Ormesher had, it turned out, a deep-rooted dislike and distrust of banks, but, heeding the detective's warning, she had arranged that henceforth Mrs Josephine Whitehouse, who lived over the shop, should escort her home every night. And so she had, each night for six full years, this May-time night an only and a first exception. She had been away visiting friends in Southport.

The following morning, in bright Sunday sunshine, Constable Mellor, off duty, was dutifully cleaning his car, when running along the lane came Tom Cummins, the Ormesher sisters' next-door neighbour at Number 6, closely followed by a breathless Mrs Whitehouse.

Earlier that morning, at about ten o'clock, Mrs Whitehouse had carried round to Mary Ormesher – or 'Aunt Polly' as she was affectionately known by the locals – her usual morning cup of tea, and to her surprise had found the shop still locked up. Wondering whatever could be the matter, for Aunt Polly was a creature of disciplined and regular habits, Mrs Whitehouse had put on her hat and coat and set off for Asmall Lane.

Arriving at Number 8, she had knocked repeatedly at the sisters' front-door, but could get no reply. There was something vaguely eerie about the unaccustomed shroud of sabbath silence in which the normally twittering little house seemed to be wrapped. Thoroughly puzzled, and with the first twinges of misgivings gradually acceding to alarm, she called at Mr Cummins' house next door.

He agreed that so profound an absence of activity seemed unusual, and deciding to see if anything was wrong, they had gone together through the unlocked side-entry door. Stepping into the back yard, they were disconcerted to see that far from being its normal neat and well-swept tidy self, it was, not to put too fine a point on it, a shambles. A dustbin had been up-ended. Shards of broken milk bottle were scattered about. Red flecks of what looked like splashes of blood spattered part of the whitewashed yard wall. Two unopened milk bottles stood, discreet among the chaos, on the back step.

But the worst was to come. Looking in through the kitchen window, they saw the bodies of Mary and Margaret Ormesher. They were lying on the floor on each side of the big square kitchen table in pools of blood, a vagrant shaft of morning sunlight illuminating their ghastly, ashen features. With one glance, and without more ado, Tom Cummins and Josephine Whitehouse took to their heels and went to spread the terrible tidings.

Arriving at the scene of the double murder, the police were greeted by the sisters' frantically tail-wagging black and white spaniel, Trixie. She had been hiding away when Mr Cummins and Mrs Whitehouse were at the window. They had heard her softly whimpering. She had been injured by a savage kick, probably when she tried to go to the aid of her mistresses. The officers noticed that the faces of the dead women were strangely clean. Trixie had tried to lick her mistresses back to life.

The sisters had both been hideously battered about the head. A poker, a heavy brass candlestick, a kitchen mallet, and a lemonade bottle, the weapons used to bludgeon them, had been thrown down near the bodies.

From a trail of blood leading out into the yard, the detectives deduced that one of the victims had made a break for it, but had failed to escape and been dragged back into the house.

The attaché-case which had contained Saturday's takings lay upturned. It contained about fifty pounds in coins, but there were no pound or ten-shilling notes in it.

The Ormesher sisters belonged to one of the oldest Ormskirk families, and Aunty Polly was widely known in the town as something of a fairy-godmother. Not only was she ever ready with a smile and a sweet or two extra for her little child customers at the shop, but she, together with her 68-year-old sister, Margaret, had lent hundreds of pounds to help people who were in trouble trying to pay off their debts. These kindly-motivated acts of pure charity had inevitably given rise to widespread whisperings that the sisters were wealthy, and were sitting on a fortune hidden away in their house.

There was probably some truth in this, for notwithstanding that the sisters had no bank account, they were planning to spend about £2000 on alterations to the shop, and close friends knew that an old grandfather's clock was used as a safe in which to deposit the accumulated takings. It was searched and found to contain just a few shillings and to be full of empty boxes.

Chief Superintendent Lindsay, of the Lancashire County Constabulary, took command of the investigation. Later, there would be consultations between the Lancashire CID and the Liverpool CID, led by Chief Superintendent James Morris.

Dr George Manning, the Home Office pathologist, estimated that the deaths of both sisters had taken place at around midnight on 5-6 May.

There were witnesses to be examined.

Thomas Draper, who lived at 10 Asmall Lane, said that he had gone to bed at about 10.45pm on the night of 5 May. His wife, Joan, was in bed reading. He had just been dozing off when he was suddenly awakened by his wife. She had heard a noise.

"Get up, Tom. There's someone in the yard."

They both distinctly heard the 'rattling, quivering sound' of a dustbin lid being disturbed.

Slipping into his trousers, Draper went down to have a look round. He found the dustbin undisturbed. He then checked the wash-house and the coal-house. Both were securely locked. Everything in the yard seemed normal. He was on the point of going back into the house when he heard a strange low moaning noise. At first he thought it was Mr Cummins' dog, two doors down the street. Then he heard the sound of breaking glass and a woman's voice saying softly: "Mr Cummins". This was followed by what sounded like someone tipping rubbish, either next door in the sisters' yard, or a bit further off in Mr Cummins' back yard. Rather puzzled by all this nocturnal activity, but satisfied that no prowler had been in his yard, Mr Draper returned indoors, and went back to bed, dismissing the whole incident as someone having a tiff.

Thomas Cummins, a shipwright, stated that he had heard similar sounds at his residence, 6 Asmall Lane. Earlier on, after visiting his wife, who was ill in Ormskirk Hospital, Mr Cummins had gone for a drink at the Eureka Hotel, in Halsall Lane. He had stayed there until closing time when, in company with a Mrs Allinson and his brother-in-law, Frank Halliwell, who was his lodger, he walked home. This would have been at about 10.45pm. Some ten minutes later, Cummins went over the road to Mr Ashcroft's house – Number 17 – with a set of golf clubs.

Alfred Allinson, a miner, who lived with his wife in Brickmakers Arms Yard, off Asmall Lane, had spent the afternoon watching the Cup Final on television at Cummins' house, and, with his 3-year-old son had stayed on watching TV until Cummins got back from his night out at the Eureka.

It was about 11pm when Allinson left to go back home. As he was crossing Cummins' back yard with his son in his arms, he heard what he thought was the sound of a milk bottle being broken. It was the sort of noise, he afterwards explained, that a cat might make knocking a bottle over. And then, just like Thomas Draper, he heard a woman's voice saying plaintively: "Oh, Mr Cummins". At first Allinson thought that the voice was that of Mrs Houghton, with whom Cummins had been having a drink earlier on, and that he must have said something to her of which she disapproved. Later, however, Allinson changed his mind, and said that he was practically sure that the voice was that of Miss Margaret Ormesher.

Two witnesses came forward claiming to have seen suspicious characters lurking around Asmall Lane.

Eleven-year-old James Houghton, who lived at 37 Asmall Lane, right opposite the Ormesher sisters' house, said that on each of the three nights preceding that of the murder he had, at around 10pm, seen a tall man, wearing a fawn trench coat and dark trousers, in the lane. On the first occasion – 2 May – the man had been leaning on a blue bicycle against the hedge at the end of the block, some 30 yards from the Ormesher house. He had stayed there for the better part of a quarter of an hour, and kept glancing up and down the road. The boy had seen him again, at about the same time, on the Thursday and Friday nights. He did not see him on the Saturday.

Thomas Derbyshire, of Brickmakers Arms Yard, told the detectives that at about 10.20pm on the night of the murder he was walking along Asmall Lane. When he was a few yards away from the entrance to the Brickmakers Arms Yard, he saw a man on the opposite side of the road, just outside the house of his sister, who lived at 19 Asmall Lane, bending down, "as if he was looking for something he might have dropped out of his pocket".

A lad named William Brompton, who lived in Halsall Lane, and who had been out walking with his girlfriend on the night of 5 May, was interviewed. He had, he said, stopped for a while, around 10.45pm in the doorway of a livery stable, about 20 yards from the Ormesher house, but, possibly because their attentions were romantically directed to other quarters, they had, he unblushingly admitted, heard no unusual noises.

The detectives worked long and hard, and cast a wide net. An inch by inch search, involving the importation of tracker dogs from Police HQ at

Preston, was carried out over the 1000 square yards immediately surrounding the murder house. The churchyard of St Peter and Paul's was scrutinised, as were the surrounding lanes and woods, for any bloodstained articles that might have been discarded by the killer.

Hospital casualty departments and doctors' surgeries in the district were checked to see if anyone had been treated for cuts and bruises. Inquiries were made at all laundries and dry cleaners' establishments in Ormskirk, Burscough, and Maghull, as to whether they had received any bloodstained clothing. From the disordered state of the kitchen, it was obvious that the sisters had both put up a fierce struggle with their assailant, and he must have been spattered with blood.

Notices were flashed on the screens of cinemas in and around Ormskirk. A patient who had absconded from a mental home on 5 May, and been picked up at Southport on 6 May, was interviewed. Twenty-two of the sisters' relatives, scattered all over the country, were traced, contacted, interviewed, and eliminated from the inquiry.

An Army camp at nearby Burscough was visited, and checks run on all the soldiers, in particular those who had been out of camp on the night of 5 May. Passengers who were regular travellers by bus and rail between Ormskirk and Liverpool were seen. Known local villains and Teddy boys (an unruly socio-sartorial phenomenon of the period) were accorded special attention.

Local shopkeepers and the staff in public-houses were asked to keep a sharp eye out for anyone passing bloodstained banknotes. People were also asked to make contact with the police should anyone offer for sale two valuable items which had been stolen from the sisters – a ladies' watch, platinum case, small face surrounded by some 40 diamond chippings and 20 emeralds, which cost £1,000 in 1942, and a gold ring, set with sapphires and diamonds.

On Friday 11 May 1956, several thousand lined the streets to watch the funeral cortège pass to where 500 sorrowing people packed the tower-and-steepled parish church of Ormskirk to await the arrival of the coffins containing the ill-used bodies of Margaret and Mary, the much-mourned Ormesher sisters. And Canon Redwood, the vicar, addressing the congregation, gave voice for them to their sentiments.

"Nothing," he said, "so dreadful has happened in our peaceful country town before. Most of us are here out of respect for the two gentle-minded souls whom we have known for so long."

The next day, Saturday 12 May, patrons of a drill hall, half a mile from Asmall Lane, where local youths attended Saturday night hops, were questioned, and that night Chief Superintendent Lindsay went along there and interrupted the jollification, casting something of a pall over the assembled dancers with the chilling announcement: "There is abroad in

Ormskirk, a brutal murderer who should be put away."

And that is precisely the conclusion that police thinking had arrived at. The killer was a local man. They also thought that there was only one man involved. Whoever it was who had attacked the sisters must have had a good knowledge of their habits and movements.

Lindsay now let it be known that it was his intention to have every man, woman, and child of Ormskirk's 24,000 inhabitants questioned, and every male in the murder area fingerprinted. The detectives went back to square one. More house-to-housing. The forensic team began to fine-tooth-comb Number 8 all over again, room by room, and to re-examine the back yard. But it all came to nothing.

George Mellor had a theory though. Long retired and keeping a pub, the Rowditch on the Uttoxeter Road, outside Derby, he confided to an old Fleet Street friend of mine, the celebrated crime reporter, Owen Summers. He was convinced that the old ladies knew their murderer.

"Once inside their house they would very seldom open their door to anyone. I never knew them to invite anyone inside. Only somebody living, or who had lived locally and knowing their habits well, could have somehow talked his way inside or trailed Aunty Polly home."

Whatever the truth of the matter, it all happened a long, long time ago. The years have cast deep shadows over the gentle ladies' grave, and the Beast of Ormskirk was never brought to justice.

GOUDIE, THE LIVERPOOL BANK ROBBER

A young Shetlander, Thomas Petersen Goudie, will always be remembered as the man who diddled the august Bank of Liverpool out of a massive £169,500, in the days when there were 240 strong-purchasing-powered pennies to the pound.

He will be remembered, too, among his peers in criminal circles in salutary fashion as the swindler who was swindled, a living testament to the bitter truth of Swift's – paraphrased – observation that:

> Big fleas have little fleas upon their backs to bite them.
> And smaller fleas have lesser fleas, and so on ad infinitum.

Hymned, with fine grandiloquence and more imagination than behoves one of Her Majesty's judges, by His Honour Judge Parry*, Goudie

is pictured in his Shetland homeland thus:

> That strange wild land of stacks and skerries, of voes and geos, of cliffs and caves, an ardent boy hero descended from a race of Norse pirates eager to follow in the footsteps of his ancestors. Some Norna of the Fitful Head would chant to him the old sagas, casting a spell over him and implanting in his young mind a predatory desire to sail for Southern lands of promise and spoil the fair-haired Saxon. Dwelling, too, in a primitive land of knitted wool and pleasant little ponies we should see him in his daily island life a simple peasant lad, bound to be an easy prey in the later scenes of the drab conspirators of the Saxon race-course.

But His Honour is honest enough to admit:

> These things may be but fancies, and Goudie, after all, may have been nothing but a vain eccentric criminal. All we know is that he was a Shetlander, and arrived in early life at Liverpool with excellent testimonials.

Sadly, I have never been to the Shetland Isles, but I know their southern

* The Drama of the Law. His Honour Judge Edward Abbott Parry. (T Fisher Unwin, 1924).

sister isles, the Orkneys, very well indeed, having spent a considerable amount of time there during World War Two, and afterwards, and followed in the excavatory footsteps of Professor Victor Gordon Childe at the prehistoric village of Skara Bray, on the Bay of Skaill. The brochs are less plenteous in the Orkneys, but the atmospheres of the two sets of remote islands are sufficiently similar for me to be able to appreciate the sort of background which shaped Tom Goudie.

At the time with which we are concerned, the year 1901, Goudie was 29 years old, and had, after a prentice period in a Scottish bank, spent the last seven or eight years warming a high stool in the prestigious Bank of Liverpool. Over that span he had, by virtue of the operation of time and talent, acceded to the post of ledger-clerk, which position yielded an annual £150, out of which he spent one pound per week on board and lodging, and was left with two pounds in hand, a fair part of which could be salted away. Hardly riches! A bank clerk's life in those days was an involuntary exercise in Smilesian self-help.

Going by appearances, as one does, young Mr Goudie was to all intents and purposes a well-educated, respectable, decent, hard-working, suitably submissive employee, lacking only in any mark of character or perceptible grace-note of personality. He exhibited no behavioural peculiarities, lived quietly, and displayed no extravagant, or even expensive, tastes. A veritable type specimen of the uncommon 'common man', he was unquestionably the very last employee against whom an employer would have entertained suspicion or unease.

But to go by appearances is rash. They can be, often are, deceptive. Mr Goudie burned with hidden, unquenchable fires. He was a secret obsessive, compulsive gambler, whose fancy rode the gee-gees. He had begun, as gamblers generally do, in a small way. A two-shilling, five-shilling, very, very occasional ten-shilling bet. But, as the mania – and that was what it was – mounted, so did the size of the stakes, and the magnitude of his losses.

So disastrously swiftly did his betting misfortunes accelerate, that it was within a relatively short time that he found himself faced with a £100 debt, and the threat of exposure, and consequent dismissal from the bank, if due payment to his rapidly patience-losing bookie was not forthcoming.

By 1898, when this fiscal crisis burst about his far from innocent head, young Mr Goudie's reputation for steady, steadfast devotion to the mathematic columns of his clerkly duties had uplifted him to the aforesaid responsible height of ledger-clerk. This meant that he had been assigned to look after and post the ledgers containing the account details of those clients whose names fell alphabetically in the H–K category. And this was the juncture at which 'the honest Scot', as he was perceived, yielded to alarm and temptation, and, in neat and faultless copperplate, forged a £100 cheque.

This was the first step on a slippery, primrose-banked path, which, stretching to the extraordinary distance of three years of blissfully undetected ledger-mulcting, was ultimately to lead to the thorn-choked terminal road of discovery and disgrace.

On Thursday 21 November 1901, the head office of the Bank of Liverpool was the scene of great, but, as behoved so dignified and hallowed an institution, discreetly controlled and managed, uproar. Defalcation had come to light.

The rumpus had started off quietly enough with the accountant of the bank remarking to Goudie upon the curious circumstance that a cheque had been recorded in the clearing-book which was not to be found in the Hudson ledger account. Nodding sagely, Goudie had agreed that that was indeed somewhat odd, and suggested that the explanation must surely be that said cheque had been entered by mistake in a wrong account.

In an effort to substantiate this likelihood, Goudie slipped off, made an entry in another account, and presented it for the attention of the investigating accountant. That gentleman had, however, already been to the file in search of the actual cheque, only to find that it was missing.

"That," said Goudie, "is for the porter to explain."

The porter was, for the moment, nowhere to be found. Goudie, therefore, put on his hat, jammed his umbrella firmly on his arm, stepped out to have his lunch, and was seen no more in those parts which knew him.

Now the end was in sight, but behind the inoffensive-seeming little Shetlander lay an absolutely amazing labyrinth of brilliant deception – and breathtakingly stupid misappropriation of his misappropriations!

How did he do it? Like a magician's trick or a Sherlock Holmes deduction, once explained it is seen to be all too ridiculously easy. Goudie had, as we have already learned, charge of the H–K ledgers. In the H ledger was a special credit current account of millionaire Robert William Hudson, the great Victorian soap magnate, irreverently dubbed the King of Suds. This account represented the sum of approximately £200,000, and had been established as a reserve fund of easily accessible cash, available for dealing with any sudden business emergency which might arise.

Goudie began by opening a modest account at the bank. This meant that, like any other customer, he could buy blank cheque forms at the counter without any difficulty. He would fill in the cheque for whatever sum he fancied, and then, exercising a God-given gift of recent discovery, would forge superbly the soap tycoon's signature.

The cheque, having been presented and paid, would be returned to the bank of origin – the Bank of Liverpool – where it would be duly entered into the journal. This clearing-book, together with the cancelled cheque, would be routinely delivered to Goudie's desk. The first thing that he would do was destroy the cheque. He would then mark the clearing-book as if the ledger had had the appropriate deduction posted therein, but he had in fact made no entry in the ledger, so that Mr Hudson's account always showed that client's actual deposits and withdrawals.

Goudie guarded against exposure of his defalcations in the weekly sheet and the recurrent sporadic audit, by a cunningly concocted system of false entries. This was made the easier for him because it was part of his duty to assist the auditors.

Luck, which deserted him on the racecourse, was certainly a lady to him at the bank. His depredations continued undetected to the tune of £170,000.

Using the name John Style, stating that he was an oil and colour merchant, Goudie, presenting a forged cheque for £100, opened an account at the Princes Road branch of Lloyds Bank. From that time forward, the proceeds of his defalcations were routed through that bank. Goudie was now in a position to lose tens of thousands at the races – and proceeded to do so.

Judge Parry sums up the developing situation most felicitously:

> A pigeon of this plump and healthy character could not flutter abroad within the curtilage of the race-course without attracting the hawks that are to be found perched upon those queer boxes which are not 'places within the meaning of the Act'.

The first gentlemen of the track who took to plucking him were a highly dubious pair, Thomas Francis Kelly, a Bradford man, and William Haines Stiles, a whilom bookie's runner. He met them on a train, bound from Newmarket to London, and they invited him to a game of cards. Such deft manipulators and cutters of the pack, could, as you might say, read it in the cards that this was an amiable young man of immense gullibility and, from their oblique point of view, rare potentiality. They made sure that they would see more of him, and develop that potentiality to their benefit, by inviting him to join them the following day at Hurst Park Races. He readily accepted.

What Goudie was doing on these south country racecourses so far from his North Western home, we can only conjecture. The likelihood seems that he was taking his annual leave. Anyway, it was in the course of that fateful day that Kelly and Stiles 'told him the tale' – and hooked him. Stiles, Kelly confided, was a man of enormous wealth who would regularly have £5,000 or £10,000 on a race, and he was prepared to let Goudie – or, rather Scott, to use the *nom de sport* under which Goudie disguised himself in his betting activities – have a share in the bets.

Back in Liverpool, Goudie promptly began wiring bets to be placed by Kelly on horses recommended by Stiles. In cautious mode, Goudie insisted that his telegrams should mention only small sums of money, but these modest stakings should actually be multiplied by their recipient by fifty. But none of these bets of Goudie's had ever been placed on his behalf. The stake money was simply siphoned off into Kelly and Stiles' pockets.

Out of these 'winnings' of theirs, Stiles purchased a racehorse named Forse. Goudie fancied its chances and wired £3,000 on it. It won at odds of eight to one. He got not a penny of his £24,000 notional winnings. The bet had, as usual, not been placed. It was explained to the disappointed 'mug' that the lady clerk at a London hotel had not handed Goudie's telegram to Stiles until five hours after its receipt – too late to lay the bet. And Goudie believed him!

The racing world is in many respects a very close, and closed, circuit, around the inner track of which news and rumours travel faster than many a three-legged horse around the outer track. It was then, understandably, not long before glad tidings of the advent of the easily plucked 'Liver Bird', who could be relied upon to provide a rich harvest for the none-too-scrupulous reaper, were surreptitiously signalled abroad.

Those tidings were picked up, seized upon, by an evil trio, who, having observed Kelly and Stiles' grandiose scattering about of their new-found wealth, put their ears to the ground and learned of the rich-plumaged Liver Bird. These three men were: Dick Burge, a former first-class light-weight prize-fighter, now fallen on hard times of debt and difficulties; Mances, an American wandering sociopath, facultative bookie, and professional card-sharper, resident in a room in an hotel in the Charing Cross area; and Laurie Marks, a hard-up, small-time, small starting-price bookmaker in the Adelphi.

There were now two distinct, mutually antagonistic cabals with sights set implacably on the Liverpool bank robber. Burge became the prime mover of the new junta. Facing up to the problem of unmasking the beneficently prodigal Liver Bird, Mances was despatched to attend a race-meeting at which it was known that Stiles would be present.

Once spotted by Mances, Stiles was followed, pillar to post, everywhere. Never for a single second did the American take his eyes off him. Vigilance reaped its reward. About mid-afternoon, Mances saw Stiles scribble off a telegram. He afterwards tore up the draft, and threw the scraps away. Mances picked them up, pieced them together, and learned Scott's name and his accommodation address.

The conspirators, Burge and Mances, set forth at once upon a priority visit to Liverpool. And there, one October day, at the newspaper kiosk from which Goudie conducted his betting affairs, he was accosted by a total stranger. The man began with a casual request for directions to the premises of a certain Liverpool stationer's, but the questing interlocutor, vertiginously speedily changing tack, began to make it painfully clear that there was nothing in the forger's duplicit life of which he did not intimately know.

The conversation proceeded somewhat like this:

A bold statement, brooking no denial: "You go in for racing."

Goudie, wary, taken aback, does deny it.

"I've seen you – at Doncaster, Manchester and Sandown. I've seen you, along with Kelly and his partner, Stiles. You've lost a lot of money to them."

Goudie is still in denial.

"I know all about you. You are a clerk in the Bank of Liverpool, and you are in a position to command money."

Goudie visibly paled.

Mances swiftly reassured him. "Oh, don't worry, I'm not a detective."

Pour encourager le patsy, he went on to tell him that he was friendly with an American jockey by the name of Ballard, who could give them any number of winners. Gilding the carrot, he added that he was prepared to introduce Goudie to a firm of bookmakers, Marks & Co, who would let him have £5,000 on any race within an hour of starting. The bemused Shetlander began to have golden visions of recouping all his losses. The gold remained visionary.

In the upshot, the bluffing Mances succeeded in blackmailing the timorous Shetlander into carrying on for the ring of conspirators' benefit that same system which had so resoundingly enriched Kelly and Stiles. For three weeks the new arrangement went smoothly and prosperously on – for the trio; Goudie, as before, never winning. Burge and his wife opened banking accounts. Mances invested £33,000 in Consols. Marks opened a banking account with Crédit Lyonnaise.

Then ... the bubble burst.

The banks had become suspicious and made inquiries of each other. There was no time to obtain an official garnishee order, but, following upon a visit from the Chief Inspector of the Bank of Liverpool, an informal banker-to-banker courtesy agreement was reached to stop payment of any cheques issued from the suspect accounts.

Goudie, for whom the police of Britain had been hunting since 21 November, was arrested on 2 December 1901. Calling himself Johnson, and saying that he was a seaman, he had been lodging with a Mrs Harding, at 2 Berry Street, Bootle. His landlady had gone to the Bootle police, reporting that for the past ten days she had had a lodger in her house who looked to her very much like the wanted man. Apart from a couple of days' absence – and from which expedition he returned lame – he had hardly left the house during that time. Those two days he had spent in Southport, where he had had a narrow squeak when the assistant who shaved him at a hairdresser's shop suspected his identity, followed him out into the street, and told a passing constable of his suspicion. After a minute's inspection, the constable had decided that the barber was mistaken. But this time, after Mrs Harding's tip-off, there was no doubt about it. The police hurried along to Berry Street at once ... and there was Goudie.

Although the actual frauds had been committed in Liverpool, the associated scheming had been done mainly in London, and it was therefore an officer from Scotland Yard, Chief Inspector WC Gough, who proceeded with a colleague to Liverpool, and repaired from there to Bootle, where they took over the prisoner from the local police. They escorted Goudie to the main bridewell, the street outside which was packed solid with a huge crowd of people. Determined to spare Goudie the ordeal of the gaping spectators, Gough decided on a ruse to draw off the hounds by laying a false scent.

Seizing upon an entirely innocent Liverpudlian, who just happened to be of Goudie's size and trim, Gough and another detective herded him between them to Lime Street Station, followed closely by one of the largest mobs that Gough had ever seen. Arrived there, the crowd witnessed an amazing sight. Prisoner and escorts vanished into the station bar.

Ten minutes later, having downed whisky-and-sodas, the three emerged, and the waiting crowd watched dumbstruck as the 'prisoner' shook hands with his 'arresting officers', and, after seeing Gough safely aboard the London train, slipped off home. Meanwhile, Goudie had been driven by cab to the first station up the line, Edge Hill, where the train having stopped for the purpose, he was escorted into the reserved compartment where Gough was waiting to receive him.

While in custody, Goudie had not only 'coughed', as the elegant police argot has it, confessing his own guilt of the series of embezzlements, but had also made statements implicating five other men. Determined to snare them, the police cast their net wide.

Tom Kelly was caught in its meshes, and on 27 December, Bill Stiles was arrested by the Broadstairs police. He had been posing as a professional pedestrian in training for an important foot race. A stickler for realism, he was actually doing the training. His fatal mistake was buying his newspaper each morning from the same bookstall on Broadstairs railway station, where eventually the suspicions of one of the sales assistants was aroused, and he communicated them to the police.

Laurie Marks escaped to France, then changed his mind, and boarded a boat at Boulogne, but never arrived at Folkestone. He had jumped into the Channel, preferring to commit suicide rather than face the music. Richard Burge had been arrested by Gough at his suburban London home on 26 November. Mances had fled, and was never brought to trial.

What has been described as the great criminal trial of the year, commenced in the Central Criminal Court, at the Old Bailey, before Mr Justice Bingham (afterwards Viscount Mersey) on 17 February 1902. Mr FE Smith (afterwards Lord Birkenhead) led Mr EG Hemmerde (who was later to play so important a part in the celebrated Wallace case in Liverpool in 1931) for Goudie, who, bowing to the inevitable, pleaded guilty.

The simple truth was that he had no possible defence. In all, he had forged twenty-seven cheques for a grand total of £169,500. Kelly and Stiles shared, divided on a fifty-fifty basis, £72,000 of the embezzled money. The Burge-Mances-Marks cartel cleared £91,000. Forged cheques spent on imaginary bets emptied £163,000 out of the Bank of Liverpool's coffers. The £6,500 balance was never accounted for. One thing is certain: it did not remain in Goudie's slippery, feckless fingers.

As for the others, Burge, who was defended by Mr Horace Avory, KC (later the formidable Mr Justice Avory, otherwise known as 'The Acid Drop') was given a total of ten years – two years' hard labour and eight years' penal servitude. Kelly and Stiles each received two years' hard labour. Marks was beyond the Court's jurisdiction. Mances, likewise – but departed hence, not dead. It was rumoured that he had gone to France, and on from there to America, where he had his fair share of further criminal adventure, but ultimately reappeared in London, a broken, decrepit man, who hobbled about the West End living thinly on blackmail money screwed out of crooks he had known in palmier times. He is said to have ended an ill-spent life in a London poor-house.

As the six day trial drew to its close, it became obvious that the only way in which Goudie's counsel could help him was by making a powerful plea in mitigation. This Mr Smith did, but for all its excellence, the trial judge was unmoved. Addressing the unhappy Shetlander, His Lordship told him:

> I don't know in your case whether to marvel more at the wickedness of your folly, or the folly of your wickedness, for the money you obtained from the bank you appear to have squandered in a most reckless manner. I remember that you benefited personally very little from it. I see no excuse for you, no palliation.

And he proceeded to sentence him to ten years' penal servitude.

Goudie was sent to Parkhurst, where, after completing only five years of his sentence, he died in 1907. An ex-lawyer, who arrived to serve his sentence in that prison shortly after Goudie's demise, later reported that he had heard that he was very delicate, and that his sisters were present at his deathbed. He had also heard that the landlady who gave Goudie away did so for the £500 reward money, and that this infuriated her neighbours, who demonstrated their feelings by smashing her windows.

Thomas Petersen Goudie, master forger, champion embezzler, lies buried on another island, a long, long way from the smiling skies of his native Shetland, in the alien earth of the convict section of the Isle of Wight's Carisbrooke Cemetery.

THE CLOCKWORK CASK OF DEATH

When I was doing the research for my *Quest For Jack the Ripper*, I came across, a rare booklet, *"Leather Apron;" or the Horrors of Whitechapel*, London, 1888, compiled by Samuel E Hudson, published in Philadelphia, undated but very likely in the late-1880s, in which I read with some astonishment the following:

> The mysterious murders of sailors at the great Canada docks, at the port of Liverpool, are today unsolved. Day after day the bodies of seamen were found either upon the bulkheads, or in the waters of the docks, with fearful gashes, until the number reached more than half a score. Then they suddenly ceased, and the police admitted they were baffled. Robbery was not the motive here. Then, what was? Was it killing for the sake of killing? Was it the work of a monomaniac, whose blood-craving appetite was finally appeased? Doubtless such was the fact.

I must admit, I had never heard of any such series of murders on the Liverpool waterfront, and was intrigued. If they indeed took place, there ought to be some record of them somewhere in the city archives.

Strange birds of passage have come from time to time to roost in the port of Liverpool, blown in by the sea-winds of chance and, sometimes, by evil design. Surely one of the most sinister and mysterious of such ill-omened visitants was the man who called himself 'Mr WK Thomson'.

The first to encounter him, upon the very threshold of his arrival, was a good-natured, amiable and hard-working Liverpool dock labourer by the name of Sullivan. Late one autumn afternoon in the year 1875, Sullivan was making his way home from his work on the quays, when he was approached by a tall, dark man whom he had never set eyes on before.

"Forgive me for troubling you," said the stranger, who spoke with the educated voice of a gentleman, "but I wonder if you happen to know of anyone round these parts who has a room to let?"

It was not, however, any common or garden sort of room that he wanted. It had to measure up to certain very precise specifications. First and foremost, it had to be absolutely private and must not be in any way overlooked. Secondly, it had to be suitable to serve as a sort of workshop and bedroom combined.

"You see," the stranger explained, "I am an electrical engineer, and I am working on an invention of mine, something to do with the docks, and it's still very secret. I hope to make a lot of money out of it eventually, and I don't want anyone to steal my idea."

Now it just so happened, the long, flexed arm of coincidence being what it is, that Mr Sullivan himself had just the very place that the stranger was looking for. And it just so happened that he had been looking for a tenant. The room was not everybody's choice. In fact, it was a sort of garret, large in area, but with a low ceiling, and lit only by two skylights in the roof. Only pigeons could look through and, in short, it was paradise for a secret-hugging inventor.

Highly delighted, the stranger, who now introduced himself as Mr WK Thomson, went home with Mr Sullivan there and then, inspected the garret, expressed his entire satisfaction with it, immediately forked out two weeks' rent in advance without a murmur, and moved in, with assorted gear, the very next day.

The Sullivans nodded sagely to each other when their exotic lodger showed no taste for stirring out of his eyrie, and worked late into the nights. Hadn't he told them exactly what he was up to? Besides, he paid for everything on the nail, like a real gentleman. He sent Mrs Sullivan out for his food. She was glad to oblige, and only too happy to cook it for him. If the truth be told, the Sullivans were rather proud of having an inventor in their house, and they listened with awe to the appropriate noises aloft – hammerings, filings, and a peculiar whirring sound, like clockwork suddenly set off.

After two or three weeks, the symphony of sounds from the attic ceased. He must have finished his invention. Then … BOOM! It was like ten cannons. A terrible explosion rocked the whole house and filled it with choking fumes and thick smoke. Upstairs in the eyrie, shattered skylight glass lay like a snowfall of glittering, lethal-edged ice. Mr Thomson emerged from the smoke and smother unscathed, but with ruffled feathers, parroting frenzied apologies. Some chemicals had ignited accidentally, he explained. And, yes, of course he would pay for the damage, every last penny of the cost.

When their upright hair had settled down again, the reassembled Sullivans forgave their perilsome lodger. After all, inventors were eccentric, weren't they? And accidents would happen, wouldn't they? Thomson told them that he had nearly finished his work and would be off soon anyway. Meanwhile, he fixed a tarpaulin over the roof, to keep out the relentless Merseyside rain.

The explosion seemed to have summoned up strange creatures out of the pit! The Sullivans' hermit-like lodger turned out to have unsuspected acquaintances in Liverpool. A succession of furtive, unappetising figures slunk upstairs after dusk, stayed all night, and slunk away again before the sun was up. The Sullivans were hard put to find an explanation for all this sudden clandestine nocturnal activity, and could only suppose that these were secret-sharers with a vested interest in their extraordinary lodger's invention.

Mr Thomson's welcome was by now wearing a little thin. To make matters worse, gossiping neighbours were having a field-day, and the antennæ of the local police were beginning to quiver. A constable called. He half expected to find a coiner's den, but the tableau in the attic did not fit. Thomson was sitting at a long, low table on which were strewn pieces of clockwork apparatus in different stages of manufacture. There was a big tin trunk in a murky corner of the room, and the constable opened it both cautiously and hopefully. It was crammed with little packages of a substance that looked like compressed oil-cake. The constable picked some up. It was sticky. He sniffed it. It smelt terrible – like sulphur. He dropped it back in the trunk – obviously harmless – and took a civil leave of the stranger, with profuse apologies.

But birds disturbed in their nests never feel safe there again. That night Thomson decamped, taking with him most of his belongings, and the Liverpool garret lay bare and untenanted again, the only relic of its late occupant, a hole in the roof and a lingering smell of sulphur on the air. Mephistopheles had fled.

He went to ground in Preston – in a locality known as 'The Dust Hole', which, as its name implies, was a twilight world through which even a Jack the Ripper could have flitted without remark. When he felt the hounds were off, the foxy Thomson moved on to Southampton. There he donned a new mask. The explosive inventor was transformed into a rich American antique collector, a connoisseur of paintings, intaglios, old engraved gems, and suchlike costly collectables.

In this new guise, he strode confidently into a shipping agents' office, deposited with them several heavy cases containing, he said, valuable antiques, and arranged for them to forward them to New York, via the steamship *Mosel*, of the North German Lloyd Line. The *Mosel* was listed to call at Southampton on 12 December 1875, having set sail from Bremerhaven, Germany, on 11 December. The consignment of antiques to be put aboard at Southampton was heavily insured. That was the crux of the whole devilish plot.

Thomson then travelled to Bremerhaven, where he had had confederates take a villa for him on the outskirts of the town. His workshop this time was a coach-house attached to the villa. He ordered a puzzled local cooper to make a curiously-shaped oblong cask for him. Delivered to the coach-house, it was promptly filled with his clockwork apparatus and sulphur-reeking packages. On 10 December, he arranged for the cask to be shipped to New York on the *Mosel*. At the same time, he booked a passage on the *Mosel* for himself – but only from Bremerhaven to Southampton.

That December night, one of the worst frosts in living memory struck Bremerhaven. It spread an iron-hard glaze over streets and quays. A skidding, straining dray-horse arrived safely at the docks with his cart loaded with Thomson's cask. It drew alongside the *Mosel*. Then, as the horse leaned back in the shafts, his feet slipped from under him, the cart tilted, and the cask toppled out with a crash. The explosion which followed was like an erupting volcano. A dazzling white light plumed high up in the air like shooting lava. Horse, cart, driver – simply disappeared. Where they had stood, yawned a great crater, all of 30 yards in circumference. About 80 people on the docks, mainly relatives and friends seeing off departing passengers on the *Mosel*, were killed outright in the holocaust, and more than 100 injured. The *Mosel* itself was a listing wreck, its decks plastered with groaning victims.

Down below in his first-class cabin, Mr WK Thomson lay mortally wounded. He had shot himself when he realised that his elaborate plan had misfired. He died after five days of agony – a fitting end, surely, for this merciless dynamitard. For the mysterious packages in his clockwork cask of death were, of course, of dynamite, which was not so well understood here in those days as it was in the Wild West! He had manufactured an immensely powerful, primitive bomb, of the accuracy of whose clockwork setting he was so confident that he was prepared to travel part of the voyage, from Bremerhaven to Southampton, knowing that his infernal machine, stowed in the hold, was clicking away the minutes, until it was set to explode in mid-Atlantic, long after he had left the *Mosel*, and his bogus antiques had been loaded at Southampton. Then all he had to do was … collect the insurance money.

The magnitude of this little-known crime is amazing. What makes it all even more sinister is that the *Mosel* plot may not even have been the first trial run. A clockmaker named Fuch, who lived in the German town of Derenburg, told the police that two years previously, in 1873, he had made a clockwork machine to Thomson's order, which was so strange that he made a duplicate model of his own, and kept it. It was found that it could be set to go off up to ten days in advance.

Two machines to this specification, one after the other, had been delivered to Thomson by Fuch. And in that year of 1873, two fine vessels were lost without trace in calm waters. The *SS Ella*, bound from London to Hamburg, and the *Scorpio*, bound from Cardiff to Charente, and all who sailed in them, had been swallowed up as mysteriously as if they had been in the latter-day Bermuda triangle.

After the *Mosel* disaster, it needed no Sherlock Holmes to check out that both the *Ella* and the *Scorpio*, had carried aboard them cases of 'antiques' – heavily insured. In their holds, we may be sure, was a clockwork cask of death.

THE VANISHING MP

Liverpool's Northbrook Street could not, by the most generous exaggeration, be described as a distinguished thoroughfare. Neat, clean, respectable, it is all those things, but it is also, not to mince words, drab, as it wends its out-at-elbows way from Kingsley Road, across Granby and Mulgrave Streets, to Princes Avenue.

And yet ... like many another ordinary-seeming Liverpool street, it has strange tales to tell. Murder, a most bizarre murder, as we have already seen in considering the curious affair of the Strangling Teddy Bear, once passed that way. It is also the cradle and grave of a world-famous mystery. An utterly inexplicable disappearance.

On a September's day in 1920, a handsome, smartly-dressed man turned the corner from Northbrook Street into Princes Avenue ... and stepped out of the world. To the end of her days, his grieving mother waited in vain in her small house, 137 Northbrook Street, for the knock on the door that never came.

The son who did not return was 39-year-old Victor Grayson, MP. Members of Parliament do not, as a rule, simply vanish. More's the pity, say their opponents. Sometimes, like John Stonehouse – the runaway Labour MP for Walsall North, whose clothes were found on a Miami beach, but who was himself found, fit and well and accompanied by his attractive young secretary, Sheila Buckley, in Sydney, Australia, in December 1974 – they fade usefully away, for a time, but, as a class, they are survivors, tenacious characters. Victor Grayson, however, was an honourable member who proved the rule by becoming, and remaining, the exception, and the story of his disappearance has become one of the most puzzling enigmas of the last century. A perplexing mixture of fact and liberally ornamented legend.

First, the legend. It has been said that at six o'clock one September evening Victor Grayson walked out of the bar of the Georgian Hotel in London, leaving his change and an unfinished whisky on the counter ... and vanished into eternity. Somewhere under the bright lights of the bustling Strand, his colourful life came to the end of its chequered road, simply petered out in an obscurity even deeper than that in which it had begun.

This, I have every reason to believe, is nonsense.

Now, the facts. Albert Victor Grayson, was the son of a Yorkshire carpenter, William Grayson, and a Scottish mother, Elizabeth, *née* Craig. The couple had three sons and two daughters. Albert Victor, named after the Duke of Clarence, was born on 5 September 1881, at 8 Taliesin Street, off Scotland Road, in Liverpool.

The Grayson family was poor. Albert Victor's childhood, spent at

15 Elstow Street, Kirkdale, was pinched. Hand-me-down clothes, a board school education, at St Matthew's Church of England School, in Scotland Road. At 14, a six-year apprenticeship as a turner at a factory bench in JH Wilson's Bankhall Engine Works. And lucky to get it.

But within the lad's frail body there glowed a spark of that divine discontent which men call ambition; a determination that factory walls should not a prison make. It was pure chance – as, indeed, most momentous things in life prove to be – that pointed his first faltering steps on the road that was to lead to impossible success.

That road ran though the unlikely purlieus of the undenominational Bethel Mission, in Edinburgh Street, and, a couple of years later, the Hamilton Road Mission, both in Everton, where, attending its lively debating society, Grayson, still in his teens, discovered that he had the gift of tongues. He was a verbal spellbinder. He could clothe the vague feelings of the brooding malcontents and the burning passions of the frustratedly inarticulate in a shining raiment of words.

But words, however glittering, are a poor currency without the solid backing of ideas. For a time, though, the richness of his eloquence seemed enough. Then, at Hamilton Road, young Grayson came into admiring contact with the Reverend JL Haigh, pastor of the Anfield Unitarian Church, and decided that, in emulation, he would like to become a preacher.

Befriended by his rôle model, the Reverend Haigh, he went to study theology at Owens College, in Manchester. And that was where that small spark within was suddenly fanned into a flaring red flame. The flame of Socialism, in which he was to be hammered and forged into the shape of a proletarian demagogue. Now, the words took on meaning. They cascaded from him in a red-hot torrent on the street corners of Liverpool and Manchester. His pulpit a soapbox, he became a preacher, not of Unitarian doctrine, but of the dogma of militant revolutionary Socialism's New Jerusalem. The convinced and converted alike, christened him 'The Voice of the People'.

He quit Owens College, and in July 1907, at the age of 25, Victor Grayson toppled the Liberals from their safe seat at Colne Valley, Yorkshire, and entered Parliament as the first real, uncompromising, hard-line Socialist MP. He became the darling of the workers. The *enfant terrible* of the House. His name blazed from every newspaper in the land. He was even tipped as a future prime minister. Children were named after him – among them Victor Grayson Feather, who was to become a great stalwart of the TUC. Sadly, his father did not live long to savour his son's triumph. William Grayson died in 1908.

As he triumphed and prospered, the squalor and poverty against which Victor Grayson had taken up unrelenting cudgels became, for him, a fast-receding memory. There were rumours. They said that his private lifestyle belied his public avowals, that he had gone soft, abdicated to the fripperies of over-elegant dress and feather-bed pleasures; the good cigars, the fine wines, the luxurious bourgeois London flat. The Voice of the People seemed to be losing its authority. The charisma appeared to be wearing thin. The comet had reached its zenith. It began to sputter. In 1910 he lost his seat.

On 7 November 1912, at Chelsea Registry Office, he married Ruth Nightingale, an actress, her stage name Ruth Norreys, the 25-year-old daughter of John Webster Nightingale, a Bolton bank manager, and his wife, Georgina, a former actress. They settled into a flat in Cleveland Mansions, Stockwell Park Road, Brixton. Life was not easy for the newly-weds. The trouble was that politically things were not going well, but The Voice of the People refused to be stilled. He did not number the word 'defeat' in his dazzling vocabulary. He stomped the country rallying and railing. He beavered unceasingly from platform to platform, trumpeting his message from the four points of the compass, assuaging his concomitant fatigue with whisky. Too much whisky. He was slipping almost imperceptibly into chronic alcoholism.

Even the modest upkeep of the Brixton flat became too much for him. The couple moved to a single room in the scarcely salubrious area of Theobald Street, SE1, where they slept on the floor, and were reduced to using a sugar-box as a table. Hardly 'bourgeois luxury'!

Teetering on the brink of bankruptcy, they were rescued by Ruth's worried father. Grayson kept on drinking. In the end, he had what was politely described as a nervous breakdown – an alcoholic collapse, more likely.

In February 1913, political friends and party colleagues launched a national appeal for funds that would permit the Graysons to embark upon a medically recommended, long, recuperative sea voyage, and by May a sufficient sum had been garnered in. The couple journeyed to Italy, then on to a one-roomed bungalow on Long Island, and finally to a small flat in Manhattan, of which a visiting friend said that "to describe [it] as austere, would be to pay it a compliment".

The Graysons returned to England at the beginning of 1914. A daughter, Elaine, was born to them on 13 April 1914, and they lived for the next twelve months or so at 15 Manor Gardens, Larkhall Rise, Clapham.

In the spring of 1915, Ruth secured a contract with the Allan Wilkie Shakespearean Company to go on tour to the Antipodes. She was accompanied to Australia and New Zealand by her husband and baby Elaine.

Seemingly restored in health, Grayson enlisted with the Anzacs, as a private, and was wounded at Passchendale, in October 1917. He came limping back to London in 1918.

In February 1918, his wife died after giving birth to a second daughter.

The baby, Elise, died too. The widowed Grayson took 3-year-old Elaine to Bolton, to live with her maternal grandparents. And then, the bereft, hard-done-by, hard-drinking Grayson tried to make a comeback. He was still a magnificent orator, alcohol had not corroded his powers of speech-making, but it had poisoned the minds of his political brethren against their former darling. Labour would have none of him. He paid a visit to his native city, and, as 'Private Grayson', addressed recruiting meetings at the Shakespeare Theatre and at the Metropole Theatre, Bootle. There, at least, they cheered him. But travelling on to further venues, further platforms, it was a dismal Odyssey. He had to concede defeat.

Returning alone to Liverpool, visiting again his mother's house, it was as if the years between had never been. But you cannot put the clock back. Liverpool, Northbrook Street, his mother, were the same ... but *he* was different. Then, on that September day in 1920, telling his mother and sister that he was going to London and would be in touch with them the following day, he just walked out, round that corner, into oblivion.

Actually, he did keep his promise, and communicated with them the following day ... and that was the last that they ever heard from, or of, him.

I do not think it likely that Grayson would have wilfully contrived his own disappearance. He was a kind man. Surely he would not willingly have inflicted the agony of unknowing upon the little daughter whom he loved and the mother who loved him. I am convinced that somewhere around that corner of Northbrook Street, death was waiting to meet him.

How did he keep the appointment? By accident? By intention? By murder? No man knows.

Oddly, it was not until seven years after his disappearance that, in 1927, the 'case of the vanished MP' received any publicity. On 20 March 1927, the *World Pictorial News* ran the story of:

> A grey-haired, sweet-faced old lady ... [who] sits waiting for news that never comes. She is the mother of Victor Grayson, MP, who mysteriously vanished seven years ago. During all those weary years Mrs Grayson has hoped against hope that her son might be alive, but the continued absence of definite news has caused hope to almost die within her breast.

She told the paper's representative:

> I am now beginning to give him up for dead. If Victor is alive, which I strongly doubt, he must be wandering about suffering from loss of memory. Shortly before he disappeared from London, we received word that he had

had an accident and injured his arm and head. How the injury happened I do not know, but the injury to his head is the only way I can explain Victor's disappearance. He was a very highly strung man and the blow on his head may have impeded his memory. But I am afraid there is a very slim chance of his being alive. He was as proud as Lucifer, and if he is still alive and in his right senses he must be in very reduced circumstances. If this is the case, his proud spirit would prevent him writing to his relatives and so revealing to them his condition. The shock of his wife's death was a very great blow to him, as also was the death of his brother Jack, who was killed in France while serving with the Grenadier Guards. He was deeply in love with Ruth and she with him.

In April 1929, Mrs Elizabeth Grayson died, aged 73. Up to that time there had been no mention whatsoever of what we may term the 'Strand incident at the Georgian Hotel'. This was subsequently further embellished. Grayson had not, it was now said, taken the train to Hull at all. Instead, he had booked a room at the Georgian Hotel, walked out and never returned for his luggage.

Then, in 1970, Donald McCormick entered upon the scene. Those who have made a study of the nefarious goings-on of Jack the Ripper will need no introduction to Mr McCormick. His reputation for truth and accuracy wasnot of the highest. On the other hand, his powers of unprincipled invention do rate highly, and it is largely upon these that he based his solution of the Grayson enigma.

He began well by recognising that there was not, and apparently never had been, in central London, any Georgian Hotel. There was, however, at the material time, a Georgian Restaurant at 43 Chandos Place, and it was, he said, from the bar of this establishment, where he was enjoying drinks with a group of New Zealand Army officers, that Victor Grayson strode out, walking stick in hand, into eternity. What lured him out was, McCormick alleges, a message saying that his luggage had been delivered in error to the Queen's Hotel, Leicester Square.

Now the Queen's Hotel had been frequently used in his counter-espionage days during World War One by a most curious, not to say sinister, character, Maundy Gregory.* Professionally suave, immaculately tailored, aristocratic monocle screwed in eye, this son of the vicar of the Parish of

* For an enthralling account of this fascinating and mysterious man see The Quest for Corvo. AJAS Symons (Cassell, 1933). Also, Honours for Sale. Gerald Macmillan (Richards Press, 1954) and A Playful Panther: The Story of J Maundy Gregory, Con-Man. Tom Cullen (Houghton Mifflin, 1975).

St Michael's, Southampton, unsuccessful actor-manager, almost certainly the successful murderer of an actress, Edith Marion Rosse, gifted entrepreneur, Government broker and tout for the sales of honours and titles, is thus tenuously linked by McCormick with Grayson.

In furtherance of his case, McCormick also conjured up a new witness, a British artist, George Flemwell, conveniently dead, who, claims McCormick, saw Grayson sailing up the Thames with another man in an electric canoe, and enter a bungalow, 'Vanity Fair', owned by Gregory, on Ditton Island. Gregory's motive for murdering Grayson? Grayson had found out about Gregory's dubious activities in connection with the sales of honours and titles, and was blackmailing him. There is not a shred of real evidence for any of this.

That Gregory and Grayson did, in fact, know one another is perfectly true. We have it on the authority of Hilda Porter, who, it seems, really was the last person to see Victor Grayson. She was the 26-year-old manageress of the exclusive block of service flats, Georgian House, in Bury Street, off Jermyn Street, near St James' Palace, where, between the latter months of 1918 and September 1920, Grayson occupied Suite 42, on the fourth floor.

Grayson was living here in some style. His rent was automatically paid for him, and every two weeks a package of money was delivered to him by two men in uniform or livery. This does, admittedly, savour of the involvement of Maundy Gregory, whose practice it was to dress up his attendants in uniforms which would suggest that they were official Government employees. What is more, Miss Porter also stated that Robert Blatchford, J Havelock Wilson, flamboyant and autocratic leader of the Seamen's Union, the notorious Horatio Bottomley, owner of the popular magazine, *John Bull,* and swindler, who was subsequently jailed, and Maundy Gregory, whom, she maintained, Grayson particularly hated, were among his regular callers.

Miss Porter recalled how, one morning in mid-September 1920, two strange men arrived at Georgian House asking for Mr Grayson. They sent up a visiting card and he invited them to his rooms. They were up there with him for most of the day, sending down for some drinks in the afternoon. Towards evening the two men came down in the lift, and called a taxi. A few minutes later, Grayson descended in the lift. He had two very large suitcases with him. Leaving them in the hall, he ascended the few steps adjacent to the lift shaft, went into Miss Porter's office, and told her, "I am having to go away for a little while. I'll be in touch very shortly." He then rejoined the two strangers and went with them out to the taxi. Apropos of the taxi: Maundy Gregory owned his own taxi, driven by his special employee, Tom Bramley, whom I actually met, many years ago, when I was investigating the life and times of his wily employer.

In July 1983, the National Museum of Labour History, at Limehouse, acquired a batch of a dozen or so letters written by Grayson, mostly between 1905 and 1918, to a fellow Liverpool Socialist, Harry Dawson, which make plain the existence between them of a homosexual relationship. Both Joseph Havelock Wilson and Arthur John Peter Michael Maundy Gregory were homosexuals. This evidence of Grayson's bisexuality may provide a significant clue as to the reason for his fate – that is, if we are to believe the late Donald McCormick, which is a dangerous thing to do.

As David Clark reported in his book on Grayson,* The New Zealand Ministry of Defence revealed in 1980 that Grayson's World War One medals had been collected from the High Commission Office in London on 25 August 1939. There is a strict protocol about the handing over of medals, and if Private Grayson was dead, proof of death would have to be provided. This had not apparently been done. The presumption must therefore be that either Grayson himself, or his wife, had collected them. But Ruth Grayson died in 1918. The only other authorised persons into whose hands the soldier's medals could officially be delivered were those of his immediate family – his parents, brothers, sisters, or children. Grayson's parents were both dead. So were his two brothers. His two sisters were living in Canada. His daughter, Elaine, did not even know that her father was eligible for any medals. It looked as if the only person who could have gone to the High Commission in London and collected the medals was Grayson himself. Unfortunately, the signature of whoever it was who had signed the release form for the medals had not been retained.

This, taken in conjunction with certain other circumstances, persuaded Elaine to a definite conclusion.

One such circumstance was the persistent behaviour of her grandmother, Mrs Georgina Nightingale, who had brought her up. That lady, a Victorian Scot, of that ilk and demeanour, always refused, and with some degree of detectable disdain, to discuss her missing son-in-law with his child, her granddaughter. At the time of Elaine's engagement to Raymond Watkins, Grandmother Nightingale worked herself up into a fine state upon hearing of the Watkins family's placing of an announcement of the betrothal in the *Daily Telegraph*, and insisted upon its immediate withdrawal. She seems to have feared that it might have been seen by Elaine's father, who she was sure would be a bad influence on Elaine. That she strongly suspected, or even definitely knew of, his survival, is indicated by the fact that she made a point of telling Raymond that if ever Elaine's father turned up they should not have anything to do with him.

Another circumstance was how, shortly after their marriage in 1936, when Elaine and her husband paid a visit to her mother's grave in Kensal Green Cemetery, they found, somewhat to their surprise, that it was beautifully

* *Victor Grayson: Labour's Lost Leader. (Quartet Books, 1985.)*

attended – the grass cut around it, fresh flowers placed upon it. When they got back to Bournemouth, where they and the Nightingales were all then living, they told old Mrs Nightingale of their visit to the cemetery and discovery of the immaculate grave, and she, to their amazement, flew into an instant tantrum, angrily denying any knowledge of the grave and the state of its upkeep.

Then, one evening, Elaine thought that it was in 1941, she and her husband found Mrs Nightingale zealously burning the contents of an old deed box, and from that time on her grandmother's attitude towards the mention of Victor Grayson completely changed. Throughout the 1920s and 1930s, she had been alternately hostile and defensive, but constantly and unfailingly secretive, about him; she was now relaxed, although still, and, indeed, to the end, maintaining that she knew nothing whatever about him or his fate.

Elaine's conclusion? That her father had survived until 1941.

Victor Grayson is long gone now. But not forgotten. He is remembered by men in grey cloth caps – in grey valleys, in bars and club rooms, and around the kitchen fires of grey stone houses, nestling in the shadows of the mills beneath the wind-tossed moorlands of the Pennine heights.

He is remembered, too, by Elaine, the little daughter he left, grown now into an old lady, older, much older, than her father when he vanished off the face of the earth. Married – Mrs Raymond Watkins – she lived in Hove, and over the years I had many a long talk with her about her lost father. In the end, she was comforted by the thought that no man is really dead so long as one mind or heart remains in which his cherished memory survives, and is still, like a small unquenchable flame, lovingly kindled.

The Curious Luck of the Engraver's Hand

Mr John Hollis Yates, solicitor, of Liverpool, was excited; definitely excited. It had come to his attention, in the way that things do come to the attention of shrewd-eyed, sharp-nosed, pricked-eared solicitors, that a £200,000 fortune was, as the saying has it, going begging, and he had quietly resolved that its appeal should not go unanswered, ignored. Indeed, he was this very day laying careful and practical plans for its salvation from the menacing shadow of the ever-open maw of the clamant Crown coffers, where unclaimed monies statutorily end up.

Such speculators as Mr Yates have thrown the dice down over the centuries, playing a hand for life-cushioning stakes. Without question, the Crown Prince of these optimistic fortune-hunters was a 24-stone butcher from Wagga Wagga, New South Wales, the *ci-devant* Arthur Orton, of Wapping, East London, who, in 1866, attempted to pass himself off as – at the last weighing nine stone – Sir Roger Charles Tichborne, presumed drowned when the *Bella*, of Liverpool, went down off South America, in April 1854. If insolence had had its reward, Orton ought to have succeeded to the rich lands and title. It did not. He did not. He was jailed for fourteen years for perjury.

Then there was the odd business of the duke and the dead draper, which in many respects echoes the Tichborne case.

Mrs Anna Maria Druce, aged relict of Walter Druce, whose father, Thomas Charles Druce, was the self-made proprietor of a flourishing Victorian drapery emporium in Baker Street, got it into her head that her dead husband, Walter, had been the rightful Duke of Portland. This brought out of the woodwork a carpenter from Down-Under, George Hollamby Druce.

The claimant, in quest of ducal robes and the cash that went with the coronet, was *bona fide* to the extent that he was undoubtedly the grandson flowing from Thomas Charles Druce's first marriage – to Miss Annie May Berkeley – and he went about matters with a cunning hand. Knowing well of the law's long delays and heavy costs, he floated companies to finance his £16 million (that was the estimated value of William John Cavendish Bentinck-Scott, the fifth Duke of Portland's worldly estate) fortune hunt.

The investors, appetites sharpened for a taste of the fiscal action when the ducal cash came chinking home, shelled out liberally. But there was one severe inconvenience. His Grace had shuffled off his earthly coil in 1879. The draper had been dead since 1864. This deadly 15-year discrepancy had been explained away by Druce's old widow. The duke, she said, wearying of the prospering career as a tradesman which he had embraced under the identity of Druce, had arranged the old merchant's 'death', and an empty coffin, weighted with an appropriate corpse-weight of lead, had been stowed away in the Druce family vault at Highgate Cemetery.

For a time, all seemed to be progressing well in the Australian claimant's favour; then the Court decided to sanction the opening of the Druce grave. The coffin-lid creaked back, revealing ... surrounded by shroud and sweet-scented sawdust, the well-preserved body of Thomas Charles Druce. And that was the end of the affair.

A possible nominee for Crown Princess, is a Liverpool children's nurse of whom I have heard tell. She was Mabel Margaret Prebble McKillen, who, in 1873, was claiming the rank and title of Princess Solykoff, and, later, was calling herself Lady Muriel Paget. I have as yet to delve into her story. *

The genesis of John Hollis Yates' enterprise dates further back than either the Tichborne or Druce-Portland endeavours. In the Year of Our Lord One Thousand Eight Hundred and Nineteen, there was stationed in Dublin a dashing young English Army ensign (which term denoted, until 1871, a soldier of the lowest commissioned rank) named Blake. During the time of his service in Ireland, Ensign Blake fell irrecuperably in love with a sweet-faced, nature to match, colleen, Helen Sherridan. The daughter of a West of Ireland family of the small farmer or peasant class, she had come to Dublin, and was resident there.

It was a liaison upon which Ensign Blake's uppercrust English family was scarcely likely to look with wedding-bell-carilloned rejoicing, being perfectly well aware of which familial obstacle, the couple in consequence hied themselves off across the Irish Sea to Scotland – it is said to the old forge at Gretna Green, in Dumfriesshire. The union thus struck upon the Scottish anvil – or wherever – flourished happily over the years. Risen to the rank of lieutenant-general, Blake died, childless, in 1850, leaving his widow extremely well provided for. It was upon this considerable fortune that the eye of Mr Yates gleamed.

Helen Blake survived her husband by twenty-five years. She never remarried, and when, in 1875, she died in Liverpool, she left neither children nor a will. No close relatives either came forward or could be traced. There were, of course, dozens of nominal Sherridans back in Ireland, and in the city that has been facetiously described as the capital of Ireland – Liverpool, but nary a one that came within legal grabbing distance of the crock of gold.

In 1883, the whole of the Blake property, by now valued at about £200,000, was, for want of heirs, adjudged to the Crown. Actually, a fair number of hopefuls had come forward endeavouring to justify their claims to being the late Mrs Blake's next-of-kin. The majority of them were poor members of the original Sherridan family, still living in the West of Ireland, but there were among them also members of the same original family who had moved to, and were currently living in, Liverpool.

* See A Pair of Liverpolitan Jades

Now it seemed to Mr Yates an unconscionable shame that so vast a sum should go, unchallenged, to be salted away by the Crown, and it occurred to him that if only he could manage to establish the claim of a Sherridan to the presently free-floating money, he might well so contrive matters that he himself came in for the lion's share of the plunder.

Mr Yates had not always lived in Liverpool. He had, as a matter of fact, been born in Gloucester, and trained to become a teacher, but, in 1888, he had started up instead in business as a solicitor. There are indications that he had not always been a shining pillar of strict legal observance. *Au contraire*, the direction of certain blown straws hint strongly at the performance of transactions which were, to say the least of them, unethical.

He had borrowed £50 from a young man whom he knew, and when the promissory note which he had given him became due, Yates not only refused point-blank to meet it, but actually charged his young creditor with the forgery of his signature on the document, and the young man's father with uttering the allegedly forged note. He prosecuted both father and son at the Gloucester Assizes. They were honourably acquitted, and Yates' costs disallowed. He was then made a bankrupt.

All this had played a significant part in the occasioning of his hasty departure from his native Gloucester, and somewhat precipitate arrival, via Leeds and Wigan, by the Mersey's side.

His first step in this latest transaction was to discover and make the acquaintance of a Patrick Sherridan living in Liverpool. Fairly easily done. Nor was it difficult to persuade him to make a bid for a £200,000 prize; having first signed the sort of agreement to Mr Yates' advantage that Mr Yates had from the start envisaged.

And with that agreement safely tucked away in his office safe, Yates embarked upon the second step of his well-ordered campaign – a trip to the West of Ireland, which he was determined would be sure to yield the necessary convincing proof of the fruitful relationship of the Liverpool Sherridans to the late, lamented Mr Helen Blake.

Alas! such evidence as he found it possible to secure, interviewing the 'oldest inhabitants', prowling the lush turf of ancient churchyards in the Emerald Isle, would only serve to convince the greenest of the green, and Mr Yates was too wily a bird to risk the submission of so slenderly supported a case to the scrutiny of a razor-minded Chancery Court judge. He betook himself and his slender batch of 'proofs' instead to eminent learned counsel, and asked his advice as to what further evidence he would deem necessary in order to provide further and better details to strengthen his case.

The answer, given in good faith, and with no suspicion that jiggery-pokery was being hatched, was that certificates of births, marriages, and deaths would seem certain to make the claim succeed. In the circumstances, that could have been a stop card. Not for John Hollis Yates, though.

His next step was to do as George Hollamby Druce had done; advertise for investors. This brought in £350. With this money in hand, he set off on step four.

Realising that the forging of certificates was absolutely beyond his capacity, Yates thought around possible alternatives. He thought long and hard. Then he hit on it.

He began a diligent round of all the second-hand bookshops in Liverpool, asking for the theological shelves. Patiently he hunted and hunted for what he sought. At last he found it. An old family Bible. Its cover was rather battered, its pages yellowing; but its flyleaves were blank. Many of the Sherridan families whom he had discovered had been almost illiterate, living in very primitive conditions, and it had struck him that the only record of family births, marriages and deaths was likely to be handwritten in the family's Bible.

As if by sympathetic magic, there appeared on the virgin flyleaf of the newly-discovered bible the carefully-scripted name, 'Martin Sherridan', And just below this was the painfully written record of the birth in 1800 of Helen (later to become Mrs Blake). Then, on the next line, came the all-important words:

> My daughter Helen has run away with young officer
> staying in Dublin Castle, and has married him privately
> in Scotland.

In order to square with the existence of the Patrick of Yates' inventive discovery, there had to be a Biblical record of another child, whose only son, Patrick, was to be the sole heir to the Blake fortune.

Martin Sherridan's death was duly scribed in the good book in what was a very recognisably different handwriting.

Since the sole discovery of the Sherridan family Bible might raise suspicion in suspicious minds, Yates took the precaution of purchasing several other old books, which he inscribed: 'Martin Sherridan – 'His book', and added various plausible dates. The story he then told was that he had found the Bible and all these books quite by chance in a Liverpool bookshop.

As an additional touch of finesse, Yates went to Birmingham, where he had two coffin-plates engraved with the names and details of Sherridans whose proven deaths were necessary to his deception. These he took back to Liverpool with him and buried for some time. He later claimed that he had found them when, serving his client's interests, he had excavated Sherridan graves in the West of Ireland. For good measure he produced a sketch of a broken tombstone, bearing the name of old Martin Sherridan, and the date of his death.

The meticulous Mr Yates had one more clincher in mind. He went out and bought a big, old-fashioned, silver watch. With this, he hurried to the engraver's. Yates' client, Patrick, whom he was officially backing – and putting forward – as the genuine claimant, was to be Mrs Blake's nephew, and the watch was to be a present to him from his aunt.

Yates gave the engraver the words he wanted inscribed on the inside of the back of the watch: 'From Helen Blake to her dear nephew, Patrick Sherridan, 1866.'

When he returned to collect the watch, Yates was furious. The engraver had inscribed the date 1896 – the current year – on the old watch.

"The year I told you was 1866," Yates screamed at him. "I even took the trouble to write it down for you. Put it right."

Those last three words were virtually spat at the startled engraver as Yates flounced, still in a rare paddy, out of the premises.

The engraver had been perfectly certain that the '1866' had been a mere slip of the customer's pen. What a fuss to make over a one-figure mistake! The more he thought of the excessive reaction the little error had provoked, the more it niggled him. Ridiculous! Unreasonable! He was still fretting and fuming about it, resenting it, when he met a detective friend of his and mentioned it to him aggrievedly. The detective, a shrewd officer, had observation kept on the engraver's premises, and when Yates' messenger called for the duly adjusted watch, he was followed, and led the police straight to Yates' office.

It was in this way that the clue was obtained which led to the detection of the whole of the carefully planned fraud. And so it was, as things turned out, that that trivial error, the well-intentioned substitution of the single numeral '9' for a '6', saved the country £200,000, and sent a man to penal servitude for life. Luck surely guided the engraver's instrument that day.

The family Bible, the coffin-plates, the inscribed silver watch, were all produced as exhibits in court – but not quite in the way that the canny Mr Yates had planned and visualised. When he appeared at Liverpool Assizes in May 1897, charged with attempted fraud, the beautifully faked Bible was shown to be a stupid mistake. What Irish Roman Catholic peasant family would give even house room to a Protestant Bible? And Yates' story of just happening to come upon the so conveniently inscribed Bible in a second-hand bookshop was laughed out of court.

John Hollis Yates was found guilty and sent to penal servitude for life.

An interesting coda: when Yates' office was searched after his arrest, papers were found which revealed that he had been in process of planning another similar fraud, this time in connection with a sum amounting to half-a-million of unclaimed money.

THE RIDDLE OF THE HANGING BOY

The radio was still on and the fire was blazing away merrily in the grate. A cosy kitchen scene in the big, comfortable house in Edge Lane, Liverpool. Except, that is, for one thing … the body of a young boy dangling from the rope of a clothes-rack.

A lad named Ernest Johnson made the grim discovery. Passing the house of his relatives, the Greeneys, at about 10pm that February night in 1946, he was surprised to see the front-door wide open, and all the lights in the house on, their radiance streaming out into the garden. He decided to investigate. What he saw in that familiar kitchen sent him scampering, terrified, out into the night, racing wildly round the neighbourhood in search of Mr and Mrs Greeney. He ran them to earth at a local hotel, where they had been enjoying an evening out.

They rushed back to the house, but there was nothing they could do. Their 11-year-old son, Charles, was beyond help. There was a second shock for the Greeneys that night. Their house had been burgled. But in their grief at the loss of their son, the loss of a carpet, linoleum, jewellery, furs and a marble clock was a mere nothing.

The burglary had more significance for the police, because it seemed to them to provide a reason for the death of the boy. They were not prepared to accept that this death of so young a boy was suicide. It might, of course, just turn out to be an accident. Adventurous, experimental boys had been known to hang themselves by mistake. To support this idea, on the floor, under the body, lay a book about the exploits of Boy Scouts, which Charles had been reading when his parents left him on his own earlier in the evening.

But if it were an accident, was it not a huge coincidence that burglars should have selected that very evening, and precisely those two or three hours when the boy was on his own, to rampage through the house? Suicide or accident contemporaneous with burglary? It seemed most unlikely. Murder was the best bet. The burglar or burglars must have hanged him.

Two forensic specialists, Dr JB Firth and the pathologist, Dr WH Grace, were called in. Dr Firth's main area of investigation was the kitchen. He looked first at the clothes-airer. Before the era of the tumble-dryer, no kitchen was complete without one of those dodo-like contraptions. It usually hung from the ceiling above the fireplace, and consisted of half a dozen long wooden slats which rested at either end in an iron bracket. It could be lowered to waist-level for loading by a pulley-rope at one end, and would then be hoisted up to allow the washing to dry. Two knots, held by a cleat in the wall, secured the two positions – up and down. When Charles Greeney was found, the airer was in the up position, and his neck was strangled by the pulley-rope itself, his head in the loop above the higher knot.

How did he get there? Had he put his own head in the loop? In that case, he would have had to stand on something to reach it. There was a small fireside chair underneath. But there were no footmarks on either the seat or the arms. If he had stood on the arms he would have had to hold on to something else to support himself. He could only have held on to the mantelshelf, but this was thick with dust, and it was unmarked. Equally, if it had been an accident, or if someone else had elevated him, surely there should have been signs of a struggle, a fight for life? There was not.

But Dr Grace, who performed the post-mortem at the Royal Infirmary, had a perfect answer to that. He found evidence of recent bruising in the deeper tissues of the right temporal region, in front of the ear, as the result of a heavy blow, which could have incapacitated the boy before he was hanged. He could, in other words, have been unconscious. And so the police doctors worked on the theory that when the boy disturbed some burglars, they knocked him out, realised that he had seen them, and decided to finish him off by a method which involved no messy blood-letting, no weapon to dispose of, and no fingerprints.

The police anticipated that if the burglars were found, their defence against a charge of murder would be that the boy died by accident or suicide. Therefore, those two possibilities had to be eliminated. Dr Firth did some experiments. He established that even if he had stood on the chair, Charles Greeney could not have reached the rope above the higher knot. He could have taken the rope off the cleat and let the whole airer down, but there was then absolutely no way in which he could have hoisted the heavy airer – and himself – to the up position. In order to do that, he would have to have been 'helped' by other hands. In which case, if the rope had first been removed from the cleat, it would have been difficult for only one person to manipulate ropes and boy. It would have been perfectly possible, though, just to part the double rope above the higher knot and insert the boy's head. The heavy tension caused by the loaded clothes-rack would have caused death in a matter of seconds rather than minutes.

A thousand sightseers crowded the streets for Charles Greeney's funeral: the Army was out in force to control hysterical scenes.

Within days, the police had arrested six men on suspicion of murder. All six were committed for trial on charges of house-breaking and theft, but only four of them – James Welsh, a seaman aged 25; Charles Lawrenson, also a seaman, aged 31; Henry Joseph White, a decorator, aged 24; and Thomas McGlynn, a ship's fireman, also aged 24 – were indicted for murder. Two of the men had admitted seeing the boy in the kitchen, and two others admitted knowing that he was in there. One of the accused, when arrested, was alleged to have said: "I can't understand what happened. They can't hang six for one, can they? Don't you think the kid could have done it himself?"

The four men pleaded not guilty to murder at their trial before Mr Justice Sellers at Manchester Assizes, and they chose not to give evidence in the witness-box.

The medical evidence suggested that the death could have occurred at any time between 8.30pm and 10.30pm. That meant that it was not beyond the realms of possibility that the boy was already dead before the men entered the house.

The Defence tried desperately to show that Charles Greeney was adventurous and accident-prone. Counsel for the defence, Mr Basil Nield, KC, had had the opportunity of examining a book which the boy had apparently been reading just before the tragedy, and he found in it one story about a highwayman called Brown Billy in which there were several references to hanging. But the boy's father would have none of it. His son was not accident-prone. He did did not enjoy reading thrillers. He was not adventurous by nature, and his ambition was learning to play the piano.

Well, said the Defence, suppose the boy for some reason climbed on to the polished arm of the chair, slipped, and clutched at the rope, thus pulling it down around his neck, fell, hitting his head against the mantelshelf, and was left suspended. This bruise could, of course, equally well have been caused by the boy's head having come into contact with the mantelshelf. Two of the intruders, in statements to the police, said that they had seen the boy apparently standing on the chair with his back to them and looking towards the mantelshelf. They had thought the lad was deaf, because he had not heard the noise when they burst panels in the door.

The Defence called only one witness, the celebrated pathologist, Professor Glaister. His credo was:

'Never jump to conclusions' must be a constant golden rule in forensic medicine … All possible aspects of a situation have to be fully explored before an opinion is given. Even then, opinions can differ, and this is a healthy thing because it is right and proper that in evidence-giving such differences between experts open up a wide field of interrogation and afford the Court a broader consideration in the final judgment.

It was just such a difference of opinion which resulted in Glaister's coming down from Scotland, where, following in his father, John Glaister *primus'* footsteps, he occupied the Chair of Forensic Medicine at Glasgow University, to appear at Manchester, where, in the course of his expert witness testimony, he uttered the all-important words:

> There is nothing specific to show in what way the hanging occurred. Everything is consistent with accident and there is nothing definitely indicative of homicide.

As he subsequently wrote in his autobiography*, a copy of which he sent to me for review:

> It was the first and still remains the only case in which I have been concerned where there was a charge of murder by hanging. The Crown had secured the evidence of several experienced medical men to support the theory that the house-breakers had, in fact, murdered the boy in this fashion. But I felt differently, for a number of reasons. The chair the men had mentioned had been present in the room, and, though its seat was a few inches below the level of the boy's feet, its wooden arms were on a rough parallel. The time of the boy's death was said to have been about 10pm, which came close to coinciding with the arrival of the four men. Yet I felt this was open to challenge if the boy had hanged himself. I had made some study of the incidence of various types of hanging fatalities, and sketched some of the details in my preliminary report to defence counsel.
>
> Statistically, suicidal hanging is by far the most common form and has been known to take place at all ages from boyhood to old age. It often occurs by accident. It is rare to find a case of hanging which is the result of homicide, but there is definite reason to believe that boys have unintentionally destroyed themselves by hanging from a strange principle of imitation or curiosity. Of all forms of murder, too, hanging is one of the most difficult. In most cases where a person has been hanged by others it has been found that this was done after death as an attempt to suggest suicide. The boy's body showed no evidence of a struggle, tearing or even disarranging of clothing, and no significant injury. From all the evidence defence counsel put before me, the picture was perfectly consistent with suicidal or, more likely, accidental hanging.

Glaister's belief was that Charles Greeney's death was accidental, and that:

> ... probably, like so many others, while he was carrying out an adventurous experiment which was, by a quirk of fate, to end in tragedy just before the four men broke into his home.

* Final Diagnosis (Hutchinson, 1964).

There is an interesting corollary, provided by Glaister. He tells how, a couple of days after discussing with his sister the trial at Liverpool, arguing that it was impossible for the Liverpool boy to have slipped off a chair, and adding, "I'll prove it," a 16-year-old boy of Tonbridge, in Kent, was found dead in his bedroom. He was kneeling beside his bed, his chest against a chair, a noose round his neck, and the rope attached to the bedrail. Recording a verdict of accidental death, the coroner said:

> I think it is quite likely, knowing his fondness for experimenting with ropes and following the remarks made to his sister, that this boy was experimenting with something on these lines and that, unfortunately, the experiment went wrong.

In his summing-up the learned judge hammered home the crux of the case. If the jury were to say to themselves, "Although we are not certain that it was an accident, we are not certain that it was not," then the verdict must be not guilty.

And that was the verdict they brought in.

So … the riddle of the Hanging Boy of Edge Lane remains – a riddle. Well, technically at any rate.

HISTORIC
SHADOWS

BLACK IVORY – THE LIVERPOOL SLAVE TRADE

A fragment of paper blown on the wind across the floor of a ruined cellar below a Goree Piazza warehouse; a screed discovered in an ancient sea-chest high and dry in the attic of an old house in Woolton; a dubiously-worded entry in Gore's *Annals of Liverpool*; sundry advertisements in the yellowing columns of a long-ago newspaper; those are some of the things which have contributed to a diehard tradition that pictured the black arches of Liverpool's Goree Piazzas – so named after a slave-trade island off the west coast of Africa – as the relics of a great slave mart, where thousands of hapless negroes, fettered to the rusting ring bolts of the huge stone pillars, were once sold like cattle. It is, in a sense, a romantic vision, but it is absolutely false.

That fragment of blown paper was actually a scrap from a manifesto of cargo being carried to faraway Africa. The letter was one of instruction to a slave-captain relating to a voyage he was to make to Guinea.

The hoary slander of slave sales in Liverpool has persisted for well over a hundred years. It is high time that it was publicly and finally contradicted.

The history of England's participation in that terrible traffic in 'black ivory' is an undeniably ugly one, dating back to the days of the first Elizabeth. Between 1562 and 1567, Sir John Hawkins was making regular voyages to West Africa, collecting negroes whom he later sold to the Spanish colonies.

However, in 1588, the year of the Armada, Good Queen Bess decided to limit what was guardedly referred to as the 'African Trade' to a single company – 'The Company of Royal Adventurers of England Trading with Africa'. This company's letters patent were renewed by both James I and Charles I, and, shortly after his restoration, Charles II granted the company a charter, permitting ships to sail together for mutual protection from the attacks of the Dutch, who had recently been harrying and robbing slave-trading vessels.

But the ancient privileged company got into difficulties and resigned its charter to a new company, the 'Royal African Asiento Company' – '*asiento*' being the Spanish word for a contract or undertaking. That undertaking, dated 1689, was to supply the Spanish West Indies with slaves.

During the reign of William and Mary, the Asiento Company's charter was revoked, and, in 1698, an Act of Parliament threw the trade open to all, on payment to the Chamberlain of London, the Clerk of the Merchants' Hall at Bristol, or the Town Clerk of Liverpool, of the sum of 40 shillings.

It was not until the year 1709, that the first recorded slaver set sail from Liverpool for the West Coast of Africa. It was a single ship of 30 tons, and it procured a cargo of 15 negroes. But this was a one-off. For twenty-one years thereafter no slave ship sailed from Liverpool. Then, in 1730, 15 vessels, with a gross tonnage of 1,111 tons, were sent to Africa.

By 1737, the number of Liverpool slavers had risen to thirty-three, but it was not until the second half of the eighteenth century that Liverpool began to play a really big part in the sale of human flesh.

The facts which may, in somewhat shaky extenuation, be said to have forced Liverpool merchants into the traffic in slaves, was the condemnation by Parliament, in 1747, of the flourishing trade in Lancashire cloths, which had been built up with the Spanish contraband traders at Kingston, Jamaica, as an infringement of our own mercantile laws. Finding themselves badly affected by this legislation, the Liverpool traders began to engage increasingly in the slave-trade.

Some startling statistics. During the ten years between 1783 and 1793, Liverpool traders made 878 trips, in the course of which 303,737 black slaves were transported from the coast of Africa to the West Indies, where they fetched £15,186,850.

As early as 1752, Liverpool had outstripped Bristol, the chief slaving port of the south, and had left London well behind. By the end of the eighteenth century, Liverpool was unquestionably the greatest slaving port in Europe.

Slaving was actually a three-cornered trade, each triangular trip adding up to a full year's voyaging.

One can picture the slaver slipping, all innocent-seeming, out of George's or some other Liverpool dock, its hold packed with bale after bale of Manchester cottons, dyed for the most part bright blues and greens, the colours beloved of the Africans, gay-striped loin-cloths, woollens and Indian piece-goods, some bearing exotically bejewelled names – niccanees, nillaes, cushtaes, chelloes, romales and photaes – others, more down-to-earth, designated negannepants and bejutapants. Towering columns of boxes of handkerchiefs. Bushels of beads and assorted cheap trinketry. Kettles and pans of shiny brass and copper, and iron pots. Cases of knives and spoons. Assorted plates and dishes and mugs. Looking-glasses. Scarlet, gold-laced jackets and modish felt tricorns. Copper and iron in short bars. More sinisterly: axes, hatchets, cutlasses, old muskets and kegs of gunpowder. The trade goods of the African Trade.

It is late afternoon or early evening. The ship, sails filling and lifting in the salty Mersey breeze, prow majestically rising and dipping in ritualised curtseys to each little foam-capped wave, strikes across the chopping water to the Bar. The old, comfortably familiar landfall recedes. The Custom House drops away in the background. The spire tapering out of the square tower of St Nicholas', the Mariners' Church, pierces the purplish, descending sky. The waterside tavern lights are just twinkling to life on the vanishing remembered shores. And up, up on the heights, growing ever smaller and further away, the ceaseless, whirring-sailed windmills grind the port's daily bread. One among a flock of vessels leaving the Mersey, upon widespread white wings fluttering amid the riggings, the slaver, like some giant emigrant bird of prey, rolls over the orange and indigo tinted river in the wake of the westering sun, leaving behind a shining furrow, a huge claw mark, in the rapidly darkening water of home. This is the first leg of the voyage … to the Slave Coast of West Africa.

As the slave-ship ploughed its way to Bonny, Brass, or Old or New Calabar, ports of the Niger Delta, preparations for its arrival would be going ahead.

In the early days of the trade, in the sixteenth century, the men and women sold as slaves were in the main prisoners held by tribal chiefs after inter-tribal wars. Had they not been bartered into slavery, they would almost certainly have been put to death. When the available supply of prisoners was exhausted, the African chiefs or kings would capture negroes from tribes near the coast, and would, when demand so required, top the numbers up by arresting natives on false charges of theft or witchcraft. But when, as inevitably happened, handy supplies again ran out, fresh sources needed to be found and tapped. Natives had to be caught and fetched from the hinterland.

Warriors would set out in war canoes at dead of silent night. Up the reed-grown stream they would glide, paddles dipping softly in the black water, where the mango roots started up out of the shallows like twisted skeletons, pallid in the moonlight. Only the occasional weird cries that are the night voice of the jungle – the sudden chatter of startled monkeys, the almost-human scream of a gorilla, the shrill screech of a disturbed parakeet – cut into the stillness.

Reaching the target village, the warriors would creep like ebony shadows in pantherine silence to its perimeter edge. Hard sticks were twirled until a spark jumped forth to light eucalyptus wood and palm-oil-soaked torches, which, touching the tinder-dry, round huts of the sleeping village, sent startled, shrieking men, women and children hurtling out in terror.

Every living being would be rounded up and stripped naked. Any who put up too vigorous a resistance would simply be clubbed to the ground and killed, or left, badly injured, to die. The men either chained or bound together with strong lianas, the women and children left to move freely. Herded, prodded with spears or lashed with whips, all would be marched to the coast, often a distance of two, three, or four hundred miles away. Any who fell were left to die where they fell. Pity was not of the current coinage. Journey's end reached, those who had, faint, weary, lame and halt, survived, were driven like cattle into the king's pens, to await the advent of the slave-ships.

That arrival the slavers would herald with a burst of gunfire, a salute to the African king with whom trading was to be done. He would come down the creek by ceremonial canoe to receive his comey (duty) and his dash (presents). All would be affability. Handshakes concluding bargaining, deals done over gourds of the strong palm-wine known as mimbo. The slaves of his selection would then be branded with his company's initials on breast or buttocks with a red-hot iron.

Now came the second leg of the triangular voyage: the terrible Middle Passage, taking the slaves who had been received in exchange for the exported goods across the Atlantic to the West Indies or Virginia, where they would be sold to work on the plantations.

The slave-ships varied in size from 150 to 400 tons. They were stout, full-rigged vessels, armed with 14 to 20 guns. But the accommodation provided for the slave cargo can only be described as appalling.

Typically, the hold of the ship, where the slaves were stowed, was divided into two by slave platforms, one above the other, and with less than three feet of overhead space between. The slaves were forced to lie on these shelves, chained to each other, and so tight-packed that sometimes it was impossible for them to lie on their backs. They had to lie on hip and shoulder on hard planking sparsely covered with dirty straw. When, in stormy weather, the ship rolled, hips and shoulders would be rubbed red raw.

The ventilation was also dreadful. With pathetically few port-holes, and gratings which had to be covered with tarpaulins in rough weather, the heat was intolerable. Added to which, the stench, taking into account the vomitings of sea-sickness and the cases of dysentery, was positively overpowering.

An average of about twelve per cent of the slaves died on each voyage. Often very considerably more. Some killed each other fighting and scrambling to get near the port-holes or gratings. Whenever shouting or disturbances were heard below, sailors would go down and lay into the helpless slaves with cat-o'-nine-tails. Those who died were flung overboard to feed the sharks. Often the dead were found chained to the living, shrouded in an abominable stench.

In fine weather the slaves were allowed up on deck, where they would often be heard chanting strange, plaintive songs. They were fed at 8am and 4pm, their food being given to them in small wooden buckets, ten slaves feeding from one bucket. A half-pint of water was provided at each meal, but it had to be drunk straight away from the pannikin proffered. After the afternoon meal they would be returned below decks.

In bad weather, the sweating, half-stifled, weeping and wailing negroes were permitted to come up for air in batches of ten, but for just long enough to eat their food before being sent below again.

It became the custom to fasten a chain from their shackles to a ring bolt on the deck, because so many of the slaves attempted to revolt or to commit suicide by throwing themselves overboard. When, as often happened, they tried to commit suicide by starving themselves, they were forcibly fed, and the barbarous *speculum oris*, an instrument, advertised in Liverpool and sold to the slave-ships, specifically designed to prise open a man's clenched jaws, was brought into play.

In view of the rough and cruel conditions obtaining on the slave-ships, it is astonishing to find that not all the slavers were men. 'Jack' Roberts, an 18-year-old 'lad', who had signed on as a member of the crew and downed his grog and chewed fierce 'baccy' along with the best of them aboard the slave-ship, *Anne*, was discovered before the Bonny-bound ship was out of home waters to be actually Jane Roberts. She was put ashore 'with all possible gentleness'. And, it is a fact that, according to the mate of the *Anne*, about this time several handsome young women committed themselves in the same way and some succeeded in eluding all discovery of their sex and made a voyage or two at sea.

The brutality which took place on the slave-ships was truly fearful. A certain Liverpool slave-captain was wont to relate, apparently expectant of approval, how he had dealt with a situation in which he found a female slave fretting herself and putting her physical fitness – and therefore her sale value – at threat, on account of an infant she had been obliged to take with her on the slaver.

"Apprehensive for her health, I snatched the child from her, knocked its head against the side of the ship, and threw it into the sea."

Captain Marshall, master of the slaver aptly named *Black Joke*, was another who displayed a strange kind of tenderness towards infants. He flogged a baby to death for refusing food, and then forced its mother to throw the child's corpse over the side.

One of the most scandalous affairs occurred during the voyage of the bad ship *Zong*, – owned by the prominent Liverpool banker, William Gregson – from West Africa to Jamaica, with a cargo of 440 slaves, in 1781. Due either to the drunkenness or sheer bad seamanship of her master, Captain Collingwood, they missed Jamaica and were two months at sea. Food and water were running short. Fever and dysentery broke out. Sixty slaves died, and many more were dying. The captain mustered the crew and told them that the sick slaves should be thrown overboard.

"If the slaves die on board, the owners will lose," he told the ship's company. "But if we maintain that the slaves were thrown overboard for the preservation of the ship, the underwriters will have to bear the loss."

In all, 132 ailing slaves were dragged on to deck and, still alive, thrown into the sea. Some of them, ill as they were, struggled desperately, until Collingwood ordered that they should be shackled with ankle and waist chains in order to speed their drowning.

Just occasionally the slaves got their own back. Captain Messerby, having driven the slaves in his care beyond all human endurance, was one meal-time on the fo'c'sle among the male captives when they were eating their victuals. Spying their chance, they laid hold of him and beat out his brains with the little tubs out of which they were eating their boiled rice.

Once the slaves reached the West Indies, they were carefully washed and scrubbed and made to look as fit and healthy as possible. A good, well-built, presentable and healthy looking African would fetch £50.

There were three methods of sale. Frequently planters had already made a private treaty with the trader. In which case, on landing, a selection of slaves would be taken to the planter's office, where, after a deal of prodding, and, in the case of women slaves, making them open their mouths to show their teeth, he would choose those who took his fancy, and the rest would be marched back to the ship. The slaves purchased would be set to work on the sugar, tobacco, or cotton plantations.

The second method of sale was by scramble. The male slaves would be lined up on the main deck and the women and children on the quarter-deck. A signal gun was fired, the gangplank was lowered, and the buyers who had been waiting on the quay would swarm aboard, choosing and seizing the slaves that they wanted to purchase.

The third method was by public auction in the market-place. All the slaves who remained unsold after the scramble were taken ashore to be disposed of in this way. Those who were too ill to attract a bid, were either given away or abandoned.

Slaves disembarked, the quarters which they had occupied thoroughly cleaned out, the ship, loaded up with hogsheads of rum, sugar, tobacco, spices, hardwood and the odd bale of cotton, would then return to Liverpool, where the cargo would be sold at a healthy profit.

It must be emphasised that the Liverpool slave-trade consisted in the transportation of Africans to the West Indies and America, and not in the importation of them to England.

That is not to say that there were never any slaves in Liverpool. Planters who had made their fortunes in the West Indies would, when they returned home, occasionally bring a favourite slave back to England with them as a personal servant. It was also at one time the height of fashion to have a splendidly dressed-up African boy or girl – a living gilded exotic trophy – as a decorative household object!

Sometimes the slave would run away, and then advertisements and rewards for his or her recapture would be published in the newspapers. In Williamson's *Liverpool Advertiser* of 17 February 1758, for instance, there appeared the following:

> Run away from Dent, in Yorkshire, on Monday, the
> 28th August last, Thomas Anson, a Negro man, about
> 5' 6" high, aged 20 years and upwards, and broad set.
> Whoever will bring the said man back to Dent, or give
> any information that he may be had again, shall receive
> a handsome reward from Mr Edmund Sill, of Dent; or
> Mr David Kenyon, Merchant, in Liverpool.

But that there were ever slaves at the Goree Piazzas is manifestly impossible. The Piazzas, which, incidentally, were destroyed by fire in 1802, had been built in 1793, just twenty-one years after the law out of the Somerset case came into force.

The Somerset case was brought as a result of the dedicated work of an eighteenth century philanthropist and writer, Granville Sharp. In 1765, Sharp had found a slave named Jonathan Strong abandoned and starving in the street. Sharp took the poor creature under his wing, and discovered the name of the master who had abandoned him, one David Lisle.

Two years later, Lisle had Strong thrown into prison as a runaway slave. Sharp, however, succeeded in obtaining his release, and went on to prosecute Lisle for assault and battery. Lisle countered by bringing an action against Sharp for unlawfully detaining the property of another – to wit, giving shelter to Jonathan Strong. The majesty of the law found against Sharp, relying upon precedent; a judgement given forty years before, that masters had property in their slaves, even when said slaves were in England.

Nothing daunted, Sharp continued to interest himself in cases similar to that of Strong, and finally reaped his reward. In 1772, his advocacy in the case of a slave named John Somerset led to the historic pronouncement of the Lord Chief Justice that: "as soon as any slave sets foot upon English territory, he becomes free."

As late as 1765, the following advertisement had appeared:

> To be sold by auction at St George's Coffee House
> betwixt the hours of six and eight o'clock, a very fine
> negro girl about eight years of age, very healthy, and
> hath been some time from the coast. Any person
> wishing to purchase the same may apply to Captain
> Robert Syers, at Mr Bartley Hodgetts, Mercer and
> Draper, near the Exchange, where she may be seen till
> the time of sale.

And in the following year, *Williamson's Liverpool Advertiser* announced:

To be sold
At the Exchange Coffee House,
in Water Street, this day the 12th inst.
September at one o'clock precisely
Eleven negroes exported per the Angola.
Broker.

It was in 1787 that the Society for the Abolition of the Slave Trade was founded in London. Liverpool names were sparse upon its list of members. The only two to appear were those of William Rathbone and Dr Jonathan Binns. But there were others in the town who sympathised with the Society's objectives. That most illustrious citizen of Liverpool, William Roscoe, poet, pamphleteer, painter, botanist, lawyer, banker and politician, had long spoken and written of his abhorrence of the traffic; indeed, it was in that year of 1787 that he had published *The Wrongs of Africa*, in which he had roundly condemned the transport of slaves. And Dr James Currie and Edward Rushton had also let their opposition to the trade be known.

It was, however, William Wilberforce, the Member of Parliament for Hull, who mounted the most determined attack on the slave-trade. Seeking information for Wilberforce's brief, Thomas Clarkson came to Liverpool to investigate. He found the citizenry distinctly hostile. He was jeered at and received threatening letters aimed at scaring him away. He stuck to his guns and succeeded in his objective of interviewing a number of the old slave-captains and slave-ship crew members. His enemies came within an ace of getting him though.

Keeping an appointment one dark night of typical Liverpool wind and rain to talk with a seaman whom he was to meet on one of the quays, he was just approaching the Pier Head, when suddenly from out of a pool of the darkest shadows, a gang of men came running full tilt at him. One of them struck him a stinging blow in the face, which sent him reeling backwards. No more than a yard behind him was the edge of the quay, and below it the dark, swirling water of the Mersey. It was a horribly plain case of fight or perish. Clarkson dashed forward, flung himself upon the leader of the marauders and knocked him to the ground. The others scattered as he rained furious blows all about him, and in the darkness and confusion he managed to escape.

But there can be no denying that the town was divided upon the issue of the abolition of slavery. For many a long year purses and consciences had been in bitter conflict. Handsomely-breeched Liverpool merchants railed against the folly of destroying a business which had yielded so many large fortunes. Feelings ran high. Family was divided against family on the moral question. Men, not entirely disinterested, held up their hands in horror at the prospect of the consequences of the discontinuance of the age-honoured slave-trade.

Be altruistic! Think … whatever would become of the plantations in the

West Indies were they to be bereft of slaves to tend them? What wretchedness would befall the men who made it their life's work to build the slave-ships? And what of the men who furnished and victualled them, to say nothing of the gallant sailors who manned them? Grass, said the prophets of doom, would grow up between the cobble-cracks in Castle Street, the docks would be turned into fish-ponds, Bootle organs (frogs) would croak their songs in the merchants' mansions of the wealthy. Liverpool would be ruined.

But none of these things came to pass.

William Wiberforce's Abolition Bill was passed in 1807.

Paradoxically, and for those who delight in paradox it is a passing strange fact, some of the slave-captains and their merchant employers, notwithstanding the agonies inflicted at their behest – albeit at a remove – on the defenceless African slaves, coming under cudgel and whiplash, lying chained and sick and suffocating in their hell holds, were God-fearing, just, and humane within the confines of their narrow philosophies, were even philanthropists, and, almost unbelievably, men of education and discernment. Bryan Blundell, co-founder, with Robert Stithe, of the Blue Coat School, who transported not only slaves, but also young white children to the New World to be apprenticed on the plantations, quieted his conscience by devoting a large part of his income to charity and his determined embracement of the belief that life in the New World would afford far better opportunities for the little ones that he had sent into exile.

It will, I feel sure, occasion small surprise to learn that many churchmen of the time declared that the cruel trade in human flesh was justified because it was the means of bringing the Africans in touch with Christianity! It also brought, as a by-product, riches undreamt of, which were modestly accepted as a blessing bestowed upon a chosen worthy few by a benign Providence.

One of the indulgent clergy was the Reverend Raymond Harris. He even wrote a book, published by H Hodgson, in Liverpool, in 1788, somewhat cumbrously titled: *Scriptural Researches on the Licitness of the Slave-Trade, Shewing its Conformity with the Principles of Natural and Revealed Religion, Delineated in the Sacred Writings of the Word of God: to which are added Scripture Directions for the Proper Treatment of Slaves, and a Review of Some Scurrilous Pamphlets.*

The work was dedicated to the 'Mayor, Recorder, Aldermen, Bailiffs, and Other Members of the Common Council of Liverpool.'

The Common Council awarded the Reverend Mr Harris One Hundred Pounds, in recognition of his conveniently approbatory services, and, his great work done, he shuffled off his mortal coil the following year and ascended, presumably to reap his reward in heaven.

One of the bitterest-tipped darts ever directed at Liverpool and its slave-trading citizenry was that of the well-known and exceedingly popular actor, George Frederick Cooke (1756-1812). Playing Richard III here on the night of Thursday 28 August 1806, so overcome was he by the beauty of Lady Anne – and with, according to his habit, something a deal stronger – that in attempting to recover himself from his kneeling position, His Majesty lost his equilibrium. Richard was not himself again! He was hissed, and retorted:

> What! do you hiss me? Hiss George Frederick Cooke? You contemptible money-getters! You shall never again have the *honour* of hissing me. Farewell! I banish *you*! There is not a brick in your damned town, but what it is cemented by the blood of a Negro!

This speech was greeted, in typical Liverpool spirit, with ironic applause!

And irony is, at the end of the day, the ruling emotion that emerges from any sustained contemplation of the slave-trade and its concomitances and consequences.

Is it not ironical that Liverpool, directly responsible for the deaths of so many thousands of black men, should, at the end of the nineteenth century, have set up its now world-famous School of Tropical Medicine, dedicated to the saving from death by disease of the descendants of those who had previously been treated so callously. Incidentally, a great-uncle of mine was Dr Albert John Chalmers, author with Doctor Aldo Castellani of an elephantine, *Manual of Tropical Medicine*. One of the pioneer men against tropical diseases, he spent many years on the coast of West Africa and became Director of the Wellcome Tropical Research Laboratories at Khartoum. My grandfather, his brother-in-law, always called him 'The Medicine Man of the East'! He died suddenly and mysteriously in Calcutta, in April 1920. His widow, my Aunt Alice, remained convinced to her dying day that his demise was the result of a curse put upon him by a hostile Arab when they were travelling on a boat up the Nile.

Is there not irony, too, in the fact that so many of the long-departed merchants and slave-captains' old houses in the Upper Parliament Street and Grove Street areas are now in the occupation of Liverpool's black citizens?

And, a final irony, where the Goree Piazzas once stood on the quayside of George's Dock, from which so many slavers set forth upon their voyages from hell, there rises today a modern office building which bears the proud name of Wilberforce House, a repentant city's tardy tribute in the 1960s to one who has been designated in the eye of time, the Arch-Apostle of Abolition.

Mind Your Eye Crow

Side by side, cheek by jowl, with the tall, sky-grasping Liverpool, that has arisen, concrete-white and shining glass, on the coral-bone bedrock of the old seaport city, there still lives and breathes at the far reaches of cobbled roads and tumble-down streets – each with its beer-brown pub, sticky counter and frosted glass – the old Sailortown.

Where once the forests of mast and spar cluttered the horizon, an Atkinson Grimshaw painting made flesh, now cranes and gantries stretch, like the long skeletal necks of prehistoric animals, in silhouette against a ragged, cloud-torn sky. And on quiet nights, when the moon sails high, and the mist wreathes in, swaddling the empty streets that run, crooked, beside the river, imagination, held to the mind's eye like a telescope in reverse, diminishes the landscape of the here-and-now, and brings into nostalgic focus the there-and-then old days of the tall ships – and the men who sailed in them.

Walk, as I have so often walked, down Park Lane and the furthermost ebbs of Paradise Street during the long watches of a lonely, bright-starred night, and, faint and far-away on the river breeze there seem to ride snatches of sailor song and the plaintive wheezings of a concertina.

On such a night the phantom shellbacks seem to be ashore, back home in their old port, money-belts bulging, full-sail in pursuit of grog and Liverpool 'ladies'. And, lurking, creek by jowler in wait for them, the ladies' bully-boys, who'll blow a poor sailorman down for his golden ballast of bright, shiny, hard-won sovereigns. For Liverpool was – could be – a bloody port for unwary sea-lubbers.

On such a night … voyaging on the waters of the moon, you might well chance upon, among the other sea-bound wraiths, the old slave-captain, 'Mind Your Eye' Crow, rolling, telescope under arm, blind eye clapped sea-doggedly water-frontwards, down Lord Street.

A man worth meeting, old Captain Crow.

Hugh Crow was not a Liverpudlian born. But he was what you might call a cousin-once-removed – removed by the stretch of Irish Sea that lies between the Pier Head and the Isle of Man.

Even as a child, the sea and ships fascinated him. Toddling beside his mother on the beach at Ramsey early in the 1770s, he pointed to a full-rigged vessel ploughing towards the harbour.

"Some day I'm going to command a bigger ship than that," he said.

His mother smiled a mother's doting incredulous smile, and squeezed his little hand.

"Of course you will, darling, of course."

The years passed. Spring tides rose and neap tides fell. The child grew into a sturdy lad. There was an accident. He lost an eye ... but never his ambition to go to sea. And, in the fulness of time, young Hugh Crow was launched upon his seafaring career; a great career, rich in colour and romance, the real-life stuff of boys' adventure books.

His first voyage was as the apprentice of a Whitehaven merchant, and his first voyage was nearly his last, for he fell foul of a bullying fellow-apprentice, who, one dark night, tried to throw him from the maintop-gallant yard down into the boiling sea. Young Crow fought like a tiger, forgave the attempted murder, and never so much as whispered a word of what had happened to the master.

Already one sees in the youth the mark of strong and individual character which was indelibly to stamp the man. That eccentric individuality of his was often to land him in trouble.

Those proving days at sea were heavily cargo'd with adventure. A captain, liking the cut of the lad, offered him the place of second mate aboard a ship bound for Honduras. Stealthily, at dead of night, he crept off the ship upon which he was already berthed, and, complete with quadrant and sea-chest, made his way to the ship whose captain had offered him so splendid an advance.

His defection having been rapidly discovered, Crow's legitimate captain immediately set off in pursuit of him with, bailiff, constables and soldiers. There was a scuffle. Crow was run to ground hiding in the pump-well, all but suffocated with filth and heat. Dragged, more dead than alive, up on deck, he was threatened by his old captain, "I'll cleave you with the cook's axe if you make trouble, me lad." And he meant it.

Crow was no fool. He made no trouble. Tightly handcuffed, wearing only his shirt and trousers, he was bundled into a boat, rowed ashore, and flung into prison. And there he lay, without food, and tormented by rats, for 48 hours.

One of Crow's little oddnesses was his habit of suddenly breaking into song at the most unexpected and inappropriate times. On one occasion at least it stood him in good stead. It was in December 1787, that the 22-year-old Crow sailed as a passenger aboard a ship bound from Cork to Kingston, Jamaica. He paid a fare of one penny. That was the custom, as otherwise a sailor, even though he was a passenger, might claim wages.

The passage was a stormy one, marked by a succession of frightful gales, which greatly disheartened the crew – until Crow began to sing. The louder howled the wind, the louder bellowed Crow. And his determined caterwauling always seemed to rally their drooping spirits. Especially appreciated was his merrily discordant rendition of *Ye Gentlemen of England*, which invariably cheered everyone up.

During the latter years of the eighteenth century the Liverpool slave-trade was at its height, and for some time Crow had been receiving offers to go as second mate to the coast of Africa, but, and it was regarded by his fellow-voyagers as a great eccentricity in him, he always expressed a great hatred and contempt for the traffic in human cargoes.

Then, one day in 1790, with a bewildering suddenness as patently eccentric as his previous intransigent attitude to slavery, he blithely announced that he was perfectly willing to engage in the trade. Thus it came about that, throughout the next eighteen years, this quaint and contradictory man played a leading rôle in the flourishing commerce in 'black ivory'.

He made his first trip to the Slave Coast aboard the *Prince*. Four years later, in 1794, he was promoted chief mate of the *Gregson*. The voyage which followed was to be an ill-starred one. A few days after leaving Guernsey, where she had called to pick up spirits, the *Gregson* was attacked by a large French ship, and Crow was taken prisoner. He remained in prison until the middle of November, and was then marched 500 miles, and put in hospital at Pontoise, 17 miles north of Paris. That was in February 1795.

One day, three months later, having fixed a large tricoloured cockade in his hat, he made his escape. He had put about 50 miles between himself and the hospital, when he was stopped by a French officer and a file of soldiers. The officer kept barking questions at him, but Crow, who knew barely half a dozen words of French, stood mute.

Then, desperate, not knowing what to do, he began to gabble out furiously all the words of all the languages of which he had picked up a smattering in the course of his travels, topping the performance off for good measure with a positive torrent of his native Manx.

The French officer stood open-mouthed, looking at him as though he had gone mad. Then burst into an enraged display of foaming and roaring, to which Crow reacted unperturbably, just keeping on repeating over and over again in fractured Spanish, "No entiendo! No entiendo!"

This was too much for the irascible French officer. All semblance of patience gone, he gave Crow a tremendous whack across the stern with the flat of his sword, swore he must be a so-and-so ignorant Breton, and told him to get going. And Crow, thanking him profusely and repeatedly as loud as he could – in Manx – ran like a redshank.

The weary trek to freedom dragged on. Missing his way one day, Crow landed up close to a camp of soldiers. That gave him a terrible fright. He took to his heels in the greatest alarm, and never stopped running and walking for the next 60 miles.

By this time his 'poor old hull was in so sad a condition from stem to stern' that he just had to 'put into the first port', which happened to be a house, and cast himself upon the mercy of its inhabitants. Luckily, they turned out to be friendly, and while they were giving him brandy and popping his feet in warm water, to their consternation he slumped insensible across the tub. They put him to bed. He slept soundly, and next morning, after a good breakfast, he plodded determinedly off again on his journey.

Eventually he reached Rouen, and a couple of days after that arrived at Le Havre, where he was lucky enough to meet up with a generous Danish sea-captain, who gave him a passage to Deal, at which place he literally kissed the good Kentish soil in gratitude for his deliverance. The Dane paid his fare to London, where Crow managed to raise the money to take a coach to Liverpool.

During the next couple of years he was back and forth between Bonny, on the Slave Coast of Africa, and Liverpool, and became very friendly with two dusky old villains, King Pepple and King Holiday, who supplied him with his human cargoes.

Captain Crow was that rare thing among the slave-captains, a merciful man, who treated his poor, helpless cargo with kindness. Every morning they were routinely brought up on deck from below. There, they washed their hands and faces, and were given chew-sticks to clean their teeth – a method said to be more effective than our modern toothbrushes. Then they would each have a ration of lime juice, the standard protection at the time against scurvy.

After a decent breakfast, nips of brandy would be dispensed to those who the captain considered to be in need of them. Next came baths, and a massage with the favourite palm-oil. A period of recreation followed, with dancing and pipes of tobacco, before another meal at midday. Meanwhile, the slave quarters in the hold were being thoroughly cleaned, and, after another meal at three o'clock, the slaves would be returned below deck at around five o'clock.

No wonder those slaves who were shipped aboard Captain Crow's vessel thought themselves lucky. Rather touchingly, on one occasion when he dropped anchor in the West Indies, a crowd of gaily dressed negroes clambered eagerly aboard his ship. They were, it turned out, former slaves who he had carried across from Africa. They begged to be allowed to see Crow, and he invited them into his cabin, where they poured out their thanks to him for the care he had taken of them on their voyage, and enthusiastically wished him joy. He and his sturdy mate, Scott, were 'deeply affected, even to tears'.

Then, in 1798, Hugh Crow received his first command – and his nickname. Fulfilling that long-ago prophecy which he had made to his mother on the beach at Ramsey, he was appointed captain of a fine vessel, Mr William Aspinall's 300-ton ship, the *Will*.

And his nickname? Here, in his own words, is how he came to acquire it:

> Mr Aspinall, my owner, who was fond of a good joke,
> happening to meet one evening with old Mr Hodson,

merchant, their conversation turned upon the voyage we had just accomplished.

Mr Hodson observed, "I give my captains very long instructions, yet they can hardly make any money for us," adding to Mr Aspinall, "What kind of instructions, Will, did you give *your* captain?"

"Why," replied Mr Aspinall, "I took him to Beat's Hotel, where we had a pint of wine together, and I told him, 'Crow! Mind your eye! for you will find many ships at Bonny'."

Mr Hodson immediately said: "Crow! mind your eye! – Will, I know the young man well, he has only one eye."

"True," said Mr Aspinall, "but that's a piercer!"

The joke travelled to London, and I could hardly cross the 'Change there afterwards without hearing some wag or other exclaim, "Crow, mind your eye!"

It is very probable that Mr Aspinall had, in joke, told some of them that these words were the only instructions I had ever received.

So, minding his eye, and his owner's interests, Captain Crow went on plying profitably back and forth, stowing away a fortune for them both.

Then ... suddenly ... it was all over. In 1807 Parliament passed William Wilberforce's Bill to abolish the African Slave Trade.

On 27 July 1807, Captain Crow set sail from Liverpool as master of the *Kitty's Amelia*, the last of the slave-ships. The voyage to Bonny was ill-fated from the start. Seeming to the superstitious seamen like a sign of heaven's anger, terrible storms raged over the vessel, and when, seven anguished weeks later, the *Kitty's Amelia* reached Bonny, it was only to find ten or twelve vessels loading slaves before them, and Captain Crow had a long wait for his turn.

It was during this wait that misfortune struck another blow. In the hurry and bustle of getting away from Liverpool in time to cheat the Abolition Bill, a number of returned goods from a former voyage had been carelessly repacked in damp water-casks, and when these were opened at Bonny a malignant fever and dysentery broke out among the crew.

In the course of the passage out of Bonny to Jamaica, the fever continued to ravage both crew and slaves. Every day there were sea burials. Then, ten or twelve hundred miles from land, this hoodoo ship caught fire – and, what was worse, there were 45 barrels of gunpowder in the magazine, enough to blow every man-jack to glory.

Below in the holds, the terrified negroes were shrieking and hammering to be let out. On deck, panic, the sailors hacking at the ropes that held the stern and quarter lifeboats, all set to abandon ship.

Crow raced on to the deck.

"Is it possible, my lads, that you can desert me at a moment when it is your bounden duty, as men, to assist me?" he roared. "Follow me, my brave fellows, and we shall soon save the ship."

And down into the inferno plunged Crow himself.

The fire was licking and spitting just three feet from the powder kegs. Crow shouted for buckets of water. He seized the spare sails from their nearby locker, smothered the flames with the sails, and doused them with bucket after bucket of water. Ten minutes later, the fire was out. Eight weeks afterwards, the fire-blackened, fever-raked *Kitty's Amelia* limped into Kingston, Jamaica.

Captain Crow was only 43 when, in 1808, he retired from the sea. He had still twenty-one years of comfortable retirement before him. At first he went back to live on his native Isle of Man, but he found life monotonous there, and in 1817 returned to Liverpool, where he could enjoy the companionship of kindred spirits. He loved to sit in the newsroom of the Lyceum Club, and of an evening, after dinner, it was his delight to foregather with cronies who had been with him in the African trade, and with them fight his – and their – old battles against the cruel sea, and even crueller humankind, all over again.

He was a familiar figure, one of the sights of Liverpool, wandering about the docks and quays on fine days, dressed in slightly old-fashioned clothes, tetchy and querulous when the mood took him. That solitary eye of his remained 'a piercer' to the end, and, aided by the telescope he invariably carried under his arm, it missed nothing.

He died in 1829, in his 64th year. His body was taken back to the Island, where it lies in the burial-ground of his ancestors, Maughold churchyard. But his eccentric, salty spirit surely remains earth-bound in Liverpool, hovering, with so many other maritime ghosts, in that strange and eerie no-man's-land where the Mersey sky falls to meet the river ...

John Newton: Parson and Slaver

Vested in brand-new cassock and gown, the impressive-looking preacher climbed with slow dignity the long flight of steps leading up to the pulpit in Liverpool's fashionable St George's Church, which stood at the head of Castle and Lord Streets, where the Queen Victoria Monument now stands.

That Sunday morning in May 1764, was surely unique, for the newly-ordained clergyman about to deliver his first sermon was a former slave-captain, and among the cream of Liverpool Society who sat under him in the prestigeful church that was known as the Mayor's Chapel, was not only His Worship himself, but also many of the port's wealthiest and most highly-respected city merchants, who owed their fortunes to canny dealings in the slave-trade.

It was a very different figure that the new-minted parson cut from the teenage lad – himself when young – who, nineteen years before, had stood, stripped to the waist and bound hand and foot to a ship's gratings, his back a raw, scarlet welter of blood and broken flesh, being publicly flogged with the dreaded cat-o'-nine-tails aboard the man-o'-war, *Harwich*, at Plymouth.

The plain, but far from simple, truth is that the Reverend John Newton had, over the course of the years, undergone considerably more than a sea-change; the alteration in his whole character had been of the Damascan Road order, it is, indeed, tempting to see him as almost a latter-day Saint Augustine.

John Newton was born in London, on 24 July 1725. His father was a prosperous, but rigid and distinctly stern sea-captain in the Mediterranean trade. His mother, who died of consumption before his seventh birthday, was a gentle, pious woman, who had always hoped that her son would enter the ministry.

Not very long after her death, the captain married again, and he and his young wife settled at Aveley, in Essex. Very soon after the wedding, John was packed off to a boarding-school in the Essex village of Stratford, where he remained for two years, leaving a little before his tenth birthday. It was about this time that the second Mrs Newton presented the captain with a son, William, after whose arrival nobody seemed to have very much time to spare for young John. He felt that he was not wanted in his stepmother's home.

On his eleventh birthday, John was taken aboard his father's ship for the first time, and travelled with him in it to Spain. Thereafter, he accompanied his father on several of his voyages.

The captain then found a situation for the boy in the counting-house of a merchant friend of his in Alicante, south-east Spain. But the lad's behaviour was bad. He showed, moreover, an impatience with discipline and restraint which boded ill for his prospects, and after a few months' trial, his removal was decided upon.

John was rising 17 when, in 1742, Joseph Manesty, a Liverpool merchant with shares in a number of ships trading to Africa, the West Indies, and the American Colonies, who was a friend of his father's, and after whom Manesty's Lane, off School Lane, is named, offered to send the awkward youth off to Jamaica, where young Englishmen were in demand to manage the sugar plantations, and to take care of his future welfare. The offer was gratefully accepted, and John, who was also well pleased about it, made ready for his departure.

Before leaving, however, he went to pay a visit to his mother's old friend, Mrs Catlett, and her family, who lived at Chatham, in Kent. There he met their daughter, Mary, who was generally called Polly, and who was just approaching her 14th birthday. John fell deeply in love with her. Strangely enough, both his dead mother and Polly's mother had earmarked Polly from the moment of her birth as his future wife.

From that time forward, the only two constants in John Newton's extremely irregular life were his love for Polly, and his dependence upon the goodwill of Mr Manesty.

Unfortunately, so taken was he with Polly that, instead of the three days that he was originally to have stayed with the Catletts, he remained there for three weeks, thus missing his passage to Jamaica, and incurring his father's most majestic wrath.

This brought him to one of life's dangerous corners. In rebellious mood, he went as a common sailor on a voyage to Venice, fell a prey to evil companionship, and started with a will down the pleasantly slippery path to a most vicious and unprincipled way of life.

He became an out-and-out militant atheist, and was addicted to the expression of the most horrible profanities. What was worse, he matched his deeds to his words.

John was back visiting the Catletts – and Polly – in December 1743. It was while he was there that disaster struck. One February day in 1744, sauntering innocently along by the riverside, he had the bad luck to fall into the hands of a press-gang, who took him to the man-o'-war, the *Harwich*, lying at the Nore, the west part of the Thames estuary, three miles north-east of Sheerness.

After a month of suffering the stench of the common sailors' quarters, stomaching the coarse, ill-cooked food and the violence of his companions and tyrannical officers alike, he was rescued by his father's influence, and reached the salvatory sphere of the quarter-deck as a midshipman.

War had been declared against France and *HMS Harwich* was employed for the next twelve months on convoy duty.

In January 1745, she sailed to the Downs, between Deal and the Goodwin Sands, and there, along with other warships, assembled a merchant fleet. A long voyage was in prospect, taking them past Spain to the Guinea Coast of Africa, round the Cape of Good Hope, up the east coast of Africa, across the Indian Ocean to the ports of India and Ceylon, and on then to the far-distant and little-known East Indies. The gun-room talk was that it was likely to be five years before they saw the white cliffs of Dover again.

The weather turned tempestuous and contrary winds forced the fleet to anchor in Tor Bay. When they set sail again, they ran into a storm. A good deal of damage was done to the merchant ships and the admiral decided to put in at Plymouth for repairs. It was five weeks before the voyage could be resumed.

Sitting idly at an English port, Newton became thoroughly unsettled, and as the ship swung at anchor in Plymouth Sound he gazed moodily across the water and dreamt of Chatham. He also happened to hear that his father was at Tor Bay, examining some of the ships of the Royal Africa Company which had been damaged, and he took it into his head that if he could only get to see the old gentleman he could persuade him to use his influence to fix a transfer for him from the Royal Navy into a ship of the Royal Africa Company. That would mean his having to make only a comparatively short voyage before being able to return to Chatham and Polly.

It was at this point that news came that it was necessary to send a boat ashore, and the *Harwich's* commander, Captain Carteret, felt that in the circumstances – an impressed crew with a long voyage facing them – the men could not be trusted. Midshipman Newton was ordered to take charge and keep a sharp watch that no one attempted to desert. And what did he do, but desert himself.

He was picked up by a party of soldiers on the Dartmouth Road, no more than two hours from the place where he might find his father, marched back and through the streets of Plymouth, guarded like a felon, and delivered into Captain Carteret's hands.

A flogging was ordered.

"Strip," came the command, and when Newton had removed his shirt,the captain barked, "Seize him up."

Whereupon the Master-at-Arms conducted Newton to a grating to which his feet were tied. Another grating had been positioned so that Newton could lean against it with his arms over the top and his wrists tightly lashed to it. The Bosun's Mate stepped forward swinging the cat-o'-nine-tails. The entire ship's company watched as, interminably it seemed, the lash rose and fell.

An eternity later, the order came, "Pipe down."

Newton's hands and feet were untied, a cloth was thrown over his red-barred, lacerated body, and he was carried below to the cockpit.

Deprived of his rank, banished to the lower deck, it was the prolongation of his punishment to be at the beck and call of the bosun and every officer on the ship, including the midshipmen, who until now had been his fellows.

Nineteen days after finally sailing out of Plymouth, *HMS Harwich* moored in Funchal Road, on the Island of Madeira. On the morning that the fleet was to sail southwards to the Cape of Good Hope, Newton, coming up on deck, saw a sailor putting some clothes into a boat. The man was, he was told, being discharged from the Navy and put aboard a Guinea ship which lay nearby.

Newton recognised what was going on. It was a custom at the time for any troublesome member of the crew of a merchantman to be put in irons and so held until such time as a man-o'-war was sighted. The troublemaker would then be transferred to the warship.

On this occasion, the Fleet Commodore had impressed two men from the Guinea ship because they were qualified in a trade, and had ordered that two ordinary seamen from the *Harwich* were to be given to replace them.

Newton ran to the lieutenant on duty and beseeched him to intercede with Captain Carteret that he might be the other replacement. Carteret, for whatever reason, gave his consent, and within minutes Newton found himself and his sparse possessions in a boat, being rowed out of the Royal Navy.

The merchant ship of which he was now a crew member was engaged in the slave-trade, and it was aboard this vessel that Newton made the acquaintance of a slaver named Clow. This man had first come to Africa only a few years earlier as a penniless adventurer. Now, he had made a fortune. The story of his remarkable success inflamed Newton's imagination. He went to Clow and begged to be taken into his service. Liking the look of the 19-year-old sailor and foreseeing the future possibility of making use of him, Clow, without making any commitment as to the amount of wages that would be paid to him, happily agreed to the proposition.

Clow took Newton with him to the largest of the Plantane Islands, 'seven leagues south of the Bananas'. They were accompanied by a number of slaves – for it was Clow's business to buy slaves from the chieftains direct, and deliver them to a visiting slave-ship, selling them on at twice the price he had given for them – and an African black woman, who shared his bed with him. Her name is recorded in Newton's journal as 'P.I.' – because it sounded something like those two letters pronounced separately.

Unfortunately, P.I. took an instant dislike to Newton, and when he fell ill and was unable to accompany his master on a slave-foray upriver from Shenge, in Sierra Leone, and was left in her care, she treated him with jealous cruelty. His bed was a mat spread upon a board or chest and with a log of wood for a pillow. When his fever eventually subsided and his appetite returned, she, who lived in plenty herself, allowed him barely sufficient food to sustain life.

On the odd occasion, when she was in the highest good humour, P.I. would send him scraps from her own plate after she had dined, which he was obliged to eat like a dog from a platter on the floor. Once, summoned to receive such bounty from her own hand, he, being exceedingly weak and feeble, dropped the plate, and she, laughing at his terrible disappointment, refused, although her table was covered with dishes and groaning with food, to give him any more.

Hunger drove him to go by night, risking punishment as a thief if discovered, to pull up roots in the plantation and devour them raw. Such was his plight, indeed, that even some of the slaves in chains felt pity for him and secretly brought offerings from their own extremely slender rations to him. Is there not irony in this vignette of these poor, generous-hearted creatures providing food to keep the future slave-captain from starvation?

But when P.I. was about, none dared show compassion. They must despise and mock. She would force the still far from recovered Newton to his feet and make him walk. This he was unable to do, and she would set the slaves mimicking his grotesque attempts, derisively clapping their hands, and throwing limes, or stones, at him.

When, two months later, Clow returned from his slaving expedition, Newton complained of his ill-treatment at P.I.'s hands, but he dismissed it as a figment of feverish fantasies deriving from the lad's bout of sickness, while accepting P.I.'s version that he had been lazy and unwilling to work.

It was not long before Clow set off on another trip in the shallop, this time taking Newton with him. Things went wrong when an unscrupulous European trader accused Newton of stealing Clow's goods by night, or in the daytime when he was absent. Clow chose to believe him, and whenever he went ashore left Newton locked upon deck, exposed to strong gales and almost incessant cold rain, and wearing only a threadbare shirt and trousers, a couple of yards of cheap cotton cloth wrapped round him to serve as a coat, and a handkerchief for a cap.

As a day's allowance of food, he was left a pint of rice. He begged the entrails of fowls which Clow killed and cooked for his own meals, and used them as bait for a fish line. The fish which he was lucky enough to catch undoubtedly helped to keep him alive.

One day back on the Plantenes, Clow and his black mistress stood watching Newton planting some limes. The trees were no higher than a young gooseberry bush.

"Who knows," said Clow mockingly, "but by the time these trees grow up and bear, you may go home to England, obtain the command of a ship, and return to reap the fruits of your labours."

It was said with what was intended for cutting sarcasm and a sneer. But it turned out to be a true prediction. The cruel P.I. was to live to see her jeering bedfellow's prophecy fulfilled.

In Clow's service, Newton became little better than a white slave. There is no record of his ever having received any money from the trader. In what spare time he had, Newton read assiduously Barrow's *Euclid*, drawing geometric figures in the sand with a stick, and this way succeeded in mastering, no mean achievement, the first six books. He also wrote assiduously to Polly and to Manesty.

And, indeed, it was Manesty who, at Newton's father's request, eventually rescued him, sending one of his slave-captains, the master of the *Greyhound*, to find him and bring him back to Liverpool. At first, Newton was none too keen to return, for he had contrived to escape Clow's clutches and was doing well for himself in the service of another trader. The captain, by dint of a little necessary yarn-spinning deception – telling him, quite wrongly, that a relative lately deceased had left him a legacy of £400-a-year, six or seven times the pay of a ship's captain – persuaded Newton to turn his face once more towards England.

After a full twelve months of voyaging, in the course of which the *Greyhound*, upon which he was regarded as a Jonah – in large measure because of the blasphemies, really appalling even to the ears of hardened seafarers, to which it was his constant delight to give tongue – all but foundered. The idea of throwing him overboard was openly canvassed. He arrived safely in Liverpool, however, in May 1748, and hot-footed it to Chatham and little Polly Catlett. He was now 23 years old.

In the August, having been appointed mate on the slave-ship, the *Brownlow*, owned by Joseph Manesty, he sailed for Sierra Leone, and from there, carrying slaves, to Antigua and Charleston.

Back in the Mersey once more in December 1749, Newton got under way with arrangements to marry Polly, and their wedding took place at St Margaret's, Rochester, on 12 February 1750. A few months later, in the August, Newton sailed, this time in command of another of Manesty's slavers, the *Duke of Argyle*.

He dropped anchor off the place where he had himself been all but a slave, and sent a longboat to bring to him the African woman, P.I., who had so delighted in tormenting him.

> I desired the men to fire guns over her head in honour of her. ... She seemed to feel it like heaping coals of fire on her head. ... I treated her with the greatest complaisance and kindness, and if she has any shame in her, I believe I have made her sorry for her former ill-treatment of me. ... I made her some presents and sent her ashore. She was evidently most comfortable when she had her back to my ship.

Newton's seafaring career was now drawing near to its close. In 1752, he took command of Manesty's slave-ship, the *African*. And it was about this time that, filled with remorse for the atheism and profligacy of the years before, he became a devout Christian. He was taken gravely ill during the voyage of the *African*, and returned to Liverpool a far from well man.

He was due to sail to Africa in November 1754 as master of a newly fitted-out and faster ship, the *Bee*, but, two days before she was due to leave, Newton, drinking tea and talking over past events with his wife, suffered a fit. His physicians advised him that he must not sail again. He resigned his command, and, in his 30th year, with a young wife dependent upon him, felt, as he stood by the Customs House at the foot of Water Street, watching the sails of the *Bee*, under the command of another captain, growing smaller and less distinct as in the gathering twilight she began her first voyage to the Guinea Coast without him, more than a little worried about the terrestrial weather lying ahead for him

Once again, it was that good friend Joseph Manesty who saw to it that John Newton's life was set fair for its passage, this time over dry land. He used his political influence to secure for him the job of tide surveyor of the port of Liverpool.

Newton took up this appointment on 18 August 1755. It was his duty to attend the tides, and, one week, to visit the ships already in the river, as well as any that might arrive, and the next week to inspect all the vessels in the docks. His office charged him with the responsibility of discovering any goods aboard a ship over and above the captain's declaration, and to seize such goods.

The Newtons found a small house in Edmund Street, off Old Hall Street, and he spent the next six years as a Customs officer, debating the while his resolve to enter the ministry.

At last, the decision taken, he was admitted to deacon's orders on 29 April 1764, at Buckden, in Huntingdonshire. In May 1764, he preached at St George's, as we have already seen, and also at Childwall Church. On 21 May, he and his wife left Liverpool, where they had spent the previous eight years, and, following his ordination as priest by the Bishop of Lincoln, on 17 June, they went to live at Olney, in Buckinghamshire, where he had been offered, and accepted, a curacy.

In November 1766, came the sad news that Mr Manesty, with whom Newton had deposited all his savings, had gone bankrupt.

The Newtons were to spend the next sixteen years at Olney, where John Newton became a close friend of the poet, William Cowper, who had been singing the wrongs of the black Africans, whom Newton had been buying, selling and transporting, in misery to misery, across the sea in floating prisons. With Cowper he was to produce, *The Olney Hymns*.

His ministry at Olney came to an end when, in 1780, he was offered the living of St Mary Woolnoth, in Lombard Street, in the City of London, where Polly died on 15 December 1790. John Newton lived on for another seventeen years. He died, aged 82, in 1807, the year that slave-trading in English ships was abolished.

He is buried in St Mary Woolnoth where the epitaph of his own composing is incised into a memorial tablet:

> John Newton, once an Infidel and Libertine,
> a Servant of Slaves in Africa, was by the rich
> mercy of Our Lord and Saviour, Jesus Christ,
> Preserved, Restored, Pardoned and Appointed
> to preach the Faith he had long laboured to destroy.

THE PLAGUE DOCTOR

Like the terrible Black Death, the rat-and-flea-carried bubonic plague, which ravaged mediæval England in the fourteenth century, and, revisited upon London as The Great Plague of 1665, killed 68,596 of its citizens, so did the dreaded cholera, the 'new' disease of the nineteenth century, sweep in successive waves across Victorian Liverpool, a merciless invisible foe, leaving mountains of corpses in its awful wake.

The blame for the onset of these fearsome epidemics has been put upon the bowed shoulders of the Irish paupers who flooded into the town. The cause of their mass exit from the Emerald Isle was a tiny fungus, *phytophthera infestans,* to the mycologist, the pathogen responsible for the potato blight, and thus for the potato famine, which, depriving the Irish peasantry of their staple food, sent them in starveling, desperate droves out of their barren cabins, across the sea to England.

A comforting axiom is that which declares that troublous times invariably breed their salvatory hero or trouble-shooter, and when the dark curtain of cholera descended upon Liverpool, sure enough, one man stepped forward on to the deserted stage to challenge, virtually single-handed, the ogreish Giant Disease assailing his native town.

His name was William Henry Duncan.

Born in Seel Street, Liverpool, in 1805, the third son and fifth child of George Duncan and his Scottish wife, Christian, the youngest daughter of the Reverend James Currie, of Kirkpatrick Fleming, in Dumfriesshire, Duncan has left no record of his early years. He first comes into focus as a young man of 24, when he graduates as a Doctor of Medicine, gaining his MD with a thesis, *De ventris in reliquum corpus potestate,* (On the power of the womb over the rest of the body), in l829.

Returning to Liverpool, he set about building up his medical career. He took on the work of being Physician to the South Dispensary, at 1 Upper Parliament Street, where free consultations were given, and free medicines dispensed, to the poor. In 1837, three years after its foundation, he, together with Dr Samuel Malins, conducted the first course of lectures on Medical Jurisprudence at the Liverpool Royal Institution School of Medicine and Surgery, in Colquitt Street. And he subsequently also lectured there on Materia Medica and Therapeutics. At the same time, he was one of the physicians to the Royal Infirmary, then situated at Shaw's Brow.

He married Catherine, daughter of William Duncan MacAndrew, of Liverpool, and he lived at 18 Rodney Street, where he saw private patients. He made a point of taking a prominent part in the professional and social life of the town. He became a member of the Liverpool Medical Institution, towards the cost of the erection of whose building, at the top of Mount Pleasant, he subscribed, and in 1836 was elected one of the four Presidents of the Liverpool Medical Society appointed annually, each in turn taking the Chair at meetings in rotation. He was a member of the Athenæum, and one of the subscribers to the publication of Baines' *History of Liverpool*, in 1852.

From his first professional days, Duncan's social conscience had been disturbed by the conditions in which he had found the poor to be living. Although there were houses available for artisans at a rent of £12 a year, the vast majority of the poor were unskilled, sporadically employed labourers, and such an annual lay-out was well beyond the scope of their ragged purses. The accommodation that they found was in the courts and cellars of the city.

Duncan grasped every opportunity to make his views known to such civic power-wielders as magistrates and members of the Town Council. As early as 1842, he had begun to read papers before the Literary and Philosophical Society of Liverpool expositive of the predicament of the city's underprivileged.

In a paper read in 1843, he described the cellar-dwellings:

> The cellars are ten or twelve feet square; generally flagged – but frequently having only the bare earth for a floor, and sometimes less than six feet in height. There is frequently no window; so that light and air can gain access to the cellars only by the door, the top of which is often not higher than the level of the street. In such cellars ventilation is out of the question. They are, of course, dark, and, from the defective drainage, they are also very generally damp. There is sometimes a back cellar, used as a sleeping apartment, having no direct communication with the external atmosphere, and deriving its scanty supply of light and air solely from the first apartment.

The courts were only slightly less dreadful. Typically, they consisted of an arrangement of two rows of six or eight three-storeyed, three-roomed houses, facing each other across an intervening space of nine to fifteen feet. The houses were 'blind' – that is to say that they were open only at the front. One room deep, their backs touched the backs of identical houses in the next court. They were, therefore, without door, window, or indeed any outlet at the back, and there was thus no possibility of through ventilation. Each of the rooms measured perhaps eight or nine feet square. The bedroom was reached by a steep, rickety stair going up out of the ground-floor room. From here, a similar stair led up to the top bedroom. The cluster of houses forming the court was set back in a sort of cul-de-sac, the far end of the court being closed off by a high wall, and the sole exit to the main street was through an arched-over passageway about three feet wide. These courts were grotesquely overcrowded, and lacking in any sort of proper sanitary provisions. They were plague-pits waiting for a plague to happen.

The plague arrived in May 1832, an epidemic of cholera, a disease which originated in the subcontinent of India, and had never gone global until the nineteenth century. Cholera hospitals were opened in Lime Street and Toxteth Park. As the sufferers were being borne in palanquins, the bearers were frequently attacked by friends of the sick, the rumour having been mischievously bruited abroad that they were being carted off to be used in experiments or as 'subjects' for anatomical dissection. So serious was the breakdown of trust between the doctors and their patients that, stated the *Liverpool Mercury*:

> Among great numbers of the lower classes in this town
> the idea is prevalent that the cholera is a mere invention
> of the medical men to fill their own pockets.

When, by the end of September, the epidemic had abated, there had been more than 1,500 deaths in Liverpool.

The discovery of the cause of cholera lay more than fifty years in the future. It was the German bacteriological researcher, Dr Robert Koch, who, in 1884, isolated the cholera bacillus, and irrefutably demonstrated that no healthy man can ever be attacked by cholera unless he swallows the comma-shaped microbe that is only to be found in the human intestine or in highly polluted water.

But, back in the 1830s, and for many decades after, faced with the mysteries of cholera, typhus, smallpox, and the like, Dr Duncan, in company with many other respected medical men, subscribed to the Miasmatic Theory of disease. This was the belief that fevers and infectious diseases were to be attributed to miasmas or gaseous poisons in the air, exuded from such sources as putrefying animal matter, rotting vegetable material, the soil and stagnant water.

This led Duncan to the conclusion that all forms of dirt represented root causes of disease. And conditions of overcrowding clearly engendered dirt. He therefore counselled scrupulous cleanliness, the demolition of the courts, and the blocking up of the cellar-dwellings. He preached the efficacy of large-scale whitewashing, which he thought to decontaminate the miasmata, and which did actually perform a degree of antiseptic function.

Thus, topsy-turvily, he was, for the wrong reasons, proposing the right remedies.

But, as John Snow, a surgeon from York, who became London's leading anaesthetist, dealing a death blow to the Miasma Theory, was to point out in 1849, cholera could not be spread by poison in the ambient air, since it affected the intestines, not the lungs, and he sagely drew attention to the contamination of drinking water as a result of cholera evacuations seeping into wells or running into rivers from which drinking water was taken.

In 1837, another virulent disease rampaged through Liverpool. This was typhus, begotten by dirt, spread by lice, caused, as we now know, by one of the *Rickettsiae* – a group of non-motile micro-organisms, extremely minute, somewhere between the viruses and bacteria in size. During the last six months of the 1837 outbreak, 524 people succumbed, and in the succeeding two years, nearly 1000 died. The disease peaked during a return visit in 1847, on the heels of the Irish immigrants, when 21,000 (one in 15 of the population) died, nearly a third of typhus or one of its adjunctives.

Duncan, who had already established a considerable local reputation, spoke out nationally in 1840, disparaging the existence of Liverpool's courts – places which were usually provided with only one privy for the use of all the dwellers therein – 'home' to 86,000 people, and the cellars, where another 38,000 lived in squalor and misery. According to one Irish resident of picturesque turn of phrase, the smell of his home was "bad enough to raise the roof of his skull".

Duncan weighed in again with evidence for Edwin Chadwick, Secretary to the Poor Law Commission, who brought out, in 1842, his *Report on the Sanitary Condition of the Labouring Population of Great Britain*. The Poor Law Commission was at last beginning to recognise the correlative link between poverty and disease.

Empowered by the Liverpool Sanitary Act 1846, the Town Council appointed Dr William Henry Duncan Liverpool's first Medical Officer of Health. He was also the first Medical Officer of Health in the country. He took up his new duties on 1 January 1847.

Barely was Duncan ensconced in his new office, when a scarifying epidemic of typhus broke over the town. Its advent was associated with the arrival of a large batch of potato famine fleeing Irish, and indeed it was they who were, poor things, to be the epidemic's main victims.

The Irish were, of course, mainly Roman Catholics, and there were in Liverpool 24 Catholic priests, attached to eight Catholic churches, to whom would fall the sad duty of coping with this ocean of misery. Ten of the priests were marked for death in the course of their ministrations. Catholic posterity has revered and celebrated them as the Martyr Priests of Liverpool.

Remembering this fearful time, Father Nugent, who took part in it, recalled:

> The strain on the surviving clergy was dreadful; hourly
> they faced death. At night they rested on chairs and sofas

in their clothes awaiting the inevitable sick call. Sometimes they lay down beside the dying in the packed cellars to hear their confessions. In the midst of the panic created by this terrible scourge the devotion and calmness of the priests commanded universal admiration. Day and night they were with the people. Into the dwellings of the poor, in attic and cellar, in the courts and alleys, where to breathe the fetid and pestilential atmosphere was death, they went fearlessly to give the Sacraments. They were at the bedside of the dying, and where the dead were left unburied, more than one of that heroic band lifted the dead body, all covered with typhus spots, and placed it in a coffin.

Recalling 16 June 1847, the day that Father Grayston, Rector of St Patrick's, Park Place, died, Father Nugent continues:

> That day there were, if I remember rightly, forty-three sick calls. The Reverend Robert Gillow of Copperas Hill, and myself divided them. Never can I forget the scenes I that day witnessed of the dead and dying. A mother lying dead of the fever on a heap of shavings in a cellar, a baby at her breast, and two young children playing on the floor. The heavy pestilential atmosphere of that cellar was loaded with malignant poison.

His friend, Father Gillow, died on 22 August. His brother, Father George Gillow, was also at St Nicholas', Copperas Hill, at this time. One day a messenger hurriedly arrived at the presbytery, and said: "For God's sake, will some of you come to St Patrick's and bury the dead, for the church is full of corpses and people attending them, and all the priests are down with the fever." The priests round the table looked at each other as much as to say "Who will be the next victim?" when Father Gillow exclaimed quietly, "I will go if you like." Later, he caught the fever – but he recovered.

Happily, the year 1848 was a less harrowing one, although scarlatina, otherwise scarlet fever, a disease caused by a bacteria, *Streptococcus pyogenes*, and spread mostly by carriers, and by dust in which discharges from carriers' ears, noses and throats have dried, accounted for 1,500 deaths.

However, to ruin everything, there arrived, in December 1848, another desolating visitation of the Asiatic cholera. Dr Duncan came in for a severe drubbing in the persistently unfriendly *Liverpool Mercury*, wherein he was accused of murder for his refusal to accept the diagnoses and magical pills offered by Dr Hawthorne, who was one of several emergent charlatans plying an infallible cure for the cholera. The epidemic fulminated on, and Duncan embarked upon a massive series of house-to-house visits and lime-washings in an all-out effort to stem the onslaught.

The cholera struck again in 1849, a new wave of the disease arriving from Scotland, and resulting in 5,308 deaths in Liverpool. An attenuated outbreak occurred in 1854, but it came and went attaining to only a fifth of the intensity of its predecessor of five years before.

Duncan had never spared his own health in his struggle to preserve that of others. But now he was tired, beginning to ail himself. Having been for some months in a delicate state of health, he travelled up to Elgin to visit his in-laws and have a little rest.

And there, in the land of his forebears, suddenly, on Saturday afternoon, 23 May 1863, at the age of 57, he died. They buried him in his wife's – the Forsyths' – family vault at Elgin Cathedral. He had spent the last 16 years of his life fighting the good fight for the health and medical well-being of his fellow-citizens. Cholera, typhus, smallpox, scarlatina, dysentery, diphtheria, whooping-cough, measles, tuberculosis and endemic diarrhoea, had all posed problems. He had coped with them as best he could, and, given the limited resources of his time, he had not done at all badly.

THE THETIS AND THE DAYS OF DOOM

All Liverpool was holding its breath – praying, and playing the waiting game. The minds of the city's people, indeed, of all of Merseyside, were far away from their normal everyday preoccupations: they had travelled out 38 miles down river and into the deep water reaches of Liverpool Bay, to hover above the spot where the stricken submarine lay, more than five times full fathom five, trapped on the sebed, powerless to move.

Each morning, anxious eyes scanned eagerly the *Daily Post*, and, throughout the day, the latest editions of the *Liverpool Echo*. In hushed rooms people sat, ears glued to the wireless, which, in that pre-universal television epoch, was the principal dispenser of up-to-the-minute news.

For this was the time of one of Liverpool's greatest maritime disasters, which filled with tears three beautiful June days in the summer of 1939.

It had all begun in an atmosphere of triumphant optimism, with cautious gaiety and disciplined confidence in attendance. Three years before, in December 1936, there had been laid down at Cammell Laird's ship-building yard at Birkenhead, a submarine ordered by the Royal Navy.

Budgeted to cost approximately £350,000, she was the third of the new 'T' class of boat (all submariners refer to their craft as 'boats', not as 'ships'), and the first of them to be built at Birkenhead. She was 270 feet long overall, displaced 1,575 tons submerged, had a maximum surface speed of 16 knots – 9 knots dived – and a range of 8000 miles. She carried one 4-inch gun and six 21-inch torpedo tubes. She was named *Thetis*, after the Nereid, wife of Peleus and mother of Achilles.

It was at 9.40am on Thursday 1 June 1939, that His Majesty's Submarine *Thetis* slipped, proceeded out of the basin at Cammell Laird's, and by ten o'clock, decked with the White Ensign, was slowly edging her way out of the shipyard entrance into the river, to catch the high tide.

She was heading, under the command of Lieutenant-Commander Guy H (Sam) Bolus, RN, for the open water, to do her diving trials. This was also something of a social occasion, a celebration, and she had aboard her 103 souls, which was at least twice the usual complement. Aside from a crew of five officers and 48 ratings, she was carrying 9 Naval officer guests, 7 Admiralty civilian staff, 26 employees of Cammell Laird, who had official technical parts to play in the trials, 5 staff members of other ship-building companies, a Mersey pilot, Norman Willcox, and a Mr Dobells and a Mr Bath, both employees of Liverpool City Caterers Ltd, who were providing the celebratory festive luncheon traditionally put up by the builders to mark the occasion.

Little Marjorie was the 11-year-old daughter and only child of Cammell

Laird ships' fitter, Bill Watterson, who lived almost on top of Wallasey promenade, and she and her mother had promised to see him safely off. She was skipping in the road with her friends that hot June morning when *Thetis* sailed by, the family home on her port side, and Marjorie waved her father goodbye with her skipping-rope as he swept past along the Mersey in the steel tube that was to become his coffin.

At 10.45am, one of the New Brighton coastguards caught a glimpse of *Thetis* as she crossed the Liverpool line heading for the open sea.

About noon, *Thetis*, accompanied now by *Grebecock*, the Liverpool Screw Towing and Lighterage Company's tug, whose master, Mr AE Godfrey, had four passengers aboard over and above his crew of seven – two Royal Naval submariners, Lieutenant RE Coltart and Telegraphist VJ Crosby, and two men from Cammell Laird – cleared the Bar Light Vessel.

Thetis was now some 14 miles out of Liverpool and at the entrance to the main channel. Conditions were fine and clear. She was making 9 knots, and it did not take her long to reach the deeper waters of Liverpool Bay. Lunch – a splendid spread of cold meats, meat pies, and all the trimmings, and a bottle of beer for each man – was served in wardroom and on mess-decks.

The weather was idyllic. Sunlight dappled the water of the diving ground, an area which Godfrey, of the *Grebecock,* knew as well as any man on earth. Up in the wheelhouse, he was, despite the warmth of the day, regaling himself with a succulent Lancashire hotpot, which he had brought from home and heated up in the galley. On the deck, basking in the sun, Coltart and Crosby were enjoying sandwiches and mugs of tea.

It was just before 1.30pm when, lunch over, *Thetis* reached her diving position – 38 miles out of Liverpool, 15 miles west of north of Great Orme's Head, at Llandudno, on the North Wales coast – and Lieutenant-Commander Bolus instructed that word be passed round that those who wanted to disembark, should do so now. They would be transferred to *Grebecock* before *Thetis* made her dive. Most unusually, no one elected to leave the submarine. Bolus informed *Grebecock* of this by megaphone, and then, at 1.40pm, despatched a formal diving signal to C-in-C, Plymouth.

At 1.56pm, acknowledgment came from the Naval Wireless Station at Plymouth, the conning-tower was cleared, the hatch shut and clipped, and the order given, "Flood the tanks".

At 2pm, the observers, watching intently from *Grebecock*, heard the unmistakable 'whoosh' of air rushing out as *Thetis* blew her tanks. Then, almost it seemed as if in slow motion, she very gradually began to sink. She got her bow down at a slight angle, and remained in that position for all of 20 minutes. After that, she levelled off until the tops of her for'ard and aft guard rails were just showing above the water. She then sank until her gun was awash and half her conning-tower below the water.

At 2.57pm, her bow came up and she dived horizontally and fairly fast.

She had completely disappeared within a minute.

Neither Coltart, nor Crosby, nor Godfrey, had liked the look of the dive. Now they waited in a state of some perturbation. *Thetis* had been due to submerge to check trim, that is the submarine's balance; to surface and blow main tanks; to dive again to periscope depth; to lower periscope and dive to 60 feet; and then to fire smoke candles. She had done none of these things. The surface of the sea beneath which she had sunk remained inscrutable and unbroken.

At 4.45pm Coltart sent a signal by Seaforth Radio to Fort Blockhouse, at Gosport, Hampshire, asking for the duration of *Thetis'* dive. Due to the initial inadequacy of *Grebecock's* radio-telephony equipment, the message did not arrive at Gosport General Post Office until 5.38pm. It so happened that the telegraph boy at Gosport GPO was deep in the intricacies of mending a puncture on his bike. It further so happened that the telegram did not seem to senior GPO staff to be urgent. Consequence: nobody applied a boot to the appropriate portion of the lad. Further consequence: it was not until 6.15pm, an hour and a half after its origination, that the message was handed in its orange envelope to Captain S5, Fort Blockhouse.

As a matter of record, at 4.45pm the Duty Chief Yeoman of Signals at Fort Blockhouse had reported to the Duty Commanding Officer of the Fifth Submarine Flotilla, that *Thetis* had been due to surface between 4.40pm and 5.05pm, but that so far, no surfacing signal had been received. From 4.45pm onwards, Fort Blockhouse had been calling *Thetis* on wireless telegraphy every ten minutes. Culver Wireless Station and the Admiralty had been approached, but neither was able to report any contact with the submarine. A telephone call to Cammell Laird, and a signal to the Bar Lightship, had produced similar negative results.

All was silence – and apprehensive speculation.

The situation looked grave. *Thetis* was down, out of sight of land, in an area of strong tides. She had a number of persons aboard, considerably in excess of her normal complement, and would therefore be short of air reserve if submerged for any long period of time. The only vessel standing by her was the escort tug, *Grebecock*, which was without wireless or any means of underwater signalling, and had only a junior Naval liaison officer on board. And yet, it was not until 6.22pm that the first order was given to begin searching for *Thetis* by ship, and the first request for an air search was not sent out until 6.50pm. In practical terms, this meant that neither ship nor aircraft could reach the scene of the sinking until it was almost sunset.

Too late, telephone lines buzzed madly, wireless messages crackled out. Proceed with utmost despatch … two submarines for underwater signalling; a flotilla of mine-sweepers to quarter the sea bed; a destroyer flotilla from Portland; *HMS Tedworth*, the deep-diving vessel, from the Clyde; the destroyer *Brazen*, en route through the Irish Sea to Plymouth; aircraft from various bases.

Sunset was at 9.04pm. With just four minutes to spare, Flight-Lieutenant John Avent arrived at 9pm with a flight of four Ansons from the RAF Station at Abbotsinch, in Scotland. It was Avent himself who spotted the buoy marking the place where *Thetis* lay.

At about seven o'clock that Thursday evening, young Marjorie Watterson, her mother and her auntie, went down to Wallasey Promenade, hoping to see *Thetis* coming back. It was a beautiful evening of slanting sunshine, and the seats all along the prom were filled with people. Bathed in reddish-gold sunlight, Liverpool's old river looked peaceful and really quite lovely. They waited and waited, but there was no sign of the sleek black submarine skimming like a whale through the water, and eventually, as the sun sank and grey twilight fell to meet and drown in the grey of the river, Marjorie was sent home to bed. Her mother and aunt stayed out watching until the moon fell and the river turned forbiddingly dark hued, before coming home and going themselves to bed. It was not until the light broke on the morning of Friday 2 June, that they heard the dreadful news.

It was only those late owls who stayed up to listen to the eleven o'clock news on the wireless who heard this bulletin:

> The Admiralty regrets to announce that His Majesty's submarine *Thetis* ... has failed to surface.

While Liverpool at large in blissful ignorance slept, events were grimly shaping up in the coldly glittering moonlight of Liverpool Bay. By midnight, *Thetis* had been shut down for ten hours.

Truth be told, things had begun to go wrong, at least slightly, from the very beginning. That was when *Thetis* would not at first dive. And as early as that, there was, curiously enough, mess-deck gossip about the boat's being a 'Jonah'. Sailors are traditionally, and perhaps understandably, sensitive and superstitious men.

Engine Room Artificer PF Jackson had reported: "All main ballast tanks flooded, sir." This was five minutes after the order to dive had been given. She should by then have been well below the surface.

More water was admitted to the auxiliary tanks, increasing the boat's weight. But, 10 ... 20 ... 30 thirty minutes later, *Thetis* was *still* on the surface.

Could the trouble perhaps be that torpedo tubes Numbers 5 and 6 for'ard were not full of water, as they should have been? Torpedo officer, Lieutenant Frederick Woods, decided to check.

Torpedo tubes have a door at either end. The cover of the tube end open to the sea is known as the bow-cap; the inboard end of the tube is sealed by the inner torpedo tube door. On this inner door there is a small-bore cock, which, when opened, will reveal the presence of water in it by permitting a thin, tell-tale stream to flow from it. When Lieutenant Woods turned the test tap of tube Number 5, nothing happened. No stream of water.

Then he made his great mistake. He opened the inner door. What he did not, could not, know, was that by a freak accident, a tiny, half-inch plug of the black bitumastic paint and enamel with which the tube was protected against corrosion by constant exposure to sea water, was blocking the top of the test tap mechanism. As the inner door of what was therefore believed to be an empty tube was opened, the sea came bursting in with tremendous and terrible force.

The men managed to struggle through from the Torpedo Space compartment into the next compartment, the Torpedo Storage Space, taking refuge behind Number 1 Watertight Bulkhead, but experienced massive difficulty in closing the door, so that the sea penetrated right through into the second compartment. Then, suddenly, the lights went out. Soaked to the skin, freezing cold, gasping for breath, the men fought blindly in total darkness to close the Number 2 Bulkhead door. If they failed, and the water reached the main batteries in the next compartment, vast clouds of poisonous chlorine gas would immediately be dispersed over the entire boat. They did not fail. But the upshot of it all was that *Thetis* not only lost two whole compartments and their supply of air, but the additional weight of water dragged her down into a position from which she was unable to right herself.

It was now approaching eight o'clock. They were starting on the long watches of the night. There was still no panic. The men sat around, civilians – engineers, electricians and fitters, and naval ratings – stokers and the like – in small knots, talking, asking questions, providing answering explanations, occasionally breaking into quiet laughter. There had been a little chicken and some cheese and biscuits left over from lunch, and the sharing out of these – as far as they would go, which was not all that far – improved morale.

Of course, the men down in the deep did not know it, but from all over the country, ships and men were speeding through the night to *Thetis'* aid. From Liverpool, the salvage vessel, *Vigilant* was making full steam ahead. His Majesty's Submarine *Cachalot* was out there, too. And HMS *Winchelsea* and a flotilla of eight new Tribal class destroyers, led by HMS *Somali*.

In *Thetis* the air had begun to grow palpably thick, it was like breathing soup, and any kind of physical effort rapidly produced breathlessness.

Up aloft, at 1am on Friday 2 June, the Company Secretary of Messrs Cammell Laird, Mr S Woodward, came out and spoke to the ever-increasing crowd of wives and relatives, who had, for the past couple of hours, been gathering at the gates in Green Lane, Birkenhead, waiting for news. All would, he assured them, be well, and he urged them to go home to bed.

Their husbands, brothers and sons, were not perhaps so optimistic. At any rate, putting on a brave face, the boat's officers were huddled around the wardroom table hatching an escape plan. The idea was hearteningly simple really. Tighten the fore hatch, pump a supply of high-pressure air into the submarine, get the men aboard to open certain valves which would allow the air access to the for'ard compartments, and so force out the water. All it needed was one man to get the plan to the surface.

Captain HPK Oram, who was the Commander of the flotilla in which *Thetis* would serve after her trials, and who had come along on the diving trip in order to get to know her officers and to see them at work, volunteered to try to make it to the surface. He would take the plan with him, strapped to his arm in a watertight cover, so that if he did not survive, and his body was found, the plan would still be intact. Torpedo Officer Lieutenant Woods volunteered to go up with Oram. There was, Oram calculated, just about enough air left in *Thetis* to keep them alive until 3pm.

Sunrise was at 4.48am.

Steaming, at 7.50am, through the rising light of the newborn day, Lieutenant-Commander RH Mills, captain of *Brazen*, screwing his eyes tight into his binoculars, focused on an object that he had seen about three miles distant to starboard, and gave a great shout.

"There she is!"

Sure enough, there she was ... some 18 feet of the stern of a submarine sticking up out of the water.

Thetis had been found.

It was just after 8am when Captain Oram and the young, curly-haired Lieutenant Woods were, in accordance with their agreed stratagem for getting the escape plan to the surface, standing in the escape chamber. So debilitated were they both, that it had taken them nearly 20 minutes to complete what had seemed like a physical obstacle course. Up the steep slope – caused by the fact that the submarine's tail had been steadily rising all through the night – from the control-room amidships, they had positively crawled, past the men lying quietly along the deck plates, to the after escape chamber, cheered on their way by whispers of, "Good luck, sir".

And the brave jokes:

"Tell them not to flog all our farewell dance tickets till we get up topside."

"Mind you tell the accounts department to watch our overtime."

The first attempt at escape was a dud. The chamber would not fill with water. They drained it down. Just as they shut the door a second time and began flooding up, there came a series of dull, subdued c-r-r-umps. The destroyer *Brazen* had hurled 12 underwater signal charges alongside *Thetis*. The sound of a gently lapping wave of croaky cheering crept round the boat. The chamber filled. All eyes concentrated on the escape hatch. Suddenly a shaft of light struck down like a sword of deliverance into the water inside the now empty chamber. The hatch had opened. Like popped champagne corks, Oram and Woods had shot upwards to the outside waiting world.

Salvage vessel *Vigilant* saw their heads break surface, and watched as one of *Brazen's* whalers picked them up. Then, after a few minutes' wait to see if any more submariners' heads were going to bob up, *Vigilant's* commander, Captain HV Hart, had the crew of the boat that he had put down in the water hammer in Morse code on the exposed stern of *Thetis*:

'C - O - M - E   O - U - T'

The message was pounded, loud and clanging, again and again, but there came no reply.

Captain Oram had, however, reported that everyone on board was still alive. And Hope had raised its head up out of the water like a benign sea monster. As if to endorse that hope, there was a splash, and, wreathed in bubbles, leading stoker, Walter Arnold and Cammell Laird engine fitter, Frank Shaw, came shooting up, back to the sea-top world of life.

Four out. Ninety-nine to go.

At 8.55am, *Vigilant* had connected a light wire, known as a 'messenger', to *Thetis'* stern. Ultimately, its job would be to pull a heavier cable into position.

Captain Hart despatched a message to the Mersey Docks and Harbour Board for oxy-acetylene cutting apparatus – 'Send burners and burning gear at once with tug.' He planned to cut a hole in *Thetis'* steel side.

The minutes and the hours were ticking mercilessly away. All Merseyside, the whole stunned nation, was watching, listening, holding its breath.

It was two and a half hours later that Diver Frederick Orton went down. He saw through the green water the dark outline of Thetis' conning-tower and her crouching black shape.

Now, albeit somewhat belatedly, the decision had been generally agreed to make an effort to get the stern of the boat sufficiently high out of the water for a hole to be cut which would be big enough to allow the whole of the remaining prisoners of the submarine to escape. The order was given for a three-and-a-half-inch wire rope to be passed round *Thetis'* tail and made fast to the bows of *Vigilant*. The winch for'ard on *Vigilant* grunted and wheezed, the spindle chugged, and slowly, almost imperceptibly, the steel hawser began to move inboard.

By 1.30pm, *Thetis* was visibly higher out of the water, the whole of her propeller and a good chunk of her after hull exposed.

Then … suddenly … without warning … tragedy.

Giant Despair arose out of the waves. The tautening wire that held *Thetis* began to sing. The singing intensified. There came a terrifying, ear-splitting pistol-shot as the steel wire broke, its two freed ends whip-lashing high into the air and flailing back across *Vigilant's* decks. The echo of that dreadful sound figuratively reverberated throughout the whole land. Striking, particularly in Liverpool, horror into the hearts of the people.

Quietly, gracefully, leaving barely a ripple to mark where she had been, *Thetis* slid, ladylike, without fuss, below the surface. Vanished. At that moment she became the steel-walled tomb of 99 men.

The time was 3.10pm. Despair took its place upon the throne of reason.

The following morning's 10.30am news bulletin reported that divers had stated that at 2am they had heard faint tappings in the submarine, and added that salvage operations were proceeding. A further attempt would be made to raise the stern when slack water provided the next opportunity:

> There is still hope that some of the submarine's crew may
> be rescued alive.

However, at 4.30pm on Saturday 3 June, the Admiralty announced that there was no longer any justification for hope that any further lives could be saved.

Nor were they.

How could such a thing happen? It is a sorry and a shocking tale, this saga of the submarine that died; a chronicle of mismanagement, a catalogue of eminently avoidable errors, miscalculations and delays. It has been succinctly anatomised as, 'too much gold braid and too little common sense.' But bad luck, sheer bad luck, comes into the equation, too.

Were the sailors who sensed a Jonah so far out, so wrong? *Thetis* was recovered, refitted, and reborn under the name of *Thunderbolt*. Precisely a year and a day after the death of *Thetis*, *Thunderbolt* was lost with all hands in a depth charge attack in the Mediterranean. She lies 3,000 feet down, with the bodies and spirits of her two brave crews of English sailormen, asleep for ever in the cradle of the deep.

LITERARY
SHADOWS

Mr Dickens Comes to Town

One November night exactly fifty years ago, I attended in Liverpool a public reading from his own works by Charles Dickens. I remember watching him as he strode confidently into the solitary spotlight which had grown gradually centre-stage out of the darkness to illuminate the plush-covered, specially designed reading-desk.

I watched as, after carefully and with infinite dignity, removing his white gloves, he scrutinised the spines of the two green-bound volumes which he carried with him, and, clearing his throat, began to weave the vocal spell that held a packed auditorium entranced for two and a quarter hours.

The performance was masterly. As if by magic, he summoned from the shadows a procession of strange characters from the pages of his books, who seemed to pass one by one across the empty stage. The bearded man in quaint Victorian evening-dress vanished. Now in his place stood the bouncing Bob Sawyer, now his shrewish landlady; now a rumbustious Cockney showman, a pathetic dwarf, a terrified signalman in a haunted signal-box.

And, at the readings' end, I went round backstage and met the great novelist face to face.

Impossible? Well … yes. For, back in the dressing-room, Dickens had vanished into a tangle of discarded false hair and an old-fashioned tail-coat hanging grotesquely in the corner. A young-faced, grey-haired, slightly-built man in a shabby plaid dressing-gown was sitting there drinking whisky out of a tumbler. He looked hot and tired.

He was the Flintshire-born actor, Emlyn Williams, who, in November 1952, was presenting, in the guise of Dickens, his 'Mixed Bill' of Dickensian readings at the Royal Court Theatre to the great-grandchildren of those who, just eighty-three years before, had listened to Dickens himself, making his last bow at the Theatre Royal, in Williamson Square.

That Charles Dickens, although born in Portsmouth, was essentially, indeed quintessentially, a citizen of London, there can be no denying. It must, however, to those of us Liverpudlians who value and admire him, bring something of a glow to learn that, not only was he wont to say that Liverpool lay in his heart next to London, but that he actually enrolled as a Liverpool Special Constable.

He first pointed a neatly-shod foot – Dickens had, like Madeleine Smith's lover, Pierre Emil L'Angelier, neat and neatly-shod little feet, of which, dandy that he was, he was, like L'Angelier, passing proud – in Liverpool in January 1836, when he was just coming up to his 24th birthday. He was then working as a reporter on the *Morning Chronicle*, and receiving a salary of five guineas a week. He and his friend and fellow-reporter, Thomas Beard, were a professional team, and they had come to attend and report on a political dinner which was being given by the Reformers of Liverpool for the Irish nationalist, Daniel O'Connell, 'The Liberator', on 27 January 1836, at the Corn Exchange, in Brunswick Street, with William Rathbone in the chair. It was Daniel O'Connell, who, many years later, after reading of the death of Little Nell, threw his copy of *The Old Curiosity Shop* out of a railway carriage window exclaiming, "He should not have killed her".

As duly reported in *All the Year Round*, the weekly journal founded by Charles Dickens in 1859, and re-reported, or, rather, reprinted, in the series of essays and sketches from life collected in *The Uncommercial Traveller*, upon the occasion of one, unspecified, of the 19 visits which he paid to Liverpool in the course of his life, Dickens, metaphorically speaking, squeezed those neat feet of his into a pair of policeman's regulation boots.

Always a member of that exclusive brotherhood, the great nightwalkers, regularly ranging alone all over London during the small hours, with a sturdy penchant for viewing the seamier side of nocturnal city life, he was for this latter purpose enrolled as a Temporary Police Officer in the Liverpool force. Escorted by a Superintendent, he set out upon, literally, a *tour de force*, plunging into the obscurest streets and lanes, a labyrinth of dismal courts and blind-alleys, called locally, he meticulously noted, 'entries'; those sad, depressing and unchanging backgrounds to evil, which, a hundred years later, I was to see and record in a series of articles in the *Liverpool Evening Express*.

Many of the things of which I wrote, Dickens had already written about. *Plus ça change* in the Sailortown underworld. He told of the multiplicity of traps primed for poor – or, more accurately, temporarily rich, Mercantile Jack, money-belt tight with all the months at sea's wage garnerings – rolling into port, only to be rolled by the alerted, waiting harpies. He saw, as I was to see: 'the unsleeping host of devourers who never go to bed, and are always in their set traps waiting for [Croesus Jack – mercantile or naval].' Dickens was fascinated by the Superintendent's magic stick:

> He carried in his hand a plain black walking stick of hard wood; and whenever and wherever, at any after-time of the night, he struck it on the pavement with a ringing sound, it instantly produced a whistle out of the darkness, and a policeman.

The night of Dickens' circumambulatory adventure was cold:

> ... the snow yet lying in the frozen furrows of the land,
> and the north-east winds snipping off the tops of the
> little waves in the Mersey, and rolling them into
> hailstones ...

Behind latched doors, opening upon a tap, crouched over their small, mean fires, the predators – wrinkled crones, hard-faced crimps, male, female, sometimes in pairs, always then claiming union in holy matrimony, thus importing a false air of seeming safety and security to the proceedings – like patient spiders, wait.

Dickens and escort moved on to what he called a singing-house; in my day, a club. The difference lies only in the name. The fleecing was the same. But he found the singing, Mr Banjo Bones' music, and the dancing of the young lady performing the hornpipe, pleasantly diverting.

Later in the night, they came, by the court 'where the man was murdered', and by the other court across the street, into which his body was dragged:

> to another parlour in another entry, where several
> people were sitting round a fire ... It was a dirty and
> offensive place, with some ragged clothes drying in it.

And later still, they found themselves in:

> ... a nauseous room with an earth floor, into which the
> refuse scum of an alley trickled. The stench of this
> habitation was abominable; the seeming poverty of it,
> diseased and dire. Yet here again was a visitor or lodger
> – a man, sitting before the fire like the rest of them
> elsewhere, and apparently not distasteful to the
> mistress's niece who was also before the fire. The
> mistress herself had the misfortune of being in jail.

When Dickens got back to the Adelphi and went to bed, 'the vermin I had seen ... ran all over my sleep'.

Whenever he was in Liverpool, he always stayed at the Adelphi. Somewhat of an expert on the question of hotels, of all those up and down the country, the Adelphi was, he said, his favourite, and he described its proprietor as 'my faultless friend, Mr Radley'.

This was James Radley, who opened the Adelphi in 1826, in the northernmost house of a terrace which had been built upon the site of The White House – latterly known as Ranelagh House and Gardens, in imitation of the famous London pleasure gardens – demolished about 1790.

Polite and easy in his manners, gifted with a nice tact, and a rare talent for organisation, Mr Radley made it the most popular hotel in Liverpool, and the establishment's fame extended far and wide. After his death, the business was disposed of to a joint-stock company. The present Adelphi is, of course, an entirely new building, and has over the years undergone quite dramatic changes of atmosphere.

Apart from a brief second visit to Liverpool, staying at the Adelphi for the first time, in November 1838, when, between the completion of *Oliver Twist* and its publication, he had, in company with Hablot Knight Brown,* otherwise 'Phiz', illustrator of many of his novels, gone to see something of North Wales, Dickens was not in Liverpool again until January 1842.

He and his wife, Catherine (Kate), put up at the Adelphi, before sailing to America on 3 January, on the Cunard packet, *Britannia*. The passage to Boston lasted 15 days and was a stormy one. Even the buoyant Dickens harboured fears of drowning as the vessel was tossed by heavy Atlantic seas and sparks exploded disconcertingly from the coal-burning steamship's funnel.

After an extensive tour of the United States, they landed back in Liverpool six months later, voyaging peacefully this time through balmy June weather, aboard the old-fashioned American sailing packet, *George Washington*.

Two years later, Dickens was in Liverpool once more, and this occasion was to prove a most curious and romantic one.

When, in the latter part of 1843, he had been invited to take the chair at the annual Christmas *soirée* of the Mechanics' Institute in Liverpool, Dickens, immersed during the November and December of that year in the business of bringing out *A Christmas Carol* and writing *Martin Chuzzlewit*, had suggested to the Mechanics' committee that if they felt able to postpone the occasion until the following February, they could, he promised, have a speech from him on the importance of adult educational reform for the working-class.

He duly arrived in Liverpool in late February 1844, in elated mood. His old friend, Thomas James Thompson, was waiting to greet him at the Adelphi – or Randle's Hotel, as it was frequently referred to. They dined and wined, and sat late over the fire talking.

The following morning they went along to the Mechanics' Institute building (now the Liverpool Institute) in Mount Street, to inspect the hall where Dickens was to speak.

After that, having heard that the *Britannia*, the vessel in which Dickens and his wife had sailed to Boston a couple of years before, happened to be in port, lying at the same berth as she had been when they embarked on her

---

* *Whose son, Edgar Browne, practised for many years as an oculist in Rodney Street, in Liverpool.*

for America, they made their way down to the river to see her. Quite by chance, they bumped into Captain Hewett, the master of the Britannia, who, in high delight at their happenstance meeting, carried them off for champagne and biscuits aboard her. In return, Dickens invited the captain to dinner that night, and gave him a ticket for the *soirée*.

Later in the day, Dickens' sister, Fanny, and her husband, Henry Burnett, came over from Manchester to join him.

At seven o'clock on the evening of Monday 26 February 1844, Charles Dickens, resplendent in a white and black or 'magpie' waistcoat, was ushered into the assembly hall of the Liverpool Mechanics' Institute. As he made his way to the platform, the organist struck forth, *fortissimo*, with *See the Conquering Hero Comes*, and upwards of 1,200 eager faces shone with excited greeting, upwards of 1,200 pairs of hands clapped, and upwards of 1,200 pairs of feet stamped. 'Thundering and awful', was how Dickens described the tumult of sound in a letter home to Kate.

The great national success of *A Christmas Carol* hovered like a gold-lined cloud above him, its sentiments seeming to make him all the more suitable and popular a spokesman for the worthy poor and the down-trodden labouring men and women of the country. His presence created an enormous sensation.

In his speech, he praised the town of Liverpool and the founders of the Institute for their noble work in making education and enlightenment available to labouring people; for tackling ignorance and shedding light in dark places. He congratulated the founders of the Institute on their library of 11,000 books and their roll of 3,000 members, soon, he believed, to be swelled to 6,000. He was delighted to learn that women and girls were to be given the same chances as men and boys, speaking warmly of the decision to add a girls' school to the Institution, and the extension of education to "those who are our best teachers, and whose lessons are oftenmost heeded in after life." He emphasised the just rights of every man to education, and extolled the virtues of self-help and mutual forbearance between various classes.

> I look forward from this place as from a tower to the
> time when high and low, rich and poor, shall mutually
> assist, improve, and educate each other.

Adding that he would give to all the means of taking out a patent of nobility, he ended his speech, which had been often interrupted by what the shorthand reporters noted as 'laughter and applause', by underlining the theme of his message once more with apt quotation from his favourite contemporary poet, Tennyson:

Howe'er it be, it seems to me,

'Tis only noble to be good.
Kind hearts are more than coronets,
And simple faith than Norman blood.

His performance at the *soirée* had been a huge success. Dickens wrote, facetiously, to Kate that he 'spoke up like a man and distinguished himself considerably,' and gave 'a vigorous, brilliant, humorous, pathetic, eloquent, fervid, and impassioned speech,' which was wildly applauded with 'frequent, vehement, uproarious, and deafening cheers.'

He also told his wife that, to his delight, his clothes had been remarked on; he had heard people saying of his magpie waistcoat, "What is it? *Is* it a waistcoat? No, it's a shirt!" and so on, and this he took to be very gratifying and complimentary.

Following the main event of the evening, which was, of course, Dickens' speech, a programme of music had been arranged, which, in his rôle as chairman, he was expected to announce. Into his hand was thrust a piece of paper. He glanced at it, stepped forward, and announced:

I am requested to introduce to you a young lady whom I
have some difficulty and tenderness in announcing …
Miss Weller, who will play a fantasia on the pianoforte.

Her name, and the echoes which it awoke, seemed to cause him some merriment, and his amusement must have somehow communicated itself to his listeners, for he had barely got the words out, and the soloist, a frail and beautiful young girl in a fur-trimmed green dress, was poised in readiness for him to escort her across to the piano, when suddenly and unexpectedly the auditorium exploded into great gusts of laughter. The name Weller had stirred among his readers richly humorous memories of the adventures of Mr Pickwick's devoted servant, Sam. Standing there, the author, the onlie begetter of the immortal Samuel Weller, was well pleased, flattered, at receiving this exquisite, totally unpremeditated crowd tribute to his comic genius.

Glancing over his shoulder, he was, however, disconcerted to see the girl, who had been about to come shyly forward, shrinking back, puzzled and painfully embarrassed, and looking bewilderedly and beseechingly at him.

Her name was Christiana Weller. She was 19 years old. She was a native of Liverpool, living with her family in Breck Road, Anfield. Her father, Thomas Edward Weller, a clerk in the Liverpool office of the Dublin Steam Packet Company, was also an amateur music and drama critic, who, eager to elicit support for his talented young daughter, had written to Dickens bringing her name to his attention the previous February (1843), exactly twelve months before.

Actually, Christiana had been a child prodigy, appearing since 1834, when she was just nine years old, with her elder sister, and achieving immediate recognition and success for the brilliance of her execution. Strikingly attractive, her highly prepossessing appearance undoubtedly added an irresistible dimension to the stirring quality of her musical virtuosity.

Heart leaping in his susceptible breast, Dickens took the girl's hand in his own, and gently led her to the piano, whispering into her ear as she waited to make her postponed bow, his hope that – anodyne to her discomfiture, for which he felt full burden of guilt – some day she would change her name, and be very, very happy.

The peeled eye of a wide-awake local newspaper reporter recorded for posterity how, as she played, the famous novelist kept *his* eyes 'firmly fixed on her every movement'.

The fantasia ended and the *soirée* drew to its close. Dickens was formally introduced to Christiana and her father. What sally of wit he produced is not known, but he made some observation which called forth much laughter, and he was heard to remark on a more serious note something to the effect that "the last remnant of my heart went into that piano".

Later, ascending the Adelphi staircase, Dickens found himself haunted by 'that angel face' of Christiana's. The plain truth is that he had conceived an immense, and flash-point, infatuation for the girl. What must surely have hastened matters was that Christiana Weller bore – as, indeed, her own relatives were to recognise strongly – a quite uncanny resemblance to Mary Hogarth. Her sudden death in 1837, at the age of 17, had prostrated Dickens – who had taken a ring from her dead finger and worn it on his own to the end of his life – with grief.

The next morning, by determined wizardry of form unspecified, Dickens somehow contrived to arrange for himself and his friend, Thompson, to be invited to luncheon with the Weller family, out at Anfield; the occasion being celebrated, it is said, at The Breck, the house of a Mr JC Shaw.

To occupy his mind gainfully on the outward journey, Dickens set about the composition of a piece of doggerel, which he would inscribe in Miss Christiana's album. Vaguely flirtatious, questionably indiscreet, it ran:

> I put in a book, once, by hook and by crook
> The whole race (as I thought) of a 'feller',
> Who happily pleas'd the town's taste, much diseas'd
> And the name of this person was Weller.
> I find to my cost that one Weller I lost,
> Cruel destiny so to arrange it!
> I love her dear name, which has won me some fame,
> But, Great Heaven! how gladly I'd change it.

.In other words, a declaration, is it not, of how glad he would be to marry her – if he could? If he were free of Kate.

Unlike most young ladies of his acquaintance, however, Christiana kept no album, so that he was obliged subsequently to post his poem to her as a keepsake.

Although tired, having spent a lively night at a fancy-dress ball that had ended with *Sir Roger de Coverley* at 3am that morning, Dickens had to tear himself away from Liverpool and travel to Birmingham, where, on the Wednesday evening, 28 February, he was due to speak in the Town Hall in behalf of the Polytechnic Institution.

In a letter written to Thompson from Birmingham that Wednesday night, telling him how things had gone, Dickens, who had realised at the Weller luncheon that they had both fallen victim to the girl's charm, and was himself frankly surprised by the suddenness and heat of his own reaction, wrote:

> I cannot joke about Miss Weller, for she is too good; and interest in her (spiritual young creature that she is, and destined to an early death, I fear) has become a sentiment with me. Good God what a madman I should seem, if the incredible feeling I have conceived for that girl could be made plain to anyone!

There is surely a clue in that 'destined to an early death'. Dickens had the typical mid-Victorian's obsession with the image of the tragically premature gathering in of the flowers of youth; the inevitable demise of creatures too sweet and gentle and noble for the cruel glades and savage groves of this harsh world, and their spiriting away on the wings of angels. Had he not already persuaded and convinced his sentimental heart that the ethereal and beautiful Christiana was such a creature, virtually a reincarnation of his lost young sister-in-law, Mary Hogarth?

Dickens' first priority and task upon his return to London, on 1 March, was to parcel up and post off, with an accompanying letter to Mr TE Weller, the two-volume set of his poems, 'given to me by Tennyson himself', as a promised gift to Christiana, who, he had discovered, knew not his poems, and in which volumes he (Dickens) had put himself to the trouble of marking those items 'calculated to give her a good impression of the Poet's Genius'. And it was in this letter to her father that Dickens confessed that Christiana had 'started out alone from the whole crowd the instant I saw her, and will remain there always in my sight'. He had reacted spontaneously in attributing to her an ethereal quality and child-like charm that alerted his protective instincts and an impulse to encourage her.

To his sister he wrote, by the same post, 'perfectly exhausted, dead, worn-out, and Spiritless', confiding that his happy recollection of Christiana 'has its tortures'. All the indications are that his depression was the result of his having had to separate from Miss Weller.

On Monday morning, 11 March, Dickens found a bombshell on his breakfast plate. It was a letter from Thompson. In it he announced that he had fallen deeply in love with Christiana.

Dickens replied at once:

> I felt the blood go from my face to I don't know where, and my very lips turn white. I never in my life was so surprised, or had the whole current of my life so stopped for the instant, as when I felt at a glance, what your letter said.

He had, he said, been looking forward to Thompson's return from Liverpool, in order to discuss Christiana's 'wonderful endowments' with him, and he went on to set out his complicated responses to his friend's unwelcome news.

Although Dickens and his friend of five years' standing were of the same age – both 32 – and shared a common passion for liberal reform, Thompson, a widower, was free, not only to fall in love, but to act in furtherance of his desire. His situation was palpably enhanced by his having been left a fortune by his Liverpudlian grandfather on the condition that he never worked, which meant that, a comfortable, cultured man, he was able to indulge his taste for collecting books and paintings, and enjoy the best of London life and continental travel. Whereas Dickens, seven years married, and while admittedly displaying a marked disaffection with his wife, was far from being unfettered, and in decidedly straitened financial waters into the bargain.

He was, he admitted:

> ... in many points an excitable and headstrong man, and ride, O God, what prancing hobbies! – and although I knew that the impression she made on me was a true, deep, honest, pure-spirited thing, I thought my nature might have been prepared to receive it, and to exaggerate it unconsciously, and to keep it green long after such a fancy as I deemed it probable you might have conceived had withered.

All the indications are that Dickens was allowing this flow of vicarious courtship to sweep him away.

Thompson was, however, seriously worried on the score of his being a widower and considerably older than Christiana. Dickens was in no doubt, and pooh-poohed his misgivings:

> *If I had all your independent means, I would not hesitate, or do that slight to the resolution of my own heart which hesitation would imply. But would win her if I could, by God, immediately! I would answer it to myself, if my world's breath whispered me that I had known her but a few days, that hours of hers are years in the lives of common women.*

To her father, he urged, Thompson should point out that the musical career to which he was bent on devoting her 'should not be called her life, but Death'; only repose, a mind at rest, a foreign climate, might possibly save her from an end that was otherwise speedy and certain.

'I saw an angel's message in her face that day that smote me to the heart,' wrote Dickens. In phrases which echoed unerringly the last hours of Mary Hogarth, he insisted that he could 'better bear her passing from my arms to Heaven than I could endure the thought of coldly turning off into the World again to see her no more.'

Two days later, 13 March, clearly unembarrassed, and labouring under no feelings of jealousy about Thompson's courtship, Dickens was telling him not to tarry, but to dash in at once.

> *As to the father, I snap my fingers. I would leap over the head of the tallest father in Europe, if the daughter's heart lay on the other side, and were worth having ... Do not crucify yourself lest in so doing you crucify her ... Think of Italy! ... a foreign climate would be, in a springtime like hers, the dawning of a new existence.*

For he was anxious that Thompson should bring Christiana to Italy, and dreamt of:

> *... the quiet happiness we might enjoy abroad, all of us together in some delicious nook. Such Italian Castles, bright in sunny days, and pale in moonlight nights, as I am building in the air!*

All this airy talk about the Italian sun and skies was just that, airy talk; for in those early months of 1844, Dickens was shorter of cash, ready money, than ever.

Later that March, Thompson sent Dickens a letter triumphantly announcing his engagement to Miss Weller. 'It is a noble prize you have won,' he congratulated him, and then, in reminiscent vein:

> *Good Heavens, what a dream it appears! Shall we ever forget that night when she came up to the piano ... The father seems*

to have acted like a man. I had my fears of that I confess; for the greater part of my observation of Parents and children had shown selfishness in the first, almost invariably.

As he had continued to promote Thompson's cause, so had Dickens' own fervour cooled, and his fascination with Christiana passed. It was in cheerfully robust avuncular fashion that he addressed her in a letter dated 8 April 1844. He had, he told her, encouraged Thompson in his suit:

... for I had that amount of sympathy with his condition, which, but that I am beyond the reach – the lawful reach – of the Wings that fanned his fire, would have rendered it the greatest happiness and pleasure of my life to have run him through the body. In no poetical or tender sense, I assure you, but with good sharp Steel.

He was writing this from Malton, in Yorkshire, where he had again seen Thompson at the funeral of his (Thompson's) brother-in-law. At this meeting Dickens had been surprised to find his friend again despairing at the direction that his courtship seemed to be taking. The obstacle, it turned out, had not been Christiana's father at all, but the girl herself, who had depressed him by telling him that he was "premature" and that there were "other footprints in the the field".

Before the couple sailed into calm waters, and the knot was actually tied, Dickens was called upon to help on a number of occasions; once, in June, to secure a musical engagement for Christiana at the Hanover Rooms, and several times thereafter to assist the pair in overcoming various difficulties with Christiana's papa.

Finally, in mid-October 1845, Thomas and Christiana were married. Dickens attended the wedding splendidly dandiacal in a brightly coloured waistcoat, donned, he joked, for the specific purpose of "eclipsing the bridegroom!" Macready, the great Victorian tragedian, had lent him the blue or purple striped garment which he had worn when playing in Bulwer-Lytton's *Money*, that his tailor might copy it for him. The newly-weds left to honeymoon in Genoa.

In 1846 the Thompsons rented a house, the Villa Claremont, in Lausanne, for eight months, and it was here, on 3 November 1846, that their first daughter, Elizabeth, was born.

By this time Dickens was much disappointed in Christiana, and, on 30 August 1846, he wrote:

She seems (between ourselves), to have a devil of a whimpering, pouting temper. She is a mere spoiled child, I think, and doesn't turn out half as well as I expected. Matrimony has improved him, and certainly has not improved her.

Dickens' younger brother, Frederick, eight years his junior, was impatiently eager to marry Christiana's younger sister, Anna. There were difficulties. His income was insufficient to support a wife, and she was two years too young to be married. Fred was working himself up into a rancorous state of resentment at Anna's father's entirely reasonable opposition, and Dickens was seriously beginning to wish that he had never met Christiana and her family. They did, in fact, marry, in 1848, and it turned out a fiasco. They quarrelled furiously, and in the end he left her, bitterly refusing to make her any allowance. He died in 1868.

The Thompsons' second daughter, Alice, was born at Barnes, south-west London, on 22 September 1847. Both daughters were to achieve distinction. The elder, Elizabeth Lady Butler – she had married Lieutenant-General Sir William Francis Butler – became a military artist, the painter of such celebrated works as *The Roll Call* and *Balaclava*. She died in 1933. Alice, the younger, best known under her married name, Alice Meynell, was one of the most accomplished poets and essayists of her time. She died in 1922.

It would have been between the October and December of 1853, that Dickens visited the Thompsons, who were at that time living in a ruinous Albara-like palazzo, at Nervi, on the road to Portofino, in Liguria. He found their domestic arrangements somewhat unorthodox.

> We had disturbed her [Christiana] at her painting in oils; and I rather received an impression that what with that, and what with music, the household affairs went a little to the wall.

He thought her as beautiful, but as unstable, as ever, 'greatly flushed and agitated' at seeing him; 'her excitability and restlessness … a positive disease'. She, who had been of yore a kind of goddess, had become a rather ordinary young woman, somewhat remiss in her domestic duties.

Christiana had largely abandoned the piano in favour of oil-painting , for which she did not exhibit much talent. Nonetheless, she appeared too engrossed in that activity to have much time to spare for two crop-headed, stockingless, little slips of girls, who were being taught arithmetic by their father in a 'billiard-room with all manner of mess in it'.

The once-upon-a-time frail, fragile, ethereal, other-worldly, idealised and idolised young virgin, doomed, with speculative sentiment, to an early death, actually died aged 85 in 1910, outliving Dickens by forty years. Many decades before, he had made a strange request of his friend, who was going to marry her. "Ask her to save the dress – the green dress with the fur on it. Let it be laid up in lavender. Let it never grow old, fade ..." This was the dress that Christiana had been wearing the night that he first set eyes upon her. He had, in like manner, preserved Mary Hogarth's dress after her death.

Dickens was back in Liverpool in July 1847, bringing with him this time a company of amateur actors which he had put together from among his friends. They appeared on 28 July at the Theatre Royal, in Williamson Square, in a performance of Ben Jonson's *Every Man in His Humour*, with Dickens himself as Captain Bobadil. Also on the bill were two short pieces: *Turning the Tables* by John Poole, Dickens playing Jeremiah Bumps, and *Comfortable Lodgings: or Paris in 1750*, in which Dickens appeared as Sir Hippington Miff. The occasion had originally been projected as a benefit for Leigh Hunt, but, as he had since been granted a civil list pension, the £480 raised was deflected to the pathetically empty pocket of the indigent author and playwright, John Poole (1786-1872).

After the curtain came down, the entire company, together with Mrs Dickens and other ladies of the party, along with a large and fashionable assemblage of the local gentry, were entertained by Richard Vaughan Yates – the philanthropist who had purchased a tract of some 90 acres from the Earl of Sefton in 1843, and given Prince's Park to Liverpool – at a brilliant *soirée* at his residence at the Dingle. Many of the guests were in fancy-dress, and it recorded that Dickens danced there with Miss Dolly Varden!

He brought his strolling players back to Liverpool the following year, appearing on 5 June 1848, in *The Merry Wives of Windsor*, and a farce, *Love, Law and Physic*, at the Amphitheatre, in aid of the fund to establish a perpetual curatorship of Shakespeare's house at Stratford-on-Avon.

During 1852, Dickens and his band of stalwart amateur actors were twice in Liverpool. They came to earn monies in aid of Sir Edward Bulwer-Lytton's Guild of Literature and Art, giving two performances, on 13 and 14 February respectively, at the Philharmonic Hall of Bulwer-Lytton's *Not So Bad As We Seem*, and *Mr Nightingale's Diary* by Charles Dickens and Mark Lemon. They were onstage at the Philharmonic again on 3 September 1852, with *Used Up, Charles XII*, and *Mr Nightingale's Diary*.

Dickens was 46 when, in August 1858, he made his first bow in Liverpool as a public reader. It was at the Philharmonic Hall, on 28 August, that he read *A Christmas Carol*, following it up on the 19th with *Dombey and Son*, and on the 20th with *Boots at the Holly Tree Inn* and *Mrs Gamp*. On the Saturday (21st) afternoon he gave an encore performance of *A Christmas Carol*.

He was greeted on the first night by an audience of 2,300, the largest that he had ever had. Each reading lasted two hours.

He gave two further readings at the Philharmonic on 15 October 1858. In the afternoon: *The Story of Little Dombey*. And in the evening: *The Poor Traveller, Boots* at the *Holly Tree Inn* and *Mrs Gamp*.

Dickens' next Liverpool engagement was in December 1861. On Sunday 15 December, he writes from the Adelphi Hotel to William Henry Wills, assistant editor of his weekly journal, *All the Year Round*:

> I have been very doubtful what to do. [The Prince Consort had died the day before.] We have a great lot for tomorrow night. The Mayor recommends closing tomorrow, and giving the Readings on Tuesday (17th) and Wednesday (18th), so does the Town Clerk, so do the agents. But I have a misgiving that they hardly understand what the general sympathy of the public with the Queen will be. Further, I feel personally that the Queen has always been very considerate and gracious to me, and I would on no account do anything that might seem unfeeling or disrespectful. I shall attach great weight in this state of indecision to your telegram.

The readings were cancelled. They took place in January 1862, and were delivered in the Small Concert Room at St George's Hall.

Writing to Georgina Hogarth, Dickens tells her:

> *The beautiful room was crammed to excess last night, and numbers were turned away. Its beauty and completeness when it is lighted up are most brilliant to behold, and for a reading it is simply perfect. You remember that a Liverpool audience is usually dull, but they put me on my mettle last night, for I never saw such an audience – no, not even in Edinburgh! I slept horribly last night, and have been over to Birkenhead for a little change of air today. My head is dazed and worn by gas and heat, and I fear that 'Copperfield' and 'Bob' together tonight won't mend it. I am going to buy the boys some Everton toffee.*

Before the occasion of his next visit to Liverpool, Dickens was to undergo a traumatic experience which left him very unhappy about train travel for the remainder of his life. Returning, on 9 June 1865, with his light o' love, Ellen Ternan, from a shared Parisian idyll, he and his companion had been involved in a serious railway accident, at Staplehurst, in Kent. He was unscathed, and had conducted himself heroically in rendering assistance to the injured and dying, but he retained a degree of shock from which he never really fully recovered.

There were to be five more readings in the Small Concert Room in April 1866. The *Liverpool Mercury*, of 11 April, reported that:

> The reader had a book before him, but throughout he made no reference to it, and his memory during the hour that the reading occupied was never at fault. The impersonation was almost perfect. Closing the eyes and shutting out from the vision the middle-aged gentlemanly-looking man in evening dress who occupied the platform, one might easily have imagined that the speaker was a real living specimen of the 'Cheap Jack fraternity'.

In the months of January and February 1867, Dickens gave, in each month, two readings in his now favourite Liverpool reading rendezvous, the Small Concert Room. In a letter dashed off to 'Dearest Georgy' (Hogarth), during his February visit, he says:

> *The day has been very fine, and I have turned it to the wholesomest account by walking on the sands at New Brighton all morning. It is* Copperfield *tonight, and Liverpool is the* Copperfield *stronghold.*

On 9 November 1867, Dickens, waved off by Charles Dickens, Junior, Miss Dickens, Wilkie Collins and Edmund Yates, sailed out of Liverpool in the Cunard steamer, *Cuba*, *en route* for Boston and his second visit to America, on a reading tour that was to last for six months, and do much to undermine his health.

He returned on another Cunard steamer, the *Russia*, and, after one of the fastest transatlantic crossings on record at that time, was safely installed and eating his dinner at eight o'clock back in the Adelphi on 1 May 1868.

In October 1868, he was back comfortably ensconced in the Adelphi again, when he was reading once more in the Small Concert Room on 12, 13, 14. 26, 27 and 28 October.

On 7 February 1869, Dickens celebrated his 57th birthday, and he now set out on a series of Farewell Readings. His last readings in Liverpool were delivered from 5-9 April, and the demand for seats was so great that the Small Concert Room had to be abandoned and he took over the Theatre Royal, Williamson Square. The theatre had, in fact, fallen into disuse. It was in a very dirty and unwholesome state. However, a fortnight's dedicated cleaning labour, together with a liberal application of new red baize in the stalls and passages, beside the newly-scrubbed gilt, worked wonders.

The final readings included the murder scene from *Oliver Twist* – entitled

Sikes and Nancy. Describing the impact of this positively ferocious 'rendition', the *Liverpool Mercury* said:

> As the reading proceeded step by step, the interest intensified, and when the agonising cries of Nancy that her life be spared were silenced for ever by the savage brutality of Sikes, and as the murderer was confronted with his blood-stained victim when the morning sun broke through the windows of his chamber, the audience almost held their breath.

So much energy and fervour did Dickens put into this dramatic performance, that he was always absolutely prostrated after it. It was often necessary for him to lie down on a couch.

Saturday evening, 10 April 1869, was the day that Liverpool set aside to honour Charles Dickens. Just before 5.30pm, the Mayor arrived at the Adelphi Hotel to escort the much-beloved author to St George's Hall in his state carriage. A public banquet had been laid on for him. Liverpool, determined to express the high regard and affection in which he was held, turned out *en masse*, to see, be seen, wave and cheer. The balconies were thronged with spectators, the great hall, where 600 guests were seated, was hung with flags, decorated with a forest of plants, bushels of flowers, bank vaults full of fine silver, and blindingly brilliantly lit. At the magnificent organ, was the renowned, and renownedly caustic, Liverpool musician and great concert organist, Dr William Thomas Best.

Replying at some length to the toast of his health, given by Lord Dufferin, who occupied the chair, the distinguished guest said that:

> Liverpool had never failed him when he had asked the help of her citizens in the cause of literature and benevolence, and that her response had been spontaneous, open-handed and munificent.

In a private letter written from Liverpool during that April week, Dickens says:

> *One of the pleasantest things I have experienced here this time is the way in which I am stopped in the streets by working men who want to shake hands with me, and tell me they know my books; I never go out but this happens. Down at the docks a cooper with a fearful stutter put himself in my way, his modesty combined with a conviction that if he were in earnest I would see it and not repel him, made up as fine a piece of natural politeness as I ever saw.*

In the free intervals between his play actings and readings, he had always loved to walk about the Liverpool streets, particularly the dockland and the poorer quarters.

Of the central town street known as Whitechapel, this is what he had to say:

> *The busy throng tends Whitechapel way, and down to Whitechapel we must go. So great is the number of orange sellers and oranges that it would seem as if the whole of one year's produce of St Michael's had been disgorged into the narrow street this Saturday night. Furthermore, it will not be without emotion that you will become sensible that in very many of the pawnbroking warehouses my uncle is for the nonce, transformed into my aunt … The person who unties your package, names the extent of the investment therein by way of a loan, fills up the duplicate and hands you the cash, is a young lady, sharp-eyed, quick-witted, and not to be done by any means.*

He knew all about Sarah Biffin, the armless midget who painted kings, and lived until her death in 1850, at 8 Duke Street. She found her way into two of his novels.*

He wrote, too, of a visit, 'walking up a hill on a wild March morning' in 'that rich and beautiful port where I had looked after Mercantile Jack', to the wards of the workhouse on Brownlow Hill. You will find his observations in Chapter VIII of *The Uncommercial Traveller*.

On Sunday 11 April 1869, Dickens left Liverpool never to return. During his progress, on foot, from the Adelphi to Lime Street Station, he was stopped by people of all classes, who wanted simply to take him by the hand and thank him for all the pleasure that his books had brought into their lives.

A little over a year later he was dead. Worn out, he died at his home, Gad's Hill Place, near Rochester, in Kent, on 9 June 1870. He was 58.

There is no statue to him anywhere in Liverpool, but that is in accordance with his own express wish. There are, though, a number of Liverpool streets commemoratively named after characters in his novels. They are, appropriately one feels, humble streets of the homes of humble people, the sort for whom Dickens had always time and space in his heart.

The mourning of his death was truly universal. I have before me as I write a flaking leather-bound volume. It is the scrapbook of my great-

---

* See: *Liverpool Colonnade*, Richard Whittington-Egan. Philip Son & Nephew, 1955, and *Liverpool Characters and Eccentrics*, Richard Whittington-Egan, Gallery Press, 1985.

grandfather, Dr Richard Whittington-Egan, the Dublin pathologist. He was obviously a keen Dickensian, for neatly pasted into it are contemporary newspaper cuttings, page after page of them. But, most memorially effective of them all is an engraving, 'The Empty Chair'. Cut by my forebear from *Judy – or, The London Serio-Comic Journal*, of 22 June 1870, it is a representation that has haunted me all my life. The empty chair stands before a small, upright writing-desk upon the top of which are scattered three manuscript sheets, the last of them half-written, and lying upon it an abandoned quill. And all around this chair, emphasising its terrible emptiness, cluster clouds of characters given life by the dead man whose chair this was. Here are Pickwick, Pecksniff, Micawber, Oliver Twist and other fictive immortals who came teeming out of that unique brain disporting themselves in their traditional poses about the seat of a departed intelligence that shaped, bore them into a never-was kind of life, and gifted to them a special sort of magic survival that was to outlast himself and, indeed, all of us poor mortals. That, in a single picture, says it all.

THE MÆCENAS OF MERSEYSIDE

His name was James Ashcroft Noble. The chances are that you will not have heard of him, but he is worth acquaintance and worthy of remembrance.

The Liverpool in which he had his being was the literary one of the 1870s and 1880s. It was the time that created the great merchant princes; the men of sugar and oil, of cotton and shipping. It was the time which also begat the likes of Richard Le Gallienne, Hall Caine, William Watson and William Tirebuck, poets and novelists who were just starting out on their literary careers in Liverpool, and flocked to hear Oscar Wilde lecture, in December 1883, in Birkenhead. Young men who deliberately set their faces against what they saw as the cultural desert, a place where life and its values were generally based solely on the commerce and commercialism which dominated the Victorian seaport city.

It is a time that seems a lot further away now than it did when I was a boy, and many people who had walked the city streets in those decades were still around, albeit getting on in years.

It was, in fact, an old friend of mine, J Lewis May, a literary man surviving from the 1890s, who bestowed upon Noble, whom he had known well, the name of that scion of the ancient Etruscan aristocracy, Knight of Rome, and great patron of letters. May wrote of him that he was:

> ... a patron and practitioner of letters in Liverpool, a none too wealthy Mæcenas who helped and encouraged budding authors.

And that was indeed true. Noble fostered the talents of local literary lion cubs of his time, and would later take under his sheltering wing young Edward Thomas, who was to marry his daughter, Helen.

Noble in aspect as well as in name, he was of rather stately appearance, adorned with a patriarchal beard, and wearing the air of a man far more advanced in years than he actually was, he could perhaps be best defined as an intellectual journalist – one of the stamp of George Saintsbury, C Lewis Hind and HD Traill.

A dedicated and most conscientious craftsman, staunch Liberal and Unitarian, he was a frequent contributor to the *Athenæum*, and his work was to be found also in the *Academy*, *The Spectator*, *The Quarterly Review*, *The Bookman*, *The Westminster Gazette*, *The New Age* and *The World*. He wrote as well bread-and-butter pieces for the *Daily Chronicle*.

Perhaps his most famous work was his book of critical essays, *The Sonnet in England* (1893), which, following on the heels of Le Gallienne's collection of poems, *Volumes in Folio* (1889), was among John Lane's early Bodley Head publications.

Queen Victoria was only 26 years old, and had been on the throne a mere eight years, when, in 1845, James Ashcroft Noble first saw the light of day. A northerner by birth, he came of Lancashire yeoman farming stock, some of whom had spilt over into Westmorland. He had never been to any university, held no degree. An autodidact, what he had learned he had taught himself by copious and far-ranging reading during a long period of youthful ill-health.

By sheer determination and fixedness of purpose, he managed to become a published writer, freelancing at first for Charles Dickens' *All the Year Round*, and progressing to *The Spectator* and *The Academy*.

As a young man he lived in lodgings in the house of a Mrs Lunt, and he married his landlady's daughter, Ethel, whose father, Captain Lunt, was a north country whaling sea-captain in the days of sail.

James and Ethel had five children: Irene, Helen Berenice, Mary Geraldine, Philip, who died of diphtheria as a young child, and Lancelot.

In the early 'seventies, when he was in his late twenties, he started to review regularly for the *Manchester Examiner*, and had also worked for the *Liverpool Albion*.

He published his first book, *The Pelican Papers*, in 1873. Its dedication – 'To E.M.L. I offer this little volume, knowing well that what goes with it will glorify even so poor a gift.' – suggests that he had not yet married Ethel Lunt. The book is subtitled, *Reminiscences and Remains of a Dweller in the Wilderness*. The 'Wilderness' of this semi-autobiographical series of quasi-essays, is the Liverpool of the 1860s, in which, in the fictive persona of Paul Pelican, James Ashcroft Noble is seeking, especially literary, culture.

This was not quite fair. Liverpool was by no means a cultural desert. There was a long tradition of music in the thriving town – Liverpool did not become a city until 1880. The theatre had prospered here. Members of the rising wealthy 'merchantocracy' were becoming patrons of the arts and contributing handsomely to the building up of a first-class collection of paintings. The Walker Art Gallery opened in 1877. One of the first free public libraries in the country had opened in Duke Street in 1852. Prior to that, the Athenæum Club, since 1798, and the Lyceum Club, since 1803, had boasted fine libraries. And, completed in 1879, the Picton Library then opened its doors, and its huge collections of volumes were freely available. Neither must the Royal Institution, in Colquitt Street, where learned lectures were delivered, be forgotten, nor the various societies such as the Literary and Philosophical Society and the Philomathic Society.

Travelling into town from his home in West Derby in the morning, Noble would often meet, and, indeed, came to know quite well, a businessman named John Watson, who lived not far away from him in Old Swan. One morning in 1875, Mr Watson mentioned to Noble, who was by this time established as a well-known local literary figure in Liverpool, that his 17-year-old son, William, was not only extremely interested in reading poetry, but was now actually writing it, with what appeared to him to be 'some apparent talent for versification', and he (Watson *père*) would be deeply grateful to have Noble's opinion of it.

Politely, Noble agreed to meet the lad, and duly invited the aspirant poet to spend an evening at his home, and read some of his poems to him. Young Watson came, and Noble was impressed. It was the beginning of a relationship which was to last for thirteen years, and be of great benefit to William Watson.

The Watson family had moved to Liverpool in 1861 from Burley-in-Wharfedale, just outside Leeds, where John Watson had kept a general shop, and was a twine-maker, selling mainly to the local maltsters. His business had gone into decline, but in Liverpool he was succeeding as a trader in jute with Dundee and Calcutta. Things had so prospered that, in 1876, the family moved to Southport, then a fashionable watering-place, with a population of less than five thousand. Very shortly after the Watsons' departure, Noble followed in their wake to Southport, and between 1876 and 1879, William was to spend many, many more evenings at his house.

It was in 1876 that Noble was given the opportunity to make his contribution to the cultivation of the Liverpool wilderness. He was asked to undertake the production of a new weekly. It was to be called the *Liverpool Argus*. There was, it is true, no shortage of newspapers – the *Liverpool Daily Post*, founded in 1855; *Williamson's Liverpool Advertiser*, founded by Robert Williamson in 1856; the *Liverpool Mercury*; the *Liverpool Echo* – but there was an undeniable dearth of literary journals, and he was determined to make the *Argus* as culturally significant and interesting as possible.

Choosing the right contributors promised to be a worrying business, for the promoters of the paper were mainly members of the Temperance Society. They were, he knew, anxious to establish it as their new organ and mouthpiece, and he felt sure that 'the faddists would be well to the fore'.

It was his old friend, Sir Edward Russell, editor of the *Liverpool Daily Post,* who recommended a young man named Hall Caine, to Noble.

Thomas Henry Hall Caine, the son of an immigrant Manxman, had been born on 14 May 1853, at 130 Bridgewater Street, Runcorn. But the location of his birth was pure happenstance, his father, a blacksmith who had retrained as a ship's smith, was working temporarily on a repair job in Runcorn docks. The baby should have been born in Liverpool, whither within a few months the family returned to rented rooms at 14 Rhyl Street, Toxteth, which area was at that period the site of a small colony of Manx exiles.

Young Tom went first to a local elementary school and, at the age of ten, to the Hope Street British Schools. His formal education ended when he was

14. He then had the good fortune to be taken on at an architect's office as a pupil draughtsman.

Books were the teenage boy's consuming passion, the Liverpool Free Library his university. He and William Tirebuck, who had been his best friend at school, and who, like him, had developed an interest in writing, started a handwritten magazine. It was perforce somewhat amateurish, and it survived for only two issues.

Tirebuck, a year younger than Caine, and described as 'a tall, carefully-dressed young Welshman, whose twinkling eyes were the only sign of his love of the ridiculous', though forced to leave school before he was 12, managed, when he was 16, in 1870, to land the position of co-editor of a new weekly.

Meanwhile, Caine, watching enviously, succeeded, while still earning his living in the architect's office, in getting freelance contributions, mainly reviews of plays, accepted by those local papers for which he had volunteered to write them. It was a start.

Following Russell's advice, Noble invited Caine to write for the new paper. Tirebuck and Watson were also pressed into service as members of his team of Argus contributors.

The first issue of the *Liverpool Argus* came out on Saturday 21 October 1876. It contained Watson's poem *Poetæ Musæ*, his first serious claim to poetry. His next major contribution was in prose – a series of six articles on 'German Music and the German Musical Composers'.

Sad to report, for all its many excellencies, it was to be a rather short-lived journal. By 1878 it was all over.

The previous year, 1877, in conjunction with Tirebuck, and another old schoolfellow, George Rose, Caine founded a literary club, the Notes and Queries Society. It met, at first, in the schoolroom under the Myrtle Street Baptist Chapel, where the Caine family were regular attendants, but as the membership increased, the venue changed. Sometimes the meetings were held at the Free Library, and other times at the Royal Institution. They proved a very happy and successful way of bringing together the men and women of Merseyside who were interested in literature, and, inevitably, Noble and Watson were to be numbered in the Society's ranks.

Throughout the three years, 1876-1879, Watson spent many evenings in Noble's company at his seaside cottage home. He brought there in succession, for polishing and furbishment, each of the ten cantos of his long poem *The Prince's Quest*, striding up and down Noble's study reading alternately passages from it and from Milton, as if to invite comparison between them.

To the cottage by the sea there came, as well as Watson, many visitors – Hall Caine and William Tirebuck; Alexander Ireland, under whom Noble had worked on the *Manchester Examiner*, and who had been the friend of

Leigh Hunt, Carlyle, Emerson and Charles Cowden-Clarke, the friend of Keats. A rare, but specially welcome visitant was Edward Dowden, Professor of English at Trinity College, Dublin. Noble had met Dowden in 1877, when he came over to Liverpool to open the first meeting of the Notes and Queries Society.

In 1879, Watson wrote to Dowden asking for an opinion on *The Prince's Quest*. He had begun to find Noble 'a perilously partial adviser', and was clearly in search of a new mentor. Surely it was with this in mind that he wrote traitorously to Dowden:

> *I always have a feeling of perfect assurance that whatever I send you will produce in you its full and due effect – that your judgement will take no tincture from temporary moods, subjective conditions, or accidental prepossessions of any kind, such as I often observe to influence the critical verdicts (upon various matters) of our otherwise admirable J.A.N. for instance.*

As Watson full well knew, Dowden had greater influence than Noble in the literary world, and he was indeed able to introduce Watson to a number of important people.

By now, the – at least superficially – pleasant confraternity of young Liverpool *literati* was beginning to break up. For all their enthusiasm and efforts, it had turned out to be impossible to make a living and a lively literary world of their own in their home town, and they were forced to recognise that they must leave, make a move, if they wanted to succeed as writers.

The first to go, in 1880, was Hall Caine. He joined William Rossetti in London, and set his foot firmly on the path that was to lead to considerable fame, and even more considerable fortune, as a novelist. The boy from the back streets of of Toxteth was to end up owning a mock castle on the Isle of Man and a fine town house on Hampstead Heath. He died in 1931 in his mock castle.

Shortly after Caine's departure, William Tirebuck left for Leeds, to become the assistant editor of the *Yorkshire Post*. Taken ill, he returned to Liverpool, to die, aged 46 in 1900, at his mother's house, 320 Park Road.

William Watson went off to London in 1890. He achieved national eminence as a poet, and was knighted in 1917. He died in 1935 and is buried in Childwall churchyard.

Richard Le Gallienne left Liverpool in 1891. He became extremely well known for a time, but long before his death his reputation had faded into obscurity. He died, a man with a great future behind him, in Menton, in 1947.

In 1883, Noble fell victim to a mysterious, but extremely serious, illness. The symptoms were those of an intermittent paralysis, which, throughout the duration of a spasmodic attack, rendered him completely helpless. It was considered that the only satisfactory course would be to consult the foremost neurologist of the day, Dr David Ferrier. The trouble was that the great man's fee for coming all the way down from London was a formidable one; particularly so for Noble, who had given so freely of his substance in lending a helping hand to impecunious young authors that he was anything but well off.

However, Edward Hutton, the great authority on Italian language and literature, and the poet, the Hon Roden Noel, set themselves zealously to work to raise a fund for his assistance. Ferrier duly arrived in Liverpool, but when he saw the Noble family circumstances he did a most generous thing; he absolutely refused to take the cheque for his fee – 150 guineas – when Mrs Noble handed it to him. Nor would he accept any smaller amount. He did give Noble only six months to live. Happily, he survived for another thirteen years, and fathered another child before he died.

Another young literary aspirant who beat a path to Noble's door at this time was Richard Le Gallienne. His father, John Gallienne, Secretary of the Birkenhead Brewery Company, had confided to Noble that his son cherished the notion that he was a poet, and he asked Noble if he would take a look at the lad's work, and tell him candidly whether or not it displayed any worthwhile promise.

Richard arrived. Peering from their window, the Noble girls saw his coming – chiselled Grecian features, a bush of raven-black hair, dandiacal turn-out – and bearing, with the invariable gallantry of gesture which accompanied him, an enormous bunch of rhododendrons for Mrs Noble.

Le Gallienne became a regular Southport visitor. The whole family was charmed by him. He never came without a sheaf of flowers for the ladies, or left without sweetening the air with a garland of compliments. Both he and his writings made a very favourable impression, and when, in 1889, Elkin Mathews published his second book of poems, *Volumes in Folio*, Noble reviewed it in the kindest of terms in *The Academy*. The relationship between Noble and Le Gallienne was always to remain most cordial. In his *English Poems* (1892), Richard dedicated the fifth and final section of the volume – 'Of Poets and Poetry':

> To James Ashcroft Noble,
> Poet and critic, a small acknowledgment of much
> unforgotten kindness.

On the other hand, since as long ago as 1873, cordiality had been on the decline in Noble's relationship with Watson. This may, in part, have been due to the fact of Noble's undoubtedly highly-strung temperament and frequent bouts of nervous illness, but Watson must also, and in good measure, share the blame. He was a selfish, egocentric, and ungrateful recipient of Noble's many kindnesses. As we have seen, he was quick to betray him to, and for, Dowden. He was a snob without reason so to be. He intensely disliked Hall Caine. He disliked Liverpool and her people. Describing Matthew Arnold's missionary visit to the city in 1882, he wrote scathingly of the 'stiff-necked and uncircumcised Liverpudlian Philistines' that Arnold came to convert. He objected to his father's being described as a 'Liverpool merchant', for – although the phrase appealed to his snobbishness in that, as he put it, 'John Watson was, like Mr Gladstone's father, a Liverpool merchant' – it would lead some people to suppose him, as his son, 'to be a Liverpool man, which thank God I'm not'.

What led to the final break between Noble and Watson was the latter's treatment of Alexander Ireland's daughter, Ethel. In 1888, Ireland had, much to Noble's delight, moved to Southport. It was at Noble's house that Watson first met Ethel Ireland. Undeterred by the fact that she was only 16, and he (Watson) was in his 30th year, the pair became engaged. There had been a period of coolness between Noble and Watson, but his relationship with Ethel brought them close together once more. Then, in 1889, Watson suddenly and quite callously broke off his engagement, and Noble, understandably siding with the ill-used daughter of his old friend, accused Watson of lacking a sense of honour. The breach between them was never healed. Continuing his ungrateful and unyielding attitude to the very end, Watson experienced no difficulty in resisting Noble's obvious wish to renew their friendship, and it was only after Noble's death that Watson unbent to the extent of writing to a friend, 'Poor old Noble is gone'.

At a Folklore Society outing to Oxford in September 1891, Watson's friend Edward Clodd, an extremely well-known literary man, and one who wielded considerable influence, introduced him to an attractive woman friend of his, Marian Roalfe Cox. Rather tactlessly, Watson took to meeting her behind Clodd's back, and then, in February 1892, even more tactlessly, announced his engagement to her. Clodd had just about accepted this when, in May 1892 – this is where we came in! – Watson, reverting to type, repeated his earlier treatment of Ethel Ireland, and broke off the engagement. And, in another *déjà vu* episode, Clodd accused him, practically in Noble's very words, of 'lacking a fine sense of honour'.

By 1892, Noble and his family had moved away from the North West to London, so that he could be more in touch with literary affairs, and were living at 15 The Grove, a small new villa in a new road quite near Wandsworth Common. It was a comfortable place with a pleasant atmosphere, and very cosy.

It was in the book-lined back room at the end of the passage – his study –

overlooking the tiny flower-filled garden, that Noble spent a large part of his days. In the centre of the room stood his kneehole writing-table. On it, always, scattered papers, his tin of Three Castles cigarettes, and his vital supporting tumbler of weak whisky and water. Here he would sit, smoking and sipping, all day, his thin, delicate hand covering sheet after sheet of paper with his small, thick handwriting. When not at his desk, he would lie on the sofa by the window, reading a three-volume novel or whatever other book he was reviewing – for a living.

In 1893, Elkin Mathews and John Lane had published Noble's *The Sonnet in England and Other Essays*. The title essay had originally appeared in September 1880, in *Contemporary Review*, of which journal, now 136 years old, I have, for the last forty years, had the honour of being a director. The essay in question was much respected by the literary pundits.

It was the following year that Noble was introduced to the boy who was to be his last protégé. The family all went to the local Unitarian church on a Sunday, and it was the Unitarian minister who had asked Noble if he would mind taking a look at the work of a boy whom he knew, and which had deeply impressed him.

So it was that there came into Noble's study one afternoon in 1894, a 16-year-old lad named Edward Thomas, who was just completing his schooldays, and would soon be going up to Lincoln College, Oxford. But, thanks to Noble, who was very taken with the boy's obvious literary capability, even before entering the university he was to have had a book published. Although Thomas was later to achieve considerable fame as a poet, his first publication, accouched by Noble, was *The Woodland Life*, a collection of natural history essays in the mode of Richard Jefferies, and a fragment of diary, all of which had previously appeared in various magazines. Sadly, Noble did not survive to see the book's publication in 1897.

In 1895, works from Noble's pen appeared twice in *The Yellow Book*. To Volume IV, January 1895, he contributed *Mr Stevenson's Forerunner*, a study of the young Glasgow poet, Alexander Smith, his poems and essays. And in Volume V, April 1895, he was represented by a long and nicely constructed short story, *The Phantasies of Philarete*.

James Ashcroft Noble, the aspiring literary man's friend, died aged 51, in 1896. He had tuberculosis in the throat and did not survive an operation. Three years after his death, Edward Thomas married Noble's daughter, Helen. He was killed in the First World War, in 1917. His widow has celebrated the joys and sorrow of their life together in two memorable little books , *As It Was* and *World Without End*. It is an old, old story, but the tears have not yet turned to stone.

VISITING PILGRIMS

In keeping with his widely recognised somewhat grumpy and pessimistic temperament, the late JB Priestley, author and playwright, professed to find Liverpool gloomy.

He always remembered the rather grim and grimy seeming approach by rail – the descent into a sudden deep cutting for the last half-mile or so before you reach Lime Street Station … the daylight blotted out … an entry into Vulcan's kingdom; an illusion compounded by the engine's red fire glow and smoke in the blackness of the tunnel, and the echoing hammer-blow-like clanging of the railway machinery.

Out into Lime Street itself. A biting wind sweeping off the plateau. The sharp-nipped citizenry snuggling down into thick overcoats. And fog, more fog than any other city of his acquaintance, and that not excepting London and its pea-soupers, sneaking and snaking in off the Mersey.

For Priestley, Liverpool was a winter city, just as for Daniel Roserra in the *conte* in Arthur Symons' *Spiritual Adventures*, Arles was an autumn city. He was, for the purpose of writing his travel book, *English Journey*, visiting Liverpool in the early 1930s. Those were the days when it was the English seaport second only to London – 'the very weight of stone emphasised that fact' – but to Priestley it was like a city in a rather glum Victorian novel – darkish, dignified, imposing. The solemn façade of St George's Hall, where 'no birds sing', or flutter, and St John's Gardens, a place where, he wonders, does spring ever come, confirm for him the omnipresent drabness of the northern town.

He homed upon the Adelphi, 'an hotel that no producer of musical comedy would object to using for his big set in the second act.' Originally built, and luxuriously appointed, with the first-class Atlantic passenger traffic in mind, it was dealt a sort of deathblow from the start, for barely were its deep-pile carpets laid and its gold paint dry when the Atlantic traffic was diverted to Southampton.

Priestley knew, of course, the Playhouse and its director, William Armstrong, running what was 'the best repertory company in the kingdom', but his previous acquaintance with the city had not extended much beyond the proscenium arch and stage door of the theatre, and the plush interior of the best hotel.

The Liverpool of this probing literary visit was, on the other hand, a place of what seemed like a thousand corporation trams lumbering and screeching and groaning their way about the town.

Priestley was, at first, uncertain as to which Liverpool it was that he wanted to capture for his book. He had, he confessed, on one former visit experienced the Liverpool of the University Club; that is to say, the city of pleasant journalists, smiling professors and their ladies, young barristers and shipping men: civilised conversation and civilised *cuisine*. He had seen, *en passant*, and was on excellent aesthetic terms with, the city of great buildings; such palaces of stone as the Royal Liver Building, the Dock Board and the Cunard Building. He knew also the street of surgeons, late eighteenth century Rodney Street, and the dark red bulk of the rising Anglican Cathedral. Thinking about it up in his bedroom at the Adelphi, he decided that it was probably 'Liverpool the Seaport' that contained what it was that he wanted to distil, and to snare in a net of evocative words.

He found, next day, what he was looking for. It was 'the queerest parish in England', presided over by the elderly priest who coined that description for the demesne of his religious ministration. It was a picturesque and exotic slum, festering in Regency streets and squares of the decayed and decaying remnants of what had once been the charming and dignified residences of comfortable Liverpool merchants.

Priestley paints a masterly miniature of Giant Decay.

> Every bit of woodwork was fast losing its last flakes of paint. The windows were broken, boarded, raggedly curtained. The open doorways gave out a reek of unwashed humanity. The buildings were rotting away, and some of the people were rotting with them.

He thought to see among the drooping flower heads faces that had blossomed young and fair in the brothels of Queen Victoria's times. This was 1933, only thirty-two years since the old Queen died. In the eyes of slumland babes he saw shades of Port Said, Bombay, Zanzibar and Hong Kong; fleshly legacies of Africa and Asia.

Visiting the infant classes of the local school, he saw children of mixed race, the jumbled products of a jumble of latitudes and longitudes – the African's distinctive hair, the Malayan's smooth brown skin, the almond eye of the Chinese. The mixing of the races did not seem to matter in the slightest. These little beings were just children, young and often beautiful. Delightful, tender exotic fruits. That their parents were 'the riff-raff of the stokeholds and the slatterns of the slums' was of no moment whatsoever. Looking at them, a miniature League of Nations, Priestley mused:

> Perhaps we have been given a glimpse of the world of 2433, by which time the various root races, now all members of a great world state, may have largely intermarried and interbred.

Under the gentle guidance of his clerical friend, in the gathering dusk of a November afternoon, Priestley forayed into Liverpool's Chinatown. Even then, seventy years ago, it was rapidly dwindling. He saw a Chinese Republican club, the Chinese Masonic Hall, and a few Chinese shops, and then went into a Chinese café for a pot of China tea.

Inquiring as to why it was that the Chinese quarter was so quickly shrinking, Priestley learned that there were two good reasons for this. First, trade was bad. The Chinese go where there is money to be made, and there had not been much to be made in Liverpool during the past few years. Secondly, they had found that it was not possible for them to live in Liverpool in the way that they liked to live. There was too much interference with their less acceptable customs such as gambling, opium-smoking and the establishment of secret societies. For several years there had not been any of the old racial street fights, Tong wars, which used to break out.

From Chinatown the author and the priest made their way down to the docks. They struck Priestley as, his favourite Liverpool label, 'most gloomy'.

He sketched a rapid, suitably gloomy, dockland vignette:

> Trams going whining down long sad roads; a few stinking little shops; pubs with their red blinds down and an accumulation of greasy papers under their windows; black pools and mud and slippery cobblestones; high blank walls; a suspicious policeman or two.

Knocking out their pipes, dutifully alert to the hazard of fire, they entered what Priestley again categorised as a precinct of vasty gloom, doom, emptiness and decay. There were empty-seeming warehouses, the place was populated by more shadows than men, a deserted waterfront stretching in dreary isolation over a long mudbank and a grey waste of water. Something somewhere hooted. It was a melancholy sound perfectly matched to the spectral scene, upon which darkness rose rather than fell. The pilgrims walked slowly from nothing into nothing.

It was a relief to escape to the warmth and cosiness of the David Lewis Club and Hostel, where Priestley's dramatist's heart was gladdened by the little theatre there, and he felt at home in the room filled with 'bits of scenery, half-painted canvas cloths, and odd "props".' In the hostel next door, a man could live on 1s.9d. a day. Albeit, he would need to be of no very sensitive temperament, for the look and feel of the place was essentially and basically functional and grimly institutional. A good plateful of stewed steak, the dearest item on the menu in the very large, self-service dining-room, cost sixpence.

The next port of call was Paddy's Market in the Irish quarter. As Priestley arrived, it was about to put up the shutters for the day, but there was just time to get the feel of the renowned covered market where folk, particularly Lascars, would come joyously to replenish their wardrobes without demolishing their money belts.

The Irish quarter sparked no enthusiasm. The feckless charm of its denizens fell upon inhospitable ground in the Priestleyean breast.

> If we do have an Irish Republic as our neighbour, and it is found possible to return her exiled citizens, what a grand clearance there will be in all the western ports from Clyde to Cardiff, what a fine exit of ignorance and dirt and drunkenness and disease.

Bidding farewell to his clerical friend, Priestley was relieved to find himself back in the neon-flashing heart of the Liverpool of cinemas, theatres, dance halls, grillrooms, boxing matches and cocktail bars. Comfortably and safely ensconced once more in the Adelphi, he lit a good cigar and gloomily decided that 'somebody else must give a plain fair account of this great city: the task in the time was beyond me.'

Next day he left for Manchester.

Fifty years later, the diarist, James Lees-Milne, made similar pilgrimage to Liverpool.

He, too, stayed at the Adelphi – 'great hotel of Edwardian era, splendour and riches of Liverpool, White Star and Cunard glories.'

His experience of the city echoes that of Priestley. In 1984, he found it all terribly down-at-heel. The streets were unkempt, littered with rubbish. Such old Georgian terraces of Priestley's observation as were still standing half a century later had, in the intervening years, either reached the point of collapse or, after such lengthy and persistent neglect, were, instead of being restored, being pulled down.

Everywhere, walls had been disfigured by the scribblings of subversive words. Liverpool conditions were at the time hopeless, the city being bankrupt.

Lees-Milne spent a morning in the University Library, examining there some 160 letters to Viscount Reginald Brett Esher, the writing of whose biography he was about to embark upon.

He afterwards visited the Roman Catholic cathedral, which he thought 'gimmicky', observed its concrete to have weathered atrociously, covered with iron rust streaks, and adjudged the finials of the lantern to be too flimsy and skimpy. Neither was he impressed by the interior of the building, which he thought cheerless, 'in spite of large circular nave and high lantern and splodges of ugly glass.'

It is a judgment in which I cannot concur. I do, however, wholeheartedly support his view that Giles Gilbert Scott's Anglican cathedral is verily a masterpiece.

Lees-Milne also waxed enthusiastic about the Walker Art Gallery, and, over the water, the Lady Lever Gallery, and was greatly impressed by the Port Sunlight village and its layout.

Friends with whom he dined reinforced the contextual validity in modern Liverpool of the home football song, *You'll never walk alone.* You never will after dark if you have any sense. His friends, the Rathbones, summoned a taxi to take him back to the Adelphi at the evening's end. They learned afterwards that the taxi had duly arrived – and driven away again, because the driver had not dared to leave his cab to look for, and pull, the doorbell.

That was nineteen years ago … and now?

SHADOWS
OF THE PAST

THE TURBULENT PRIEST

There stands, has stood for the past 97 years, at the St John's Lane side of St John's Gardens behind St George's Hall, the bronze statue of a fully-robed priest, one arm raised in benediction, the other curved protectively around the thin shoulders of a barefoot Liverpool street arab of the Victorian days of *Her Benny*. The waifs and strays, the physically and the mentally afflicted, these were his meticulously garnered flock.

The man whose 83-year pilgrimage across the Liverpool horizon this statue represents and celebrates is Father Nugent, the Ragged Children's Friend, protector of those sealed of the sad tribe of 'The Orflings', as the Micawbers' servant, Clickett, dubbed herself, veritably the champion of those unfortunates poetically enshrined within the pedestal of Bartholdi's Statue of Liberty:

> ... your tired, your poor, your huddled masses ... the wretched refuse of your teeming shore ... the homeless.

He was turbulent only in the sense that he was ever ready to rise and smite injustice, to fight the battles of the poor and weak, fearless in facing the cruelties of tyrannous authority.

James Nugent, eldest of the nine children of the good Roman Catholic couple, John and Mary Nugent, first saw the Mersey light, a Sunday's child, on 3 March 1822, in Hunter Street, behind William Brown Street, in the heart of the city. His father, who had come over from Ireland, sprang from the Nugents of County Meath. He was in a fair way of business as a fruiterer, poulterer and dealer in game. Besides owning a shop, he had a stall in St John's Market. The family seems to have been mildly peripatetic, living at different times in Circus Street, Lime Street, and at, succesively, Numbers 4 and 9, Commutation Row, where they stayed for many years before a final move out to Great Crosby, taking up residence there, near the Church of Saints Peter and Paul.

The baby James was baptised on, appropriately, St Patrick's Day, 17 March 1822, at the church which was to play a large part in his later life, St Nicholas', the Pro-Cathedral, on Copperas Hill.

Finding a suitable school to which to send the young James presented something of a problem, for, with the exception of a handful of Poor Schools, educational facilities for Catholics in Liverpool were literally non-existent. A compromise had to be arrived at, and, on the recommendation of the Reverend James Picton, incumbent of the Protestant Christ Church, in Hunter Street, young James was sent to the Academy, a private school in

Queen Square, which was conducted by the Reverend Mr Picton's two brothers.

James was intended for a business career and, leaving school, it was arranged that he should enter the office of Messrs WG Maxwell, merchant, of King Street. However, as St Thomas à Kempis has it, *Nam homo proponit, sed Deus disponit* (Man proposes, but God disposes), and Father Walker, of St Nicholas', whose advice was sought by James' parents, told them that their son showed signs of having a vocation to the priesthood.

So it was that, in February 1838, James, just about to celebrate his 16th birthday, left home to begin life as a theological student at St Cuthbert's College, at Ushaw Moor, near Durham. Five years there was followed by a further three years at the English College in Rome. Then, returning to Liverpool, he was ordained priest in St Nicholas' on 30 August 1846.

Father James Nugent's first sacerdotal appointment was to St Alban's, the solitary Catholic church in Blackburn. He was transferred from there, in March 1848, to St Mary's, Wigan. Then, *Dies splendens*, on New Year's Day 1849, a rubric day in his life, he found himself back in Liverpool, back at St Nicholas', as a curate to Father Worthy there.

The Liverpool to which Father Nugent returned was very different from that which he had left eight years before. The population then had been about 210,000, and what were to become the suburbs, such places as Everton, Walton, West Derby, and Old Swan, were distant and distinct communities.

The year of his departure had seen the beginning of the building of St George's Hall on what had been known as the Great Heath. The site had then been occupied by a hospital, which was demolished, and a new one, the Royal Infirmary, erected in Brownlow Street. William Brown Street was at that time still known as Shaw's Brow. Its name was changed in 1860, when William Brown presented the Free Public Library and the Museum to the town, and received in exchange a baronetcy. The Wellington Column would be put up in 1863. Alderman AB Walker gifted the town with the Walker Art Gallery, completed in 1877, and the Picton Reading Room, courtesy of Sir James A Picton, was to open its doors in 1879.

The year 1847 had been one which was to import a dreadful change to Liverpool. That was when the terrible Irish potato famine was raging at its height. The price of a deck passage from the Irish ports to Liverpool was sixpence. Thousands fleeing from famine, disease and death, scraped together the few pennies that could, as they saw it, purchase deliverance and transportation to a place of safety, where many already had friends and relatives, earlier emigrants, to count upon. It was only after they had arrived, that they discovered that the immigrant families were often living in appalling conditions of poverty, in filthy, overcrowded courts, alleys and damp, foul-smelling cellars. Not for nothing was Liverpool, with its grossly swollen hibernian population, known as the Black Spot on the Mersey. By public health standards it had become about the worst town in the country. Its warrens of insanitary dwellings providing fertile soil for the incubation of frequent epidemics.

Father Nugent was genuinely distressed by the sights he witnessed every day now in his home town. He saw the streets overrun by hordes of homeless vagabond children, ragged, barefoot and starving, struggling for a precarious existence by theft, begging, street trading in all its forms. He saw the newsboys, the match sellers, the shoeblacks, the street actors, street conjurors, street musicians, of a sort, and the embryo pavement artists – girls as well as boys, some of them, not more than seven or eight years of age.

He called them 'Nobody's Children', and in a lecture he described them:

> They roam unheeded about those crowded thoroughfares and along those five miles of docks, desolate and homeless wanderers, without a heart to love them, or a hand to guide them. They prowl about the busy city, the keen and cunning succeeding by various devices to live, whilst others suffer all the hardships of hunger and absolute want. In the long, cold winter nights when the snow lies thick upon the ground, and the stormy winter's blast makes comfortable luxury draw close to the fireside, the birds of the air have their resting places, and the very dogs their warm kennels, but these poor little ones huddle together under railway arches, in empty boxes, over bakers' ovens, in fact anywhere to get a little heat and protection from the frosty and nipping night air. How many died of actual starvation, and are buried in the pauper's heap without a mourner to follow their coffin, or a single tear shed over their grave? Poor children of the streets! Already, evil in its twofold form of vice and sorrow blocks their pathway in life, to corrupt and afflict them. The streets are the schools of crime, where the girl scarce in her teens is degraded into a fallen outcast, the boy into a rowdy, duffer, thief and convict.

Many of these shepherdless sheep strayed into the prison and the workhouse. Some, and not necessarily the best and most honest, were sharp enough to steer a wide berth of both places.

Determined to dedicate his stoutest efforts to the rescuing of these straying sheep, in his first year at Copperas Hill Father Nugent decided to open a Ragged School. This, with the help of a strong-willed Catholic woman, Mrs Holmes, he did in the area called Spitalfields, long since vanished, which lay between Whitechapel and Dale Street. It was a district of evil reputation, well known for drunkenness and crime. The house that he managed to secure there was a tumbledown place, reputed to be haunted. Some good repairs and a lick of paint soon put the ghosts to flight.

Ragged Schools – there were 32 of them in Liverpool in 1853 – were all very well as far as they went, but they didn't go very far. They offered daytime shelter and food, and sometimes clothing, rather than any serious course of education, and such efforts as they made to find work for their pupils met with but indifferent success. Worst of all, the children were turned out to fend for themselves at night.

So, Father Nugent got to work and set up a Night Shelter and Refuge at 22 and 24 Soho Street, its object being to provide somewhere for the boys who had nowhere to lay their heads down except on the stone pillows of the pavements. They were also provided with the opportunity to have a good wash and clean-up, a basin of coffee, and a half-pound of bread, together with a dash of treacle. That the Soho Refuge was a great success is statistically testified to by the fact that in 1867 it provided 2,913 nights lodgings for boys, and 48,205 suppers. At one time, Father Nugent made an educated estimate that there were some 23,000 children running wild along the Liverpool dockside.

The range of the Good Father's activities over the next half-century – 1850-1900 – is truly astonishing. In 1860 he founded the *Catholic Times*. In 1863 he was appointed Chaplain to Walton Gaol, a position which he held for 25 years. He was also one of the chaplains serving Brownlow Hill Workhouse. In 1864 he played a key rôle in the acquisition and fitting-out of the Reformatory Training Ship, *Clarence*, which was anchored in the Mersey. He was largely instrumental in the introduction of the Sisters of Notre Dame to fulfil the crying need for Catholic teachers in Liverpool. He worked, too, in the giving of comfort and aid to 'fallen women', and was enthusiastic in his efforts to steer the boys and young men who came within the orbit of his influence towards the avowal of total abstinence, and to deal with the problems of the alcoholics of the city.

At the turn of the century, Father Nugent retired and moved into a house called 'Harewood', at the corner of Duke Street and Freshfield Road, Formby. He returned there after a long visit to America in the spring of 1903.

He was now 81, and it seemed unlikely that he would visit America again, but, in the summer of 1904, when his friend Abbot Gasquet made up his mind to go on a lecture tour to the States, Father Nugent insisted upon accompanying him, to show him the ropes. After touring Canada, the two friends crossed into America in September.

Father Nugent headed for St Paul, Minnesota, where he preached in the cathedral on the last Sunday in September. During October he was struck down with what he persisted in regarding as a severe attack of rheumatism. Others considered it to be an affliction somewhat more serious. Whatever, it was not until the following February (1905) that he was fit enough to return to St Louis. He was able to set sail for home aboard the *SS Oceanic* on 16 May 1905. Unfortunately, during a storm, he lost his footing, and fell heavily, injuring his head.

Once safely back in Formby, he seemed to improve, but the fall appeared to have upset his sight. Twice he made the journey to an oculist in Liverpool. He also paid a short visit to Southport.

During one of these visits he caught a chill. It developed into a serious bout of pneumonia, and despite the most devoted nursing, Monsignor Nugent – he had been raised to that eminence by Pope Leo XIII in 1892, but he was always, and still is, thought of as Father Nugent – lapsed into unconsciousness. He died at 4am on 27 June 1905, just three months into his 84th year. The flags of Liverpool were lowered to half-mast. Throughout the city there was heart-felt sorrow for the passing of 'a great priest who bestrode the life of Liverpool like a colossus for over fifty years.' He was laid to rest in Ford Cemetery.

Liverpool's Vanished Teashops

One of the highlights of my Liverpool childhood was being taken out to tea in town. Greedy memory unfolds before the mind's retrospective eye a vision of tray upon tray, plate after plate, of wonderful confections, which, along with the old-fashioned teashops that supplied them, have simply vanished.

Like Nicholas Monsarrat before me, and George Melly after me, I used, as an occasional treat, to be taken into town by my mother to have tea at Troxler and Ecker's, the Swiss-owned teashop in Bold Street. I always looked forward to seeing the beautiful carved wood bear which stood outside to greet one. Inside, past the big umbrella stand, one settled down into one of the comfortable, chintz-covered sofas to await the arrival of the glass of milk and the excited anguish of choosing just one of the mouth-watering, temptatious pastries set before us.

First, and always a prime favourite, there were the luscious éclairs, a choice of chocolate or coffee icing, melting choux pastry, cramful of the thickest cream. The nineteenth century French *pâtissière* of undoubted genius who 'invented' the éclair, well named it so – literally a 'flash of lightning', for that was just about how fast I used to find that it vanished!

Then there were cakes and tartlets embellished with memorable frangipane; cherry pies on a custard base; *millefeuilles*, their feather-light, layered puff pastry oozing cream and jam; seductive cakes covered with rainbows of hundreds and thousands; and delicious sponge-cakes, liberally crusted on top with delicious pink icing.

Monsarrat remembers in his autobiography, *Life is a Four-Letter Word*, that Troxler's:

> ... probably figured more largely in our lives than any other establishment in Liverpool ... it was a true oasis ... We were ravenously hungry, and Troxler's was our delicious answer. We had a cup of chocolate with a blob of whipped cream on top; and we were allowed two cakes each, except on or near a birthday, when the ration was three. The choosing took us three or four minutes; the spun-out eating was good for half an hour. Then Mother paid the bill – about three shillings.

Sometimes my mother would take me instead to Sisson's, higher up Bold Street on the right-hand side. The seats there were cane or basket chairs. I didn't like them as much as Troxler's sofas, and the atmosphere was not so cosy and intimate. Neither were the cakes so good, but I seem to recall the compensation that there were very splendid ice-creams produced there, which was fine in summer, but not so good on winter's days.

Occasionally, too, we might go to Fuller's Café, which stood pretty well opposite the end of Bold Street, where Church Street takes over from Ranelagh Street. The great attraction there was Fuller's Walnut Cake, with its thick layer of superbly flavoured cream filling and rather crumbly covering of powdery white sugar. You could buy one of these cakes to take home, beautifully packaged in a four-square, shiny white cardboard box. I think that they cost three shillings and sixpence or four shillings.

My mother, who had, of course, been coming to the Liverpool teashops since she was a little girl in the first decade of the last century, seemed to know all the waitresses by name. Though of indeterminate age, they were mostly unmistakably 'mature'. They were also plump, as if, by some weird process of osmosis, they had absorbed by some weird process of osmosis vast quantities of the sugar and cream by which they were all their working day surrounded. Their feet seemed invariably to be giving them either gyp, or at least 'a bit of trouble', and to that extent provided ready-made conversational material with those upon whom they habitually waited, and with whom they habitually chattered.

They always had names like Gladys and Phyllis. They were chatty and tended to have a nice line in Liverpool native wit, and verbal dexterity in the case of the necessary put-down.

There was, I recall, a very old lady customer, a regular, rather eccentric, I think, dressed in what was most conspicuously the high fashion of several decades earlier. I remember the waitress regarding her with a sort of amused affection as she made her entrance through the revolving door and remarking, quick as a flash, and very much to the point: "Here she is. *All our yesterdays!*" – which was the name of a programme of sentimental nostalgia currently running on the wireless.

I suppose that my favourite place for afternoon tea as I grew older was the Lyceum Café. It was situated in the basement of the venerable old Lyceum Club (founded *c* 1803), at the bottom end of Bold Street, and I had, of course, been visiting there, with both my mother and my grandmother, since I was a child.

As in Troxler's, there were huge, comfortable sofas to sink into. The place was always full of flowers, on tables and shelves, and at the side of the handsome wooden cashier's box, beside the revolving entrance door, there was a large silver bowl, kept constantly full of lovely fresh blooms.

Again, the cakes were superb, especially the various creamy gateaux, and the magnificent custard tarts, which were a *spécialité de la maison*, and the Welsh rarebit with a poached egg on top of it was perfectly delicious. The atmosphere was excellent. The clientele were mostly ladies, many of them well weighed down with shopping wrapped in bags bearing the names of Liverpool's best stores. Some days there would be a sprinkling of pink-faced elderly gentlemen accompanying their ladies.

Beryl Bainbridge, I remember, was fond of the Lyceum. Indeed, she specifically mentions it in her *English Journey*. In an entry under the date 13 September 1983, she reports finding a notice outside the revolving doors that led into the cosily-carpeted Lyceum. It announced that on 17 September, a Saturday, it would close for ever.

She comments: 'I don't understand the malevolent force behind the destruction of this city.' Neither do I. She adds: 'I can't believe the café doesn't pay – I've never been there and found it empty.' No more have I. And she echoes my precise sentiment, saying:

> There isn't a restaurant in England which could provide a dish as tasty as the buck-rabbit served up in that basement at the bottom of Bold Street.

The other places where one could, and did, pay a very occasional tea time visit, were the restaurants of the department stores. They provided, I am told, good, wholesome afternoon teas, well and cheerfully served. The only one of which I had any personal experience was Henderson's. For me, it did not compare with Troxler's, Sisson's, Fuller's or the Lyceum.

The whole ritual or mystique of taking 'a dish of tay' ran in the family like a wooden leg! One of my maternal grandfathers, Alphonse, a musician, son of Jakob Zeugheer Herrmann, the first conductor of the Liverpool Philharmonic, would in the early years of the last century, leave his home in Queen's Drive – 'Hazelwood'*, now Number 55, built for him in 1912, one of the first houses in Queen's Drive, Mossley Hill, which was then surrounded by corn fields – walk down Queen's Drive and across Sefton Park to the Number 15 tram terminus at Croxteth Road, and catch a first-class tram into town, where it was his invariable custom to take afternoon tea at the Kardomah Café, in Church Street, often meeting his wife, Helen, or my mother, Margaret, there.

Nicholas Monsarrat remembered:

> There was also a café called the Kardomah, with a delicious, all-pervading smell of freshly-ground coffee wafting out of its front door. But we never went there. "It's for office people," said Mother.

---

* *It was, incidentally, in the octagonal turret room there that I was delivered into the world, at about 1am on Wednesday 22 October 1924, by Dr Mort, the appropriately named Liverpool coroner, whose wife, Hilda, had been a school friend of my mother's at Huyton College.*

Mrs Monsarrat was conveniently forgetting her own family roots in trade. Her father, Sir John Turney, was rich and civically distinguished in Nottingham, but he had made his money as a dealer in leather.

There were two more branches of the Kardomah in Liverpool. The one in North John Street was decorated throughout in a sort of Moorish style; very bizarre. It was even more bizarre, partially surviving in the shop of Henry Young, the booksellers, who had taken the premises over.

The third Kardomah was in Bold Street. I very seldom went there for tea, but at one time my mother and I used it a great deal for lunching. There used, in fact, to be quite a social gathering in the downstairs, many of the regulars knowing one another. A group of doctors from Rodney Street, I remember the eye-surgeon, Mr Rankin, among them, meeting there every lunchtime to play chess.

And now there is not a Kardomah in Liverpool. All swept away. It is sad how things change – and so seldom for the better.

Nor is it only teashops that have vanished. There was in the old days, in the basement of the now also vanished, Exchange Hotel, a splendid institution, the Exchange Quick Lunch Bar, presided over by Richard, the *maître*, in snow-white, all-enveloping white apron. The lunchers sat around an enormous horseshoe-shaped counter, with Richard and a couple of white-overalled female assistants occupying the space at the centre, from which they administered to the gastronomic needs of the invariably ravenous patrons. The fare was excellent and the price relatively moderate. My mother and I frequently, and very happily and satisfiedly, luncheoned there.

Just round the corner in Exchange Street, was Anderson's, a favourite sandwich lunch and watering place for city businessmen. I would occasionally meet my uncle, Schofield Cannington, he of Cannington & Shaw, the great glass manufacturers of St Helens, there for lunch. What I remember as unique about the place was that you helped yourself to food and drink, then, as you left, stated the amount that you calculated that you owed, and paid the unquestioning cashier on your way out. I do not know, but I cannot imagine that that kind of trust can profitably survive in the brave new Liverpool of today.

The Ghosts of Liverpool Christmas Past

Close the curtains. Let the fire burn bright and fragrantly. Outside, a thin-edged wind, blowing surely straight off the Irish sea, cuts through the deserted streets and empty miles of grieving lamplight. Inside, is all cosiness. Sprigs of dark green holly with scarlet berries. A pine-scented Christmas tree, dripping tinsel, gold and silver, and spangled with hanging orbs of rich-hued, light-as-air spun glass.

That is how it should be. We are about to celebrate the mystery that is Christmas.

The rush and scurry of ritual preparation is over. The shops, so lately radiant with rainbow storms of light and stuffed plum-pudding-full with carnival shapes of tins and boxes, and all the rich treasure of presents to be given and received, stand dark and shuttered. Town stretches dead as petrified Pompei.

Now, in the brief respite, the breath-taking, before the day breaks, is the time to sit back in well-earned, warm and slippered ease to savour the atmosphere, the message, and the meaning, of Christmas.

Christmas is all things to all men. It is the sharp sweet smell of tangerines, cupped in their silver shells. The frosty glitter of mountains of mince pies. The jewel-bright tantalisation of crystallised fruits. The wrinkled brown impassiveness of little hillocks of unwinking nuts. The glistening invitation of boxes of dates, with pictures of camels browsing at balmy oases on their pastel-papered lids. The vivid challenge of unpulled crackers.

It is the sound of clear young voices carolling old, old songs about kings and shepherds and angels, in the outer darkness of the night. It is the sight of children's faces, flushed with innocent excitement as, tongue between teeth, they spell out with infinite pains and care their little letters to Santa Claus. It is a time for the gathering together of scattered families. It is a time for remembering.

Flicking back the leaves of the calendar, you will find that Liverpool has always been a city which has bubbled and fizzed with Yuletide spirit. Although, of course, like everything else, the shape of Christmas has changed over the years.

Travelling back through Time, traversing on the sledge of imagination the snows of yesteryear – *les neiges d'antan* – the inner eye can see, clear and colourful as one of this year's Christmas cards upon the mantelshelf, the olden, once-upon-a-time scene of a baronial Christmas at Speke Hall.

The great hall is swept and garnished, its floor newly strewn with leaves and twigs and rushes; huge boughs of holly, ivy, and other seasonable evergreens are festooned among the stags' antlers, the fox brushes, the armour, weaponry and tapestries on the walls. The minstrels play. Amid cheers, the mighty Yule log is drawn in upon its wheeled sleigh.

The ruddy glow from the enormous open hearth massacres the furthermost shadows and turns the panels of the dark-wainscotted walls a glowing orange-red. The cheerful flicker of the flames is caught in the shining armour, thrown off the blades of swords, halberds and pikes, and reflected by every glistening leaf, transforming everything into a festival of naked fire. Candles flare in their sconces, torches flame in the hands of the young men, who presently will dance with girls who carry provocative sprays of mistletoe.

Now comes the hour of the traditional feast.

In the great Tudor houses of England the main dish was always a boar's head, garnished with rosemary and bay, and with an apple or an orange in its mouth. But there were also magnificent side dishes of roasted swan, peacock or bustard, borne in upon vast silver salvers, their wings and tails spread wide, their gilded beaks tipped with sponges of blazing spirit.

There were traditional mince pies, too, though not compounded solely of spiced raisins, but containing also minced chicken, neats' tongues, and eggs. And all the festive meats and sweets would be washed down by goblets of strong old ale and gargantuan draughts of golden mead.

The merry scene dissolves. The centuries grind on. The Tudors pass. The Stuarts arrive – and depart. The House of Hanover comes to the throne.

> During the period which elapsed between 1775 and the close of the eighteenth century … the time-honoured festival of Christmas was commemorated in Liverpool to an extent much beyond what is now the usage …

Laments a mid-nineteenth century historian.

Not perhaps surprising, for the plain truth is that not a great many people had anything to feel festive about. For nineteenth century Liverpool was a city of uncushioned contrasts. The poor were very poor, and far outnumbered the well-heeled merchants, professional men and wealthy ship owners. For them, the Christmasses of the time of *Her Benny* were cold and drab occasions.

Out of the icy mist steaming up from the gleaming cobbles, another picture forms. Not the sort of picture you will find among your Christmas greetings cards this, but like a desolate old engraving from the pages of Silas Hocking's classic novel of Liverpool street life. We see, gaunt against the heavy, snow-banked sky, the grey and cold stone bulk of long since vanished St George's Church, down at the southern end of Castle Street. Beside it stand two shivering, ragged children. They are phantoms from the pages of fiction, make-believe waifs, never-were strays, little Nelly and her brother Benny.

But do not be misled. They are representatives of a very grim reality. Barefoot, cage-ribbed little creatures – urchins, 'Street Arabs', they used to call them – scarcely more than babies really, just such as Nelly and Benny, did scamper pathetically about the streets of Liverpool, trying to scratch a few pennies from the unyielding pavements.

Poor, sad little ghosts. Imagine the feeling of unshod feet on the sharp crusts of frozen sludge, the hunger pangs piercing the hollow stomach, the disappointment lancing through the heart as the hopeful little tray of matches is all-too-often ignored. But at least at the Christian season of goodwill, at Christmastime, the odd homeward-bound passer-by might pause just long enough to thrust a copper or two into a tiny, frozen hand. Those were the days when mercy was measured out in pennies.

Thank God, we do not see those fragile starvelings any more. Please God, one day those other sad ghosts, the underprivileged old, the old age pensioners, many of whom suffer still at 'merry' Christmastime, will be laid, too.

We may perhaps, all of us, grumble a bit. The cost of living. The iniquitous enormity of income tax. The shortfall of the National Health Service. But, looking back from the twenty-first century's cornucopian glades of plenty, we should surely, most of us, be heaving sighs of gratitude when we glimpse the lean spectres of other days – other Christmasses.

I still recall talking, only thirty years ago, to a man, not an old man, a man in his late forties, who told me how he could remember as a child scrabbling on the ground after market stalls had closed, to find among the refuse, fallen vegetables to take home for the family's Christmas dinner. Remembered his mother buying cracked eggs and broken biscuits, as special extras for their Christmas treat.

"But no matter how poor we were," he told me, "there was always one great joy for us at Christmas. That was being taken to see the cribs in the churches, and the excitement of going to midnight Mass."

Those were the days, 'the good old days', when for thousands of truly underprivileged children the fairy on the Christmas tree wore a Salvation Army bonnet; when it was only because of the good works of a handful of charitable, caring people, that they knew what it is surely the right of *every* child to know – the thrill of being invited to a Christmas party, and to go home excitedly clutching a little surprise parcel.

This looking back, to good times or to bad, is always a dangerous business. It is so easy to confuse the memory of things that were, with the memory of the lost self that was, to find ourselves mourning not the deaths of old Christmases, but the passing of our young selves.

The lesson of Time is that the wisest – and happiest – man, is he who looks neither back in regretful nostalgia, nor forward in unfounded expectation, but enjoys the present, for, after all, we are making tomorrow's memories today.

2153LILO